Tough Jews

TOUGH JEWS

Political Fantasies
and the Moral Dilemma
of American Jewry

PAUL BREINES

BasicBooks
A Division of HarperCollins*Publishers*

Library of Congress Cataloging-in-Publication Data

Breines, Paul, 1941–
    Tough Jews : political fantasies and the moral dilemma of
American Jewry / Paul Breines.
        p.   cm.
    Includes bibliographical references and index.
    ISBN 0-465-08636-5 : $19.95
    1. Jews—Politics and government.   2. Jews—Psychol-
ogy.   3. Jews—United States—Politics and government.   4.
Jews—United States—Psychology.   5. Toughness (Personality
trait)   6. National characteristics, Israeli.   7. American fiction—Jewish authors—History and criticism.   8. Jews in literature.   I. Title.
DS140.B7   1990
909′.04924—dc20
                                                            90-80242
                                                            CIP

For Wini

CONTENTS

PREFACE   IX

ACKNOWLEDGMENTS   XV

PART ONE:
Sigmund Freud's Tough Jewish Fantasy,
   Philip Roth's, and Mine   1

PART TWO:
From Masada to Mossad: A Historical Sketch
   of Tough Jewish Imagery   75

PART THREE:
The "Rambowitz" Novels   169

PART FOUR:
Toward a Conclusion   231

NOTES   241

BIBLIOGRAPHY OF TOUGH JEWISH NOVELS   265

INDEX   269

PREFACE

THE TITLE *Tough Jews* is the accidental invention of my friend Paul Piccone, to whom I am deeply grateful. Being a wordy person, I am especially pleased to have been given a title that is at once compact and suggestive. At the same time, tough Jews is also a fuzzy and ambiguous couplet, raising as many questions as answers, as many problems as solutions. It appeals to me for that reason, too. Tough Jews, but tough in what sense? Are they good or bad? And why is one discussing them now? The title evokes much but perhaps too much. While I emphatically do not want to wipe away all ambiguity, several matters can at the outset be clarified.

As I use the couplet here, tough Jews refers to Jews who fight, who are violent in the public political sphere. The term has meaning only in relation to its counterparts, which I speak of throughout these pages as weak and/or gentle Jews. With the expression "weak Jews" I refer to the image of the Jew as victim, as the frail and meek object of anti-Semitic initiatives; with gentle Jew, I have in mind those who uphold in theory and practice the conviction that Jews *must* not be violent. I am interested in the relations *between* these apparently opposite types: tough Jews on the one hand and the weak or gentle ones on the other. More immediately, I am interested in the interplay in the thinking of American Jews of historic Jewish victimization and contemporary Israeli violence, which is, of course, the most obvious of the many present-day expressions of Jewish toughness. One of the themes I want to develop in these reflections is that the tough Jew and the weak and gentle ones are not opposites but *intimates*.

The idea of Jewish toughness developed here does *not* refer to the long-standing, most often anti-Semitic stereotype of the Jew as tough in the economic sphere. Nor do I intend the term to refer to the Jewish toughness that so deeply impressed Friedrich Nietzsche, namely, toughness in the form of the capacity of Jews as a people and as individuals to endure extraordinary adversity, rejection by majorities, and persecution. Anyone interested in the full range of Jewish toughness will find the following discussion fairly narrow, though I certainly hope that what is said will justify the limited focus.

In working on this study, I often considered an objection that might be summarized as follows: Do we really need another look at and more words about the moral anguish of the Jewish soul? What of Palestinian anguish? And what, for that matter, of the dynamics of toughness and gentleness in Palestinian culture and politics? These are, I believe, serious issues to which my only response seems inadequate. I would answer that the moral anguish of the Jewish soul is worth many looks and words because it is so full of consequences, not least for Palestinians.

I write in criticism rather than in praise of tough Jews. In the hope of forestalling claims that my views exemplify Jewish self-hatred or that my anti-Zionism is anti-Semitism I offer these brief comments. We live amid an expanding global cult of toughness and a fear-ridden nationalism before which, it

seems to me, ordinary people, not to mention intellectuals—
especially in America—have capitulated. This idea of a global
cult of nationalistic toughness is expressed in the rise to prominence of Ronald Reagan, Margaret Thatcher, Ayatollah
Khomeini, and Menachem Begin, all of whom placed at the
core of their political visions the idea of toughness in just the
sense I am using it here. Thus in one respect the tough Jew
is simply a part of this larger phenomenon. In another sense,
however, tough Jews are distinctive precisely because of the
Jewish history of weakness and the Jewish claim to the moral
high ground of gentleness. This distinctive element makes the
figure of the tough Jew particularly worth analyzing not, finally, because such analysis tells us new things about Jews,
but because of what it tells us about toughness itself.

My deepest hopes in writing this book are that it will contribute to kindling thought that refuses to bow to toughness
and nationalism as the inevitable horizons of political and
social life. I willingly accept, indeed, I embrace, the label
antinationalist since I see nationalism as a curse that has been
the source of untold misery since its emergence in the French
Revolution. And when I speak of nationalism I intend not
only the nationalism of the so-called great powers, but also
that of the smaller, victimized peoples such as Jews or Palestinians: the distinction between big-nation and small-nation
nationalism is meaningful but not fundamental. In the name
of freedom, justice, and independence, nationalism has invariably bred conformity, an ideology of toughness, paranoia
in the face of difference, and violence. To think and act within
this framework is commonly referred to as realism, either by
the powers that benefit from such thinking and acting or by
intellectuals who like to serve power in its established or its
revolutionary forms.

If that framework is realistic, then these reflections should be seen as unrealistic, or more precisely as antirealistic, in trying to think through and finally transcend the framework of nationalism and toughness. This is not easy. As George Orwell showed long ago, ideas generally and words in particular are among the chief victims of modern politics. So, for example, in his successful campaign for the presidency of the United States in 1988, George Bush spoke of his desire to see a "kinder and gentler" America, and he did so in connection with a political program that is emphatically neither kind nor gentle. Similarly, the establishment of the birthday of Martin Luther King, Jr., as a national holiday can hardly be anything but a token of America's pursuit of King's pacifist and integrationist dream in the face of the negation of that dream in the massive increase of violence in our national life. I have tried to write on behalf of the victims of modern politics and in the service of gentleness.

On the matter of tough *Jews* in particular, it needs to be said that this is not a study of Israel or Zionism. Both inevitably loom large here, but more as points of reference than as objects of close analysis. I do not read Hebrew and am neither a Middle East expert nor a Jewish historian. This is, rather, a book about the thinking, feelings, and imagining of *American* Jews. If my reflections can be said to have a single thesis, it would be that a new Jewish self-image has moved to the foreground of the contemporary scene and that this new image indicates both a brutalization and an *Americanization* of Jewish political culture in this country. Or, reduced to a formula, it would be this: Tough Jews in America may at first seem not very Jewish and, in relation to Israelis, not very tough, but they are very American.

These reflections are presented in three parts. After noting the quite varied articulations of tough Jewish imagery—political, intellectual, cinematic, literary—part 1 considers tough Jewish images in America from two angles. First, it investigates relations between Jewish weakness and gentleness on one side and toughness on the other by looking closely at some fantasies about tough Jews, first of all, my own, but also those of Sigmund Freud and Philip Roth, who are themselves analysts of Jewish fantasies and characters in my own fantasies of tough Jews. My conviction is that fantasies, particularly Jewish male fantasies about bodies, are decisive in the development and itinerary of the tough Jew. Second, part 1 situates the intense and widespread emergence of tough Jewish imagery—and this book itself—in developments in American culture and politics over the past three decades.

Although part 2 reflects the American origins of this book as a whole, its focus is not limited to America. Rather, it presents a survey of general Jewish history as a history of tough Jews, as against the obvious and not altogether mistaken assumption that Jewish history is largely a story of Jewish victimization. My goal here is to debunk the assumption that I *do* believe is mistaken, namely, that Jews are by *nature* or by some religious or racial *essence* gentle or weak. With the historical sketch, however, I hope also to criticize the parallel Zionist assumption that Jews need a Jewish state in order to be tough. When I began this study, I was fairly close to both of these assumptions. I now accept neither one.

Part 3 examines some forty (mostly American) novels published during the past two decades—roughly since the 1967 Arab-Israeli War—that constitute a new subgenre of contemporary fiction: the tough Jewish novels. Though not the only expressions of Jewish toughness in America, I believe these novels are the most concentrated expression of it. They con-

front the reader with Jewish-American ambivalence and flights
from ambivalence on tough Jewish matters, and they offer a
sharp look at the processes of brutalization and Americanization. As in parts 1 and 2, so in part 3, the organizing theme
is the intertwining of Jewish defenselessness and gentleness
with Jewish toughness, and the varied political and psychological functions of that interplay.

In view of this focus, readers may be surprised to find that
the names Meir Kahane and the Jewish Defense League, certainly the most publicized of American tough Jews, appear
infrequently in these pages. That the JDL is very much in the
background here, however, does not mean that politics are.
Indeed, my exclusion of the JDL is politically motivated in
the following sense: I believe that to focus on such relatively
extreme figures would be to divert attention from the more
ordinary, mainstream, and widespread instances of American
Jewish toughness. It is, in other words, the Kahane present in
virtually all of us that really interests me.[1]

---

1. There are a number of studies of Kahane. Janet L. Dolgin's *Jewish Identity and
the JDL* (Princeton: Princeton University Press, 1977), is the work of an anthropologist
interested in the psychocultural mechanisms that structured the ethnic identities of
members of the Jewish Defense League. It pursues the story of the JDL into the early
1970s. Yair Kotler's *Heil Kahane*, trans. Edward Levin (New York: Adama Books,
1986), is anecdotal rather than analytical. Leon Wieseltier's "Kahane: The Making
of a Jewish Monster," *New Republic*, Nov. 11, 1985, 15–25, is quite the best study
available. On the more recent activities of Kahane's Jewish Defense League, see
Robert I. Friedman's articles in the *Village Voice*: "Nice Jewish Boys with Bombs:
The Return of the JDL," May 6, 1986, 21–26, and "Did This Man Kill Alex Odeh:
On the Trail of the JDL Terrorists," July 12, 1988, 19–21. On the Jewish Defense
Organization, formed in 1982 by ex-JDL members in search of tougher strategies,
see Wendy Leibowitz, "Every Jew a .22," *Present Tense*, July–August 1987, 6–14.
Robert I. Friedman's *False Prophet: Rabbi Meir Kahane, From F.B.I. Informant to
Knesset Member* (New York: Lawrence Hill books, 1990) appeared while this book
was in press.

ACKNOWLEDGMENTS

MANY YEARS of schooling taught me how private a matter writing is; working on this book showed me how social it can be. Friends and colleagues are in these pages. I can feel their presence—their ideas, inspiration, criticism, encouragement, patience, cajolings, suggestions, and also the tensions and strains among us. It is a pleasure to acknowledge their help.

Throughout their history, Jewish women have endured many things. But only Wini Breines has had to endure a husband working very slowly on, and sometimes running from, a book about tough Jewish men. As she tended to her own writing and teaching, she also made possible the completion of this work. Dedicating it to her is only a token of my gratitude not only for countless encouraging pushes and proppings-up and for an extremely helpful reading of the manuscript, but also for innumerable insights and suggestions that in major ways shaped what I have thought and written. For the attitude toward tough Jews that I develop here, Nesi and Simon Breines bear heavy responsibility. Although they often disagree sharply with many of my judgments, it is nevertheless as *their* child that I came to understand the stupidity of nationalism and the importance of gentleness. Had I not come to understand that, I would not have written this book. My parents, to and for whom I am boundlessly thankful, also scrutinized several versions of this work, providing me with extensive written commentary and much supportive conversation. From all of this I have, with pride, taken freely. My daughter, Natasha, and son, Raphael, have been sources of inspiration in ways they cannot imagine.

Tough Jews is in many respects also the outcome of three decades of discussion and friendship with George L. Mosse, who introduced me to the issues examined here, who has given me confidence when I lacked it, and whose own work, particularly *Nationalism and Sexuality: Middle-Class Morality and Sexual Norms in Modern Europe* (1985), has made me see the power of images and myths in history. Peter Weiler took time from his work on *British Labour and the Cold War* (1988) to read several drafts closely and in many places to reshape *Tough Jews* fundamentally. He also succeeded in the exacting task of teaching me the Boston College word-processing program. I have relied on him for so much. In response, he has been a fount of generosity and warmth.

For their critical readings of various drafts and for their supportive commentaries, including many major suggestions, corrections, and leads, I am deeply grateful to Rosalyn Baxandall, Jim Miller, Russell Jacoby, Anson Rabinbach, Stuart Ewen, Martin Jay, Shlomo Lambroza, Paul Piccone, Raymond McNally, Paul Buhle, John Hoberman (who is at work on a cultural history of the Jewish body), Reuven Avi-Yonah, Elizabeth Ewen (who also gave me, along with the titles of numerous tough Jewish spy novels, some especially effective criticism), and my brother, Joe Breines. Edward Said's very supportive response to an early draft was especially gratifying.

In later phases, encouragement, advice, and copious criticism of the manuscript by Sandra Joshel were particularly valuable to me. So were numerous discussions with Michael T. Gilmore, which got me to rethink my initial view of the place of the Holocaust in the story of tough Jews. I am pleased, as well, to acknowledge the support and suggestions of Mike Wilner, Allen Hunter, and of my friends at Boston College, James Cronin, Alan Rogers, Andrew Buni, Karen Potterton, Kevin O'Neill, Lawrence Wolff, Gerald T. Harvey, Lois Bilsky, Melanie Murphy, Paul Dunn, Max Pensky, and Gail Koza. Early on Eileen Farrell, a graduate student in philosophy and a consultant at the Boston College computer center, got me out of many difficulties. In the final phases Alex Wirth-Cauchon, a generous computer whiz and doctoral candidate in sociology at Boston College, was of immense assistance. In the person of Ilene P. Cohen, I was blessed with a remarkable copy editor. I am deeply grateful as well to Steve Fraser, my editor at Basic Books, who saw promise in a disjointed manuscript, challenged me to give it at least some focus and meaning, and contributed substantively to the final version.

The approaches to Jews and Jewish stereotypes in the writings of both Arthur Koestler and Philip Roth are the ones I have liked best. When I began work on this book, I was also provoked and influenced by Roberta Feuerlicht's *The Fate of the Jews: A People Torn between Israeli Power and Jewish Ethics* (1983) and Edward Said's *The Question of Palestine* (1979). By the later phases, I had been introduced to and much affected by poststructuralist feminist ideas, which were mediated to me more by conversations with Avery Gordon and Kate Gyllensvard, graduate students at Boston College, than by particular texts. George L. Mosse's *Nationalism and Sexuality* mentioned above, his *Toward the Final Solution: A History of*

European Racism (1978), Michael Bakhtin's *Rabelais and His World* (1965), Peter Stallybrass and Allon White's *The Politics and Poetics of Transgression* (1986), and Klaus Theweleit's *Male Fantasies* (1977) helped me to place bodies and fantasies about them at the center of *Tough Jews*. The assistance of all these friends and books has been so substantial that it seems ungracious to absolve any of them of responsibility for what I have written.

PART ONE

Sigmund Freud's Tough Jewish Fantasy, Philip Roth's, and Mine

Approaching Tough Jews

THE STARTING POINT of these reflections is the displacement, now under way, of two longstanding, deeply ingrained stereotypes of the Jew—the Jewish weakling and the gentle Jew—by a third, more recent (and more ancient) image, that of the tough Jew. This is a study of how and why, in American as well as in Jewish American eyes, images of Jewish wimps and nerds are being supplanted by those of the hardy, bronzed kibbutznik, the Israeli paratrooper, and the Mossad (Israeli intelligence) agent. It investigates two connected processes. There is, on one side, the waning of what could be called the Woody Allen figure, that is, the schlemiel: the pale, bespectacled, diminutive vessel of Jewish anxieties who cannot, indeed, must not, hurt a flea and whose European forebears fell by the millions to Jew-hating savagery. And there is, on the other side, the emergence in *American* culture of less whiny, more manly and muscular types, sometimes referred to as Jewish James Bonds. As part 3 considers in detail, these latter kill their enemies and take their women to bed with neurosis-free, seemingly un-Jewish alacrity, as if to avenge all

3

the helpless Jewish victims of history. These are, in other words, reflections on images or stereotypes of Jews, particularly of Jewish bodies, for the most part bodies of Jewish men—with bodies being understood as physical bearers, literally embodiments, of community experiences, fantasies, and ideals. I am interested in the political and cultural impacts of those bodies. This is a book, then, about Jewish body politics and Jewish moral identities.

This shift in images prompts reflection on the remarkable cultural fact that many young Americans, including many young American Jews, will grow up without viable images of gentle, disheveled Jewish intellectuals and saintly schlemiels. Their visual sense of who and what Jews are will instead be shaped significantly by the mostly Israeli images appearing on the television screen, in *Time* and *Newsweek*, and in the daily press: Israeli soldiers and settlers shooting, beating, or screaming at Palestinians. Regardless of how one interprets such events, it is striking that there is now emerging a generation for whom the phrase "weak Jews" will be as odd and oxymoronic as the phrase "tough Jews" would have been to previous generations of American Jews, indeed, to many Jews virtually everywhere for nearly two thousand years. Not only Palestinians, who bear the material brunt of this shift, but anyone who had internalized the ideals of Jewish gentleness and tried to sustain them will find their present erosion striking and disconcerting.

Today's scene is replete with signs of the emergence of the tough Jew. One meets the new type in Ariel Sharon's recent autobiography, *Warrior*; its dramatic back cover features a photo of the commander-author shortly after he incurred a head wound in the 1973 Yom Kippur War.[1] Or one meets

4

tough Jews by way of Israeli journalist Chaim Pearl, who commented in 1984 that "not so very long ago, the ideal picture of the Tora-observing and believing Jew was one who had great room in his heart for the pursuit of peace. He took seriously the exhortation of the rabbis to be of the disciples of Aaron, loving peace and pursuing peace." But today, Pearl continued, "that picture has drastically changed. Today the orthodox Jew is frequently represented by a young man with a full beard, knitted kippa [yarmulke], tzitziot [the fringes of the prayer vest worn by the Orthodox] hanging out, who totes a gun over his shoulder as he walks along the streets of the West Bank."[2]

Sergio Leone's film *Once upon a Time in America* (1984), starring Robert De Niro, a stylized, romanticized depiction of Jewish gangsters on New York's Lower East Side in the 1920s, and *Raid on Entebbe* (1977), the film based on the remarkable Israeli hostage rescue mission in Uganda in 1976, are among the major cinematic representations that drew their inspiration from *Exodus* (1960), the film based on Leon Uris's novel of the same title (1958). The successful and much-publicized Israeli rescue mission did more than any other single event to generate in America a full-blown myth of the Jews as nearly superhuman in their bravery, physical strength, and military skill. Tough Jewish impulses are also present throughout the pages of the influential magazines *Commentary* and the *New Republic*. In the immediate aftermath of Israel's triumph in the 1967 Arab-Israeli War, for example, Milton Himmelfarb spoke in *Commentary* of Jews learning that, while "they can be pretty good with a fountain pen and a briefcase, they can also if necessary be pretty good with a rifle and tank."[3] These words would serve as a kind of leitmotif for *Commentary*, which remains the major intellectual voice of Jewish toughness.

And those impulses find direct and substantial political articulation in organizations such as the Jewish Institute for National Security Affairs, whose advisers include Michael Ledeen, Jeane Kirkpatrick, and Jack Kemp. JINSA was formed in 1973, when the Yom Kippur War demonstrated to the founders that (as one of the group's brochures puts it,) Israel could not defend herself against the Arab nations without military resupply. All of JINSA's main activities aim at fostering an ambience and attitude of toughness: bringing major Jewish American donors to meetings with Pentagon officials, hosting retired American military officers on visits to Israel, and sponsoring various seminars and mailings that promote the idea of Israel's strategic importance.

Another political-intellectual expression of the tough Jewish theme can be found in the Jonathan Institute, a right-wing think tank that sponsors programs and publicity in the area commonly called antiterrorism. Typically that means supporting Israeli military power and fostering negative views of the Palestinian cause. The Jonathan Institute takes its name from Jonathan Netanyahu, commander of the storming unit at the Entebbe Airport in 1976. Netanyahu was killed in the assault. His brother, Benjamin Netanyahu, a founder of JINSA, was Israel's ambassador to the United Nations in the mid-1980s. He has served as a major political voice of Jewish toughness in his frequent interviews on network television.

The American Israel Public Affairs Committee, known as AIPAC, or the Jewish Lobby, is doubtless the tough Jew's most important political outlet. In the service of Israeli national security needs, AIPAC raises funds, lobbies members of Congress, supports and opposes candidates, sponsors seminars and lectures, and advises college students in the art of challenging critics of Israel on college campuses. Although Edward Tivnan does not speak of tough Jews as such, his recent analysis of AIPAC indicates that the term captures much of the Jewish Lobby's ideals, strategies, and sensibility.[4]

Tough Jews also appear in the nooks and crannies. One finds them in a recent Giant Coloring Book for children, *The Story of Chanukah*, the final page of which offers a towering depiction of Judah Maccabee. Sword at the ready, this mighty defender of the Jews bears a notable resemblance to the evil warriors of the Syrian king Antiochus who appear in the book's opening pages—an easily overlooked moment in this children's book.[5] And one comes face-to-face with tough Jewish images not only in the texts but also on the covers of the roughly forty novels of Jewish toughness examined in part 3—covers depicting the rugged faces, strong, brave glances, and athletic bodies of what is represented as a new Jewish type.

My Tough Jewish Fantasies

With an eye to clarifying the flurry of terms and issues just introduced—tough, gentle, and weak Jews, body politics, moral identity, image, stereotype, representation, as well as distinctions and connections between American and Israeli Jews—something should be said about the author of these lines. Like many readers, I am not a detached observer of the matters at hand. While bearing in mind the call of postmodern literary criticism for a skeptical approach to confession and personal testimony as paths to truth, I nevertheless choose to write in roughly those modes in part 1, out of a belief that this is the best way to introduce the assumptions, convictions, and goals of these reflections.

To start, then, a confession. In earlier drafts of this work I had sought a position outside if not above the fray. I made use of scholarly formulations here or efforts at subtle irony there in order to render invisible my own entanglement in the issues raised by the appearance on the scene of what I have called the tough Jews. I tried to stow behind rhetorical screens my ambivalence in the face of Jewish toughness. Although I rewrote the manuscript several times, I continued, until this version, to avoid exploring that ambivalence in its personal aspects. Although I have not resolved everything in the interim, I have at least come to believe that the moments I had previously considered highly private, and thus to be excluded from a work with critical, historical pretensions, are actually quite social moments and, as such, interesting forms of evidence. The personal roots and cast of this work will, I hope, encourage *all* who have things to say on the subject of tough Jews—and who has nothing to say on the subject?—to think historically and critically about *their own* experiences of stereotypes, identities, and differences, and in so doing to risk gaining in understanding and generosity what they may lose in certainty. My experiences and responses may at times be atypical or marginal; but at other times they may be representative of significant currents among Jewish Americans.

One of the connections between intellectual, political, and bodily experiences that this study tries to demonstrate was present at the moment—1982—the idea for the study was hatched from what can only be called a psychosomatic womb. At that time, a bout of insomnia had set me in search of corrective measures, one of which was a friend's prescription: regular doses of spy novels, a genre that had until then not interested me. "Even with a bad spy novel," she had said, "you don't really notice you're awake." Though it failed to restore restful sleep, my first encounter with a spy thriller—*Triple*, by Ken Follett—changed my life.[6] The hero, Nat Dickstein, is in nearly all respects the prototype of the new, tough Jewish image I am examining. His itinerary is roughly this: He lost his family to the Nazi Final Solution. He survived the death camps and made his way to Palestine after the war. By the time of the novel's main action in the late 1960s and early 1970s, Nat Dickstein is a Mossad commander. His mission is to prevent Egypt from gaining, with Soviet support, the nuclear capacity that can pose a mortal threat to Israel. In carrying out this task, Dickstein kills, often in hand-to-hand combat, a substantial number of Arab and Soviet operatives.

Follett's *Triple* turned out to be but the first of what I soon realized was a fictional subgenre: the tough Jewish novel. I have gathered more than forty, only a portion of which are spy thrillers. Others include historical novels about both ancient Jewish warriors and modern Zionist ones, family sagas running from the Jewish Pale of Settlement in tsarist Russia in 1890 through Manhattan's Lower East Side in 1910 and Palestine in the 1940s, to Scarsdale, New York in the 1970s, and so forth. The unifying element is the positive, often highly idealized, representation of tough Jewish characters. One finds the imagery of Jewish toughness articulated across a broad cultural and political field, but it is in these novels that the tough Jew finds his, and often her, most sustained and detailed expression. Part 3 of this study attends in detail to the tough Jewish novels.

The present reflections were generated by Nat Dickstein's numerous killings, by the importance—in the novel—of bodies, and by the present author's ambivalence. Follett's novel set off what I would call my own personal primal tough Jew experience. The crux of it—a token both of Follett's skill as a spy novelist and of all that I brought to the reading of *Triple*—was that I was seduced by Nat Dickstein. I delighted in his killings and warmed in ways I was neither prepared for nor pleased with to the great and, in my eyes, altogether un-Jewish exploits of this remarkably lethal Jew. The achievements of Dickstein's Jewish body brought on adrenalin rushes and raised goose bumps of excitement. This arousal—it amounted to that—was as lively as my understanding of its intensely ideological, even racist, source. I was aware that the other bodies in the novel, those of the largely incidental Russian and the more central Egyptian characters, were the stock figures of Anglo-American cold war ideology and Arab-fearing bigotry and were thus nonpersons even before Dickstein did them in. Yet as Dickstein finished them off, I experienced a visceral pleasure.

I have noted that Dickstein was in *nearly* all respects a prototype of the new tough Jew. I emphasize *nearly* because he is, in fact, atypical in one respect, namely, physically. Among contemporary images of tough Jews, Dickstein's body is distinguished by its insignificance, its near frailty: he is approaching his fifties, balding, with a smallish, if wiry, body. He is far from the essentially Greco-Aryan model of masculinity typical of much of the imagery of Jewish toughness, a model examined in part 2 (pp. 139–67). Rather, Follett's hero looks the part, not of a new Jewish warrior, but of an earlier, even slightly meek Jewish victim. His name is notable in this regard as well. As Follett depicts him, one imagines—because one has been culturally conditioned to imagine—precisely a Nat Dickstein rather than an Ari Ben Canaan, the complete, tough Jewish hero of Leon Uris's vaunted *Exodus*. Ben Canaan is the beast to Dickstein's gnat. With a Dickstein one imagines a clarinet; with a Ben Canaan, a trumpet. One of Dickstein's arms bears the tattooed number from the Nazi camp. I do not know if Follett had in mind a model for his hero. In any event, I brought to the book a model of my own choice: Isaac Bashevis Singer. My mind's eye read the Jewish storywriter and novelist into the figure of Nat Dickstein.

Reading the Polish-born, Yiddish American writer into Nat Dickstein is an imaginative and a moral strategy. Singer, the writer, had created an unmatched galaxy of gentle Jewish characters, and he himself seems the very essence of Jewish gentleness—in the author photos on the dust jackets of his books and in his public lectures and occasional essays on mysticism, vegetarianism, pacifism, and Yiddish as a language peculiarly expressive of today's frightened humanity. The merger of the images of Singer and Nat Dickstein resulted in the gentle and tough Jew in one, the schlemiel as terminator. This particular fusion was neither arbitrary nor odd. In 1982, when I encountered Follett's *Triple*, Singer was at the peak of his popularity. (His best-selling novel *Shosha* had appeared in 1978, and in the same year he received the Nobel Prize in literature.) It was a fashionable time to be reading Singer, and I was reading him with great enthusiasm, above all the hymns to the ethos of Jewish gentleness sung by many of his stories and novels.

Yet at just that moment, I experienced the lure of the anti-Singer: Nat Dickstein. This was unsettling for an educated, nonreligious, non-Zionist, middle-aged, middle-class male American Jew on the political Left who had ingested as a youth and continued to cherish as an adult ideals of gentleness and nonviolence, seeing them as *the* Jewish values par excellence. Nevertheless, my agitated identification with Nat Dickstein should not be seen as surprising or unusual. Such a response, after all, is precisely the aim of any successful spy or action thriller, namely, to create an atmosphere of suspenseful sadism that draws the reader into a clash between good (in this case, the Israeli, the Jew) and evil (Arabs, communism, anti-Semitism) on the side of the former.

My response to Follett's Nat Dickstein was also in keeping with what has amounted to a mass phenomenon among American Jews. And here I make this study's pivotal assumption that not only is my particular primal, tough Jew experience— my seduction by Nat Dickstein—not unique, but it is today virtually a *pan-Jewish experience*. I assume that my private excitement was a piece of a collective excitement; that all Jews, as it were, have their Dickstein. In my reaction to *Triple*, I was sharing a passion for toughness among American Jews that has ruptured the nearly two-millennia-old Jewish cultural heritage based almost entirely on persecution, physical and military weakness, and principles of gentleness. Because I have thought much about my own tough Jewish fantasies and because they are in at least some respects representative, I will use them as one among several case studies to receive extended comment.

Thus, these pages reflect on the passion of the primal, tough Jew experience, on what could be called the Jewish goose bumps, the Jewish adrenalin of revenge and power induced by the world's Nat Dicksteins. I investigate that passion—here is a secondary assumption—because in important ways it shapes a vital segment of contemporary world affairs: the Middle East and the role of the United States there. Yet, for all its importance, that passion is a virtually invisible factor, barely recognized, not discussed, as if there were an unwritten but widely endorsed prohibition on speaking of such things. My argument, then, is that when American Jews (and non-Jews) talk or write about such topics as Israel, the Jewish Holocaust, anti-Semitism, world politics, Arabs, the Middle East, U.S. policies, terrorism, or relations between Jews and blacks in America, they are also speaking with the passions aroused by images of tough and weak Jewish bodies that come into play in the primal, tough Jew experience. They are not, in other words, speaking only on the basis of rational political interests and aims. I would argue further that to speak and write as if those passions were above scrutiny and criticism because of the history of Jewish victimization, is to contribute (perhaps unwittingly, in which case, all the more unfortunately) to the brutality of the present. One of the goals of this study is to lessen that contribution.

Admittedly, 1982 was an odd year for a first tough Jewish awakening. It came so late in my life. And that was the year that the Israeli invasion of Lebanon and the Israeli role in the mass murder of Palestinians in the Sabra and Shatilla refugee camps opened, for the first time since 1967, some cracks in the consensus of American Jewish enthusiasm for Israeli military might. After Sabra and Shatilla, even a few Jewish American devotees of Israeli toughness began raising some questions. Nonetheless, what had eluded me at the age of seven, when Israel was founded, and again at twenty-six, with Israel's victory in the June 1967 Six Day War, when the largest number of American Jews were drawn to Israel's Jewish toughness, finally struck me in 1982, at the age of forty-one.

One could certainly object to my assumption that every Jew, surely every American Jew, is going to have his or her primary, tough Jew experience. But that is what I assume: that every Jew today has some sort of primal, tough Jew, or Nat Dickstein, experience, not as a matter of nature or destiny, but as a matter of history, politics, and culture. My *questions* concern what to *do* with the experience once one has it, for have it every American Jew—and some non-Jews as well—will. My own intense response to Nat Dickstein was not only late in coming, it was also brief, lasting only for some days. The moment was indeed jarring and not without ambivalence, arousing in me feelings about being a Jew I had not known I had. The experience resulted, however, not in an enduring commitment to the Jewish toughness of the Mossad, of Israel, but in this book.

Consider the specifics of my infatuation with Nat Dickstein, the specifics, that is, of my ambivalence. His impact on me was not simple. He attracted *and* repelled, but in both instances for the same reason: my own commitment to the ideals of gentleness. At the immediate politico-ideological level, then, Dickstein's violence and ruthlessness should be repellent. The gentle Jew condemns him. Promptly, however, the gentle Jew (this particular gentle Jew) is dazzled by the force of Dickstein's phenomenal success in this violent and ruthless world—the world before whose blows Jews had for centuries fallen, help-lessly, even pathetically. My very commitment to the ideals of gentleness violated by Dickstein made me, at least for an important moment, *more* rather than less open to the appeal of his transgressions, to his Jewish toughness and violence.

For it was not from the outside but from within me that a voice drove the argument toward its logical conclusion: What did gentleness, generosity, or kindness ever do for those count-less Jewish victims? What is truly pathetic is not the Jews who fell defenselessly to the Jew haters, but the very principles of gentleness and nonviolence. Had there been fewer like me and more Dicksteins in Europe after 1933, or in Odessa in

1900, or at the time of the Crusades . . . Shamed by this inner voice and thus feeling the pull of Nat Dickstein, the avenging angel, I wavered.

And then I capitulated, thrilling to the brutal melody of Dickstein's executions. But my elation at having been liberated from the albatross of a conscience and a mildness that could save no lives was short-lived. It may even have been tainted by conscience from the outset, for my imagination, guided by my conscience, changed the novel's Egyptian and Soviet agents into embodiments of every anti-Semite that ever lived and Dickstein's killings into acceptable, even admirable examples of retributive justice. I want to emphasize that this was an act of *conscience* in a double sense: the action was carried out by conscience, and conscience was, in effect, putting on an act by fooling itself into thinking it was still a conscience.

This imaginative reading strategy has two broad components that mesh well together. First, the transfiguration of Arab and Soviet characters into universal Jew haters means that such characters simply *cannot* represent a legitimate cause or interest. As embodiments of every anti-Semite who ever lived, they simply must be killed. Second, there is my blending of Nat Dickstein and Isaac Bashevis Singer, which unifies a fictional tough Jewish character and a living creator of fictional characters, the finest of whom are gentle Jews who bear no moral resemblance to Nat Dickstein. But *Triple*'s description of Mossad commander Dickstein could easily be used of Singer as well: "He was a thin man, small-boned, with narrow shoulders, a shallow chest, and knobby elbows and knees" (p. 34). Follett encourages this sort of imaginary rewriting by placing a virtual golem, or Jewish superhero, into the body of an apparent weakling. So clever a fusion of the old, frail and the new, fighting Jew almost necessitates further imaginings by readers, especially readers like myself, who bring to a book such as Follett's a great need for such revisions.

My own particular revision required Isaac Bashevis Singer. For me to accept and eventually embrace Nat Dickstein, he *had* to become Isaac Bashevis Singer, and my need for a Singerized Dickstein only mirrored the ideological necessity within the novel itself. For if Dickstein is to have any moral stature at all, he must have the body of a schlemiel, of a victim. Only such a body—those "narrow shoulders, . . . shallow chest, and knobby elbows and knees"—can imbue Dickstein's killings with some sort of moral sanction. For that *body* crystallizes the history of hapless Jewish suffering. Only such a body could vindicate Dickstein's actions, transfiguring him from a killer who is merely highly skilled into one who is moral as well.

If he embodies the *whole* history of Jewish suffering, looking very much like the next victim, Dickstein is, in particular, the living embodiment of those, including his own family, who had fallen to the Nazis. One of his wiry arms bears the brand of the death camp, as does his heart, which for much of the novel is closed to the calls of love. In my reading of *Triple*, Dickstein embodies the Jewish victims of Nazism in another sense as well: his "narrow shoulders, . . . shallow chest, and knobby elbows and knees" transform him into one of the skeletons come to life from the piles of skeletons, from one of the seemingly countless visual documentations of the Jewish Holocaust that I had seen and internalized over many years. The body of Follett's Mossad commander is suggestive; indeed, it is a metaphor for the most potent Jewish bodily image of all— the Jewish corpse in the Nazi death camp. This may seem to be a hallucinatory reading of *Triple*, but in many respects the entire web of relations between tough and weak, or gentle, Jewish stereotypes *is* overshadowed by Nazism's dead Jewish bodies.

Dickstein is at once that image and its cancellation. He will not be the next victim; on the contrary, he is the Jewish skeleton enlivened, armed, and ready to kill. He is the deadly dead Jew, his skeletonlike body full of lethal surprises for the anti-Semites. Dickstein will kill them, often and deftly. Part of me accepted, even embraced, this. For to *see* Nat Dickstein as a skeleton awakened from the heaps of the dead at Auschwitz or Treblinka is to extend moral efficacy, or at least moral acceptability, to his killings of Arabs and Russians. Whether intentionally or not, Follett has surely persuaded many a reader, Jewish and not, that the still-visible blue numbers on Nat Dickstein's arm are his *license to kill*: after Auschwitz, *no one* can tell Jews what is or is not moral.

To put the matter bluntly, this strategy of justification, which evokes the Holocaust's Jewish corpses in order to rationalize Israel's Palestinian corpses, is a most ironic result of the Holocaust. I know the strategy firsthand. Look how automatically I summoned up the images of Jewish corpses from Nazi death camps while reading Follett's *Triple*, even as the Israelis were invading Lebanon. And this strategy is familiar to other Jews as well. No less a figure than Israeli Prime Minister Menachem Begin reasoned basically as I did in connection with the bombing of West Beirut in the summer of 1982: Beirut was Berlin, and Yasser Arafat in the PLO quarters of the Lebanese city was Hitler hiding in the secret bunker in Berlin as the Allies advanced. To be sure, this caused a stir, as numerous Israeli and some American Jews rejected his claims as erroneous and cynical, which they are. My assumption is nevertheless that even Jews who expressly reject

Begin's distortions, myself among them, are *not* deaf to them.
On the contrary, we are attentive. My goal here is to challenge
that attentiveness, which I believe is a source of much trouble.

Such casuistry is, moreover, an integral part of the primal,
tough Jew experience, the sign of the tough Jew's ambivalence,
which can be summarized this way: The trauma of Nazi mass
murder made the Jewish yearning for toughness especially
strong, while nearly two thousand years of self-definition according to an ethos of meekness and gentleness made toughness
unacceptable. Unwilling to reject either fully, the Israeli and
the post-Holocaust American Jew have sought to have *both*.
They want, in Israel, a moral *Machtstaat*, a conquerer state
with a conscience; they want to subordinate others or to kill
while themselves remaining the chosen people, "a light unto
the nations."

To a large extent, this is what I sought, and found, in *Triple*.
By blending Singer and Dickstein, I vindicated both. That is,
Dickstein, who derives moral capital from his frail body, is
purified further by my infusion of Singer, the physically weak
and philosophically gentle Jew. And the other side of this
relationship—that the weakness of the Singer figure, his *failure
to protect* the Jews, is vindicated by being made powerful and
tough through the merger with Dickstein—plays an equally
decisive role in the primal, tough Jewish experience. I believe
that many Jews are ambivalent not only about being tough
and violent but also about their own commitment to the principles of gentleness that the Jewish people are often said, and
often claim, to embody, indeed, have historically exemplified
in many ways.

Triple triggered childhood and teenage memories that exemplify some of this ambivalence toward gentleness. This is
a testament to Follett's craft, but the very fact that his novel

evokes memories of long-lost *formative* moments is itself also an index of the intensity of what is apparently my quite modest tough Jew experience. Through osmotic rather than directly instructive processes—to turn now to the content of one such memory—I not only understood that Jews do not engage in physical fights, but I understood that this in effect summarized for our secular home what it meant to be Jewish at all, namely, to be rational, kind to others, and not violent.

I also recall, however, the sense of excitement and security I felt at the age of seven or eight, when my father, sleeves rolled up, exposing to my view quite sizable (and untattooed) forearms, strode from our house to challenge an infamous neighborhood crank who had been intimidating my playmates and me. To the best of my recollection, anti-Semitism played no role in the episode, but I nevertheless *perceived* it as having Jewish significance, as being a kind of test of our Jewish mettle—this in the mind of a boy with no religious training in a home that was more interested in Henry Wallace's presidential campaign than in the founding of Israel. As I listened to the shouting between the two men, I knew that if things came to blows, not only would my father return them, but he would surely vanquish our tormentor, who, as it happened, was repulsed, scowling, prior to actual fisticuffs. I never discussed the matter with my father.

This memory suggests that Oedipal dynamics played a role in my later attraction to Nat Dickstein; I may have been drawn to Dickstein/Israel as a son to a powerful and protective father. Yet, if such dynamics were operative in drawing me to Dickstein, they were doubtless operative in my fairly prompt rejection of him as well. This brings me to a different, if still Oedipal, aspect of my memory of my father as a tough Jew, namely, to what it suggests about Jews', at least some Jews', ambivalence toward their own principles of gentleness. My father actively joined my mother in imparting those principles to me, yet he was not prepared to be supine. For my part, I did not find this at all inconsistent. Rather, I took great pleasure in my father's behavior, his evident readiness to fight physically to protect his child. It did not trouble my sensibilities that this behavior was at variance with the nonviolent, gentle norms that guided our family.

My enthusiasm for what seemed to me my father's heroism and my lack of concern for the inconsistencies both sprang from hidden doubts about the nonviolent values I accepted without question. Those doubts arose from fear, from a small boy's recognition that the refusal to fight was not a value shared by everyone else in the neighborhood. For me as a child, especially a Jewish child, then, my father offered protection, an alternative to intimidation, and security. This childhood memory was retrieved with Dickstein; he (and a powerful Israel) offers to Jews the same benefits my father once provided. The childhood memory in turn intensified my attachment to Dickstein (and to Israel) by linking him with my very deep emotional layers.

Follett's novel also recalled my one more or less serious fight as a youth of fourteen or fifteen. It took place on the playing field of my suburban school. What began as a playful wrestle turned into a real and unnervingly hostile battle. Painful and frightening, it was also—certainly in memory—compelling. The fear and tears; the suddenness of being where my values said not to be; madly working not to be subdued; the grunting, muddy physicalness of the situation; and the fact that I finally managed to pin my friend to the ground all left me quite pleased to have acted wrongly, that is, in so unJewish a manner, by fighting.

As in the previous childhood episode I recalled while reading *Triple*, so this one ostensibly had nothing to do with Jewish matters. But for me it *was* a Jewish matter. My friend was Catholic, and although he was a good friend, it occurred to me during our fight that I could be adversely affected by both the reputed anti-Semitism of Catholics and the Jews' reputed avoidance of, and lack of skill in, physical combat. I was sure a Jew would do badly in a fight. I recall as well returning home, unable to hide my muddied, disheveled, and bruised appearance and sheepish about my pleasure in the battle's outcome. And finally I recall that my parents shared the pleasure, for all their looks of concern. It is, of course, the same compellingly perverse pleasure I felt on reading of Nat Dickstein's battles. Like its Proustian prototype, Follettian recall is always coherent.

Although it is even smaller in scale and lightly amusing, the third of my *Triple*-provoked recollections is no less exemplary than the others as an indication of the ambivalence of the American Jew. Again, my father is the central figure. It was 1953 or '54, and I was roughly twelve or thirteen years old. My younger brother and I were the principal watchers of our family's first television set. My father, an architect and an avid reader, indulged only occasionally. Yet, whenever "Texas Rasslin" (the forerunner of today's televised professional wrestling extravaganzas) featured the one Israeli among its stable of fighters, my brother and I, aware of the irony in our rational-minded and peaceful father's enthusiasm for a wrestler, would summon him to the screen. Once seated, his attention was riveted and, like the black listeners to the broadcasts of the Louis-Schmeling fights, he would move with each of his hero's feints and leaps, wincing with each blow or fall his hero took, as if the fate of his people lay in the balance. Again, I recalled my father's display of the gentle Jew's secret enthusiasm for Jewish violence because I was feeling the same secret enthusiasm for Dickstein's exploits.

Philip Roth's Minimal Fantasy

To pursue further the matter of Jewish ambivalence toward gentleness (and the role within it of father-son dynamics), I take the immodest step of comparing notes with Philip Roth and Sigmund Freud. In his recent novel, *The Counterlife*, Roth acerbically registers the ambivalence and its apparent resolution. The voice belongs to Shuki Elchanan, a not altogether disillusioned left-leaning Zionist intellectual, here angrily interpreting what he deems the representative response of American Jews to the Israeli scene: " 'The American Jews get a big thrill from the guns. They see Jews walking around with guns and they think they're in paradise. Reasonable people with a civilized repugnance for violence and blood, they come on tour from America, and they see the guns and they see the beards, and they take leave of their senses. The beards to remind them of saintly Yiddish weakness and the guns to reassure them of heroic Hebrew force.' "[7]

Follett's *Triple* indicates that American Jews need not travel to Jerusalem and circulate among the Israel Defense Forces and Hasidic rabbis in order "to take leave of their senses." Indeed, Nat Dickstein is available now at the neighborhood bookstore, in a "two for one" sale: he gives you both "saintly Jewish weakness" *and* "heroic Hebrew force." The divided American Jewish conscience to which Roth's Elchanan refers is not unhappily divided at all. Far from being troubled over it, significant numbers of American Jews are in fact elated with what is often seen as a uniquely Jewish fusion of violent tough-ness and victimization that yields a new position, one that is at the same time protected and morally elevated. This is, of course, the same strategy I employed in identifying with Dick-stein's achievements. And the strategy is at the heart of the dynamics of tough Jewish consciousness. For the divided con-sciousness, the ambivalence, is quite *functional*. This is central to my argument, that the ambivalence lends great flexibility to the moral foundation of Jewish American support for Israel.

The ambivalence observed by Elchanan is present as well in Roth's own youth. In *The Facts: A Novelist's Autobiography* (1988), Roth, a genius of Jewish stereotypes, recalls how he and his pals at Weequahic High School used to flee from the anti-Semitic violence perpetrated by toughs from neighboring, non-Jewish schools in Newark, New Jersey, at the end of the 1940s. Not only did such experiences *not* arouse in Roth a hunger for tough Jews or Jewish revenge, but they seem rather to have sustained his allegiances to what he considered then, and evidently still considers, to be the Jewish ideals of non-violence and gentleness. "The collective memory of Polish and Russian pogroms," he writes, "had fostered in most of our families the idea that our worth as human beings, even perhaps our distinction as a people, was embodied in the *incapacity* to perpetrate the sort of bloodletting visited upon our ancestors" (emphasis in original).[8]

He then reports on what appears to have been the start of his own youthful tough Jew experience:

For awhile during my adolescence I studiously followed prizefight-ing, could recite the names and weights of all the champions and contenders, and even subscribed briefly to *Ring*, Nat Fleischer's colorful boxing magazine. As kids my brother and I had been taken by our father to the local boxing arena, where invariably we all had a good time. From my father and his friends I heard about the prowess of Benny Leonard, Barney Ross, Max Baer, and the clown-ishly nicknamed Slapsie Maxie Rosenbloom. (p. 28)

For the young Roth, the appeal of Jewish pugilists was apparently weak, however; even more than my own, his tough Jewish experience was fleeting. For he continues:

And yet Jewish boxers and boxing aficionados remained, like boxing itself, "sport" in the bizarre sense, a strange deviation from the norm and interesting largely for that reason: in the world whose values first formed me, unrestrained physical aggression was considered contemptible everywhere else. I could no more smash a nose with a fist than fire a pistol into someone's heart. And what imposed this restraint, if not on Slapsie Maxie Rosenbloom, then on me, was my being Jewish. In my scheme of things, Slapsie Maxie Rosenbloom was a more miraculous Jewish phenomenon by far than Dr. Albert Einstein. (p. 28)

Gestural though it is in its muted and transitory form, Roth's youthful fascination with Jewish boxers nevertheless registers precisely the ambivalence toward gentleness and nonviolence I have been underlining.

Sigmund Freud's Tough Jewish Fantasy

Quite different from Roth's is what is surely the most renowned recollection of a childhood tough Jew experience and a most emphatic instance of Jewish ambivalence toward gentleness, namely, Sigmund Freud's "cap in the mud" story. It appears in chapter 5 ("The Material and Sources of Dreams") of *The*

Interpretation of Dreams (1899) and highlights the ways in which episodes from one's childhood find their way, often in well-concealed form, into adult dreams. In this context, Freud turns his attention to what are known as the "Rome dreams" for having been occasioned by his own anxious anticipation of a trip to Rome. His concerns were in part those of a Jew (with a passion for Roman and Christian histories and myths) about to enter the capital of the Roman Empire and the center of Catholicism—the heart of two cultures not known for their friendly treatment of Jews. Freud's report thus reminds us more vividly than even Roth's (and certainly than my own childhood recollections) that tough Jewish episodes are as interesting and as important as they are—indeed, occur at all—only because there is fear and hatred of Jews in the first place. He reminds one that outside the history of anti-Semitism there are no tough Jews; nor are there weak ones, either.

In the context of the dreams connected to his impending trip, then, Freud writes of

the event in my youth whose power was still being shown in all these emotions and dreams. I may have been ten or twelve years old, when my father began to take me with him on his walks and reveal to me in his talk his views upon things in the world we live in. Thus it was, on one such occasion, that he told me a story to show me how much better things were now than they had been in his days. "When I was a young man," he said, "I went for a walk one Saturday in the streets of your birthplace; I was well dressed, and had a new fur cap on my head. A Christian came up to me and with a single blow knocked off my cap into the mud and shouted: 'Jew! get off the pavement.'" "And what did you do?" I asked. "I went into the roadway and picked up my cap," was his quiet reply. This struck me as *unheroic conduct on the part of the big, strong man who was holding the little boy by the hand.* I contrasted this situation with another which *fitted my feelings better*: the scene in which Hannibal's father, Hamilcar Barca, made his boy swear before the household altar to take vengeance on the Romans. Ever since that time Hannibal had had a place in my phantasies. [emphasis added][9]

Freud identifies with the bold and tough Hannibal not only because the "semitic general," as Freud calls him, was valiant, but because Hannibal had also had several abortive journeys to Rome. The account offers a sharp glimpse into the psychological dynamics of what I have been calling the primal, tough Jewish experience, which arises from anti-Semitic persecution and Jewish fears of it. What is of great interest here is that Freud's father, whose thoughts we have only through his son's presentation, evidently did *not* consider his own behavior unheroic. On the contrary, he appears to have considered it entirely reasonable, very much what any self-respecting Jew would have done. Had he known the story would make him appear to be unheroic in his own son's eyes, Jakob Freud would not likely have chosen it as a vehicle of paternal instruction. Had the father learned of the son's Hannibal fantasy, moreover, he might well have found it quite un-Jewish. This is one of the historical aspects of Freud's story toward which he is largely oblivious.

Jakob Freud's behavior would very likely have been repeated by the great majority of Jews not only in the mid-1860s in eastern Europe, but in Sigmund Freud's own Vienna in 1899, in Spinoza's Amsterdam in the seventeenth century, in Rabbi Jacob ben Meir's France in the twelfth century, or, for that matter, in Philip Roth's Newark in the 1940s. Jakob Freud's behavior was guided by the norms and ideals of gentleness that had been regnant among Jews for centuries, norms of nonviolent mildness and restraint considered to be the most appropriate Jewish response to Gentile bestiality. The altogether *typical* character of Jakob Freud's behavior should serve as a reminder that the ideals of the meek and gentle Jew are central in any study of tough Jews. It reminds us as well that under discussion here is the phenomenon of the Jews' ambivalence toward the very ideals of gentleness they embrace. In Freud, who is profoundly disappointed by his father's "unheroic" behavior, the ambivalence had clearly become a more single-minded discontent with Jewish gentleness. By contrast, the elder Freud appears to have had rather little ambivalence, but for the opposite reason, namely, that he had no doubts regarding Jewish ideals of restraint and nonviolence.

But what if he did have such doubts, even if, as it seems, he never communicated them to his son? Speculative as the effort may be, I want to probe Jakob Freud's hypothetically divided mind regarding Jewish gentleness in order to highlight the extent to which the image of the tough Jew, by virtue of its very otherness, has always *appealed* to the weak or gentle Jews who rejected it. It is curious that although Freud's father acted (as the son saw matters) unheroically and my own acted in a notably more Hannibal-like manner, in both instances, the outcome was the same: the sons yearned for Jewish toughness. Or, to put the matter differently, the tough Jew had *never* been essentially foreign or unfamiliar to Jews. The tough Jew is a Jewish figure even though he may appear only in the form of a yearning.

Could it be that Jakob Freud envisaged a Hannibal of his own or imagined himself his own Hannibal, if only for a fleeting moment of reflection? In *The Golem Remembered*, 1909–1980: *Variations of a Jewish Legend*, for example, Arnold L. Goldsmith notes that "throughout their history, the Jews of the Diaspora looked for heroic figures who could mitigate their suffering and lead them to the messianic redemption their religion taught them to expect." Goldsmith examines twentieth-century literary versions of the greatest example of such longings: the tale of the golem. Near the end of the sixteenth century, against a backdrop of intense persecution of the Jews of Moravia, the revered rabbi of Prague, Judah Loew, is said to have employed kabbalistic formulas to call into being what amounted to a tough Jewish redeemer, the golem, a mystical force materially incarnated from clay as a gigantic Jewish genie capable of beating back the tormentors of the Jews.[10]

Or might Jakob Freud not have had feelings similar to those of Jews in Poland in the 1660s, when the extraordinary Jewish messianic movement led by Sabbatai Zevi blossomed in the period following the pogroms led by Bogdan Chmielnitski's Cossack brigades? For Zevi had resurrected as a prophetic forerunner of his own battles the figure of Simon Bar Kokhba, the warrior who led the last of the Jewish revolts against the Romans in the second century A.D. Some participants believed that Bar Kokhba's soul had been reincarnated in Sabbatai Zevi. Gershom Scholem, the great historian of the Sabbataian movement, suggests that although talmudic legend insisted that the ancient fighter had been executed on orders from the sages, "popular tradition did not subscribe to the rabbinic disparagement of Bar Kokhba's memory. He remained a kind of hero-saint . . . and kabbalists . . . rehabilitated the messianic dignity of his soul."[11]

As regards Jakob Freud, I assume that he *did* have fantasies of this type; indeed, in one or another form, every Jew does. Had the elder Freud's son later been more interested in the Jewish and historical dimensions of the "cap in the mud" story than in its psychoanalytic dimensions, he might have pursued, or at least wondered about, his father's fantasies. There may, of course, be sound psychoanalytic explanation of why Sigmund Freud chose not to fantasize about his father's fantasies; namely, to have done so would have called to the son's attention the extent to which he might have *resembled* his father. For after all, as he himself unintentionally emphasizes, he did not actually confront the anti-Semite who insulted his father. He turned instead to a Hannibal, to a tough Jewish *fantasy* in which he contrasted his father's story with "another which fitted my feelings better. . . . Ever since that time Hannibal had had a place in my phantasies."

For a Politics of Gentleness

My point is to *emphasize* not to minimize the significance of fantasy, yearning, or desire. I remarked above that the figure of the tough Jew is Jewish *even* when he appears only as a yearning or as a fantasy. From the standpoint of the historically dominant (if presently eroding) ideal of Jewish gentleness, however, this claim would have to be revised to read as follows: the tough Jew is Jewish *only* when the tough Jew appears as fantasy or yearning—only when the Jew who yearns to let the Jew hater have it *refrains* from entering the Gentile world of violence and refuses to renounce ethics for brute force. According to the gentle Jew, in other words, the tough Jew is not really Jewish.

When I began this study, I was an insistent partisan of that view. Israeli behavior toward Palestinians and American Jewish fantasies about that behavior, for example, seemed to me not merely cruel and stupid, but fundamentally un-Jewish. I can no longer agree with the last point. For as I tried to unravel my own reactions to Nat Dickstein, I found myself less and less able to accept the conviction that Jews are *essentially* gentle, nonviolent, nonmartial. These reflections themselves amount to an extended explanation of this change of perspective, and they thus conclude with remarks on what I would substitute for the conviction about Jewish gentleness.

In rethinking this conviction, it is worth recognizing its historicity, which is the aspect of the "cap in the mud" story that Freud had neglected. The first matter to note is that Jakob and Sigmund Freud, father and son, were both very Jewish men, but precisely in the years between Sigmund's birth (1856) and the publication of *The Interpretation of Dreams* (1899) notions of what it meant to be Jewish changed radically. Indeed, Sigmund Freud's revision of the "cap in the mud" story is itself both a reflection and a constituent element of those changes. While Jakob Freud correctly observed a decline, at least in a city such as Vienna, in the personal anti-Semitic assaults of the sort he had spoken of to his son, neither he nor any of his contemporaries anticipated the gestation in the 1890s of highly politicized anti-Semitic mass movements. The Vienna in which Freud had grown up was, in fact, one of the seedbeds of such movements, which were laying the ideological foundations for Hitler's Nazism. Paris, site in the mid-1890s of the extraordinary Dreyfus Affair, was another. From this maelstrom of xenophobic nationalisms, moreover, Zionism also emerged.

The decades around 1900 in Europe constituted a turning point in the history of tough Jews: Zionism amounts to *the* historic break with the culture of Jewish meekness and gentleness and the beginnings of a tough Jewish counterculture. (This whole development will be addressed in more depth in part 2). Freud's reworking of the "cap in the mud" story is itself part of this historic rupture and is also nurtured by it.

He was not alone in having lost patience with the deferential model; nor was he unique in his search for "another which suited my feelings better." His disappointment on learning of his father's behavior was not that of an isolated son; it was the feeling of a generation—in any case, a vocal portion of a generation—of European Jews. In this context Zionism was a collective Hannibal.

We appear to have moved, at last, beyond Jewish ambivalence into the more univocal and decisive world of Zionism, but the move is only apparent. One must acknowledge Freud's ambivalent relation to Zionism, our focus here, not to mention the rich complexity of his relations to Jewish matters generally. We have just seen both Freud's yearning for Jewish conduct more befitting "the big, strong man who was holding the little boy by the hand" and his fulfillment of the wish through an identification with Hannibal. We know, too, that Freud had a number of dreams in which he identified with no less a figure than Moses and that he also dreamt of his Viennese contemporary, Theodor Herzl, the founder of the Zionist movement, as a modern Moses.[12] Moreover, according to Marthe Robert's fine study of Freud's "Jewish identity," "though his interest in the Jewish homeland was neither militant nor public, it was deeply ingrained."[13]

At the same time, however, serious reservations kept Freud from Zionism. One that is especially fascinating concerns the role of fantasy, dream, and image in politics and society. In a 1913 interview with Hans Herzl, the son of Theodor Herzl, Freud commented: "Your father is one of those people who have turned dreams into reality. This is a very rare and dangerous breed. It includes the Garibaldis, . . . the Herzls. . . . I would simply call them the sharpest opponents of my scientific work." Freud meant, as William McGrath aptly notes, that the Herzls did the opposite of what Freud himself did. In Freud's words: "It is my modest profession to simplify dreams, to make them clear and ordinary. [The Garibaldis and Herzls] on the contrary, confuse the issue, turn it upside down, command the world while they themselves remain on the other side of the psychic mirror. It is a group specializing in the realization of dreams. I deal in psychoanalysis; they deal in psychosynthesis."[14] This brilliant and poignant insight applies not only to Herzl but, no less sharply, to the leaders of the larger wave of generally anti-Semitic mass political movements of the turn of the century.[15] Herzl himself, who will be discussed more fully in part 2, would likely have agreed with Freud's remark on their differences, although his own evaluation of them would of course have contrasted radically with Freud's.

What finally interests me about Freud's insights into Zionism, however, is a less-visible dimension of his thinking. To get at it, I propose to examine Freud's criticism of Zionism as a dangerous politics of "psychosynthesis" in relation to the "cap in the mud" story. In connecting these two moments of Freud's thinking, we immediately catch a sharp glimpse into our main theme: the dynamics, particularly the ambivalence, of the tough Jew experience. Freud's "cap in the mud" story reveals a man with tough Jewish yearnings, deeply discontented with his father's deferential behavior in the face of anti-Semitism, and moved by a real passion for an alternative. "Ever since that time," he had written in 1899, "Hannibal had had a place in my phantasies." If we emphasize the name of Hannibal, we meet Freud, the incipient tough Jew, fantasizing vengeance on the anti-Semites. If we emphasize instead the final phrase, "in my phantasies," we notice that his later (1913) criticism of Herzl and Zionism was *already present* even when he was in a maximally tough Jewish mood (and conversely, in a mood of minimal attachment to the moorings of Jewish gentleness or meekness).

We gain something else as well when we put the "cap in the mud" story alongside Freud's subsequent critique of Zionism: *Freud himself becomes an image*, an image like those others that constitute my own tough Jewish experience with *Triple*. The founder of psychoanalysis has entered my galaxy of tough and gentle Jewish character images, which includes Dickstein, Isaac Bashevis Singer, my father, and myself in the playground fight. I *imagine* Freud, not as a man of action like Dickstein, Hannibal, or my father, but as a man imagining; imagining such things as his father, the "cap in the mud" story, Hannibal—and thinking (thinking *in* images and *about* them). It becomes clear that I very much need Freud here. Like Isaac Bashevis Singer and me (but unlike Nat Dickstein), Freud is an intellectual, a writer. That common ground noted, however, my Freud and my Singer follow different paths. Where I had been able, with little difficulty, to blend Singer into Nat Dickstein, creating a uniquely moral Jewish killer, I am unable to do this with Freud, who represents neither Jewish frailty nor violence. He refuses to be merged with Dickstein and Singer.

Freud stands apart from Dickstein and Singer in other ways as well. Although Singer is an intellectual, he is specifically a literary psychosynthesizer, a maker of images, whereas Freud is their critical analyst. Precisely because Singer *plays* with images, his own image within my tough Jewish experience is more pliable than is Freud's—and Dickstein's. That Singer is at his most brilliant with gentle Jewish types and images only makes him a more perfect rather than a more paradoxical match for Nat Dickstein. I cannot envision Singer, the pacifist and vegetarian, shouldering arms to help fend off a pogrom, though I easily imagine the Freud of the biographies, photographs, and correspondence doing so. Yet within my Dickstein fantasy, it is Freud who resists fusion with the great Mossad agent, whereas Singer seems to merge with him effortlessly. For me, that merger helped to prolong the Dickstein-induced high of Jewish goose bumps and adrenalin. To Dickstein's license to kill—in the form of a wispy body and death camp numbers—I brought additional moral vindication by fusing him with the gentle Isaac Bashevis Singer.

Accordingly, Singer (the familiar gentle Jewish part of my own conscience) was not a counterweight to the attraction of Dickstein (my own strange but insistent tough Jewish desire), but *part* of that attraction: its essential ethical glow. Furthermore, both the Mossad commander and the Yiddish novelist are, each in his own way, unproblematic Jews. They differ radically from one another as Jews, but, simply put, both are spontaneously and unhesitatingly Jews. For them, being a Jew—whether Israeli warrior or gentle, Yiddish-speaking mystic—is innate, rather than something external with which they are proud to associate.

Freud, by contrast, is the virtual paradigm of the problematic Jew: the Jew for whom being Jewish is itself a problem, if often a productive and creative problem. As anti-Semites, particularly in the medical profession, never ceased to remind Freud, he was a Jew. Moreover, his writings, especially his letters, are full of warm, often fervent statements of pride and pleasure in his membership in the Jewish race, as he often put it. For Singer and Dickstein, such statements would be superfluous. Isaac Deutscher rightly included Freud in the ranks of the "non-Jewish Jews," those cultivated, cosmopolitan nonconformists such as Marx, Spinoza, Einstein, and Rosa

Luxemburg, for whom being a Jew was an issue rather than an impulse. In Freud's case, aside from his renunciation of Judaism, one thinks of his anguished relations with Carl Gustav Jung, whom he lionized as the great Aryan hope of the largely Jewish psychoanalytic movement. Or one thinks of his only slightly less complex connection to the figure of Moses, with whom he had a strong Jewish identification. This makes all the more poignant and problematic Freud's argument, in *Moses and Monotheism*, that the father of the Jewish people was an Egyptian, not a Jew. The non-Jewish Jews, Freud among them, forsook Judaism for philosophy, science, or social revolution; they generally stood on the margins or crossroads of several cultures, tied to each but anchored in none. According to Deutscher, that uprootedness was a source of their pathbreaking creativity.[16]

The Freud element in my tough Jewish experience is the piece that serves to keep that experience at the level of fantasy. It allows me to feel that experience, to embrace it, to think through it, and, finally, to distance myself from it, as Freud did. Freud—neither a Zionist nor an embodiment of Jewish meekness, neither a tough Nat Dickstein nor an unheroic Jakob Freud—is, instead, a third possibility: the Apollonian Jew. Not the Dionysian Jew of Singer and Dickstein, Freud is the rationalist-cosmopolitan Jew who, with many ties to the Jewish tradition of gentleness and few if any to that of Jewish weakness, sailed with remarkable courage directly into the bad winds of anti-Semitism. This Freud has become a serious contender for my affections. Indeed, I doubtless evoked him in the first place precisely because he could halt my rush toward the remarkable Dickstein-Singer duo: he was the model of a rationalist who had experienced the desire for the tough Jew yet had refused to translate that desire into politics.

But my Freud strategy neither decisively neutralized the power of that Dickstein-Singer combination, nor failed altogether to do so. Given Freud's ambivalence, and my own, it is not surprising that my use of his image yields ambiguous results. Freud, the critical rationalist, has a definite appeal, but, having died in 1938, he, if not his theory *tout court*, has been rendered partially obsolete by the Nazi attempt to exterminate Europe's Jews, by the creation of a Jewish state, and by postwar American society, especially during the past two decades, which is the immediate context of the tough Jewish imagery I am studying here.

For my purposes, the Freud strategy as an alternative to the tough Jewish Singer-Dickstein image was also undercut by recent feminist and homosexual perspectives. Those perspectives suggest consideration of the fact that Freud, Singer, and Dickstein, not to mention Philip Roth, my father, and myself, share a significant plot of common ground: we are all (Jewish) men who do not want to appear to be women.

Thanks to the insights of feminism, it would be difficult today to overemphasize the significance of this particular male and Jewish male desire, especially, of course, in a discussion of tough Jews. As I mentioned earlier and will examine more closely in part 2, the modern, tough Jew imagery was formed exactly when Freud was imagining his father and his Hannibal. That, in turn, occurred in a time of crisis for many males— the 1890s through the 1920s. It was a period of anti-Semitic rhetoric proclaiming the effeminacy of Jewish males, and a broader, non-Jewish (and Jewish) Western, heterosexual, male crisis of masculinity occasioned by such challenges as the emergent women's rights movements (the suffragettes and the "new woman" of the turn of the century) as well as the openly homosexual subcultures that were starting to appear. It is not surprising that men in the West, Jews among them, were preoccupied with asserting what was perceived as their manhood. A yearning for particular images of masculinity—images that have prevailed in the dominant, non-Jewish culture—is, I am proposing, part of the very formation of the tough Jewish idea. As indicated below (pp. 65–69), the blossoming of tough imagery among American Jews during the past two decades is also bound up with male concerns about a perceived threat of emasculation provoked in part by contemporary feminism.

For the moment, the focus is more simply on Freud, who was distressed by the "unheroic conduct on the part of the big, strong man who was holding the little boy by the hand." Freud took for granted that an authentic man would have conducted himself in a more warlike manner (or, as gentle Jews might argue, a more goyish manner). It did not occur to him that his father's refusal to confront, directly and physically, the anti-Semite who had insulted him may have entailed great strength and courage—the strength of his resolve not to use violence, or the courage to resist established (Gentile) terms of conduct.

From Freud's theme of the childhood origins of adult fantasies in *The Interpretation of Dreams*, we can derive insight into our own fantasies. His identification with Hannibal, he suggests, did not actually originate in the "cap in the mud" story, but in an even earlier fascination with a history book on the Napoleonic era. "I can still remember," he writes, "sticking labels on the flat backs of my wooden soldiers [common among some children of middle-class Jewish families] with the names of Napoleon's marshals written on them. And at that time," he adds, "my declared favorite was already Massena (or to give the name its Jewish form, Manasseh)." Moving from Napoleon's officer Massena to Hannibal was "only . . . a question of a transference of an already formed emotional relation onto a new object," facilitated by the fact that both Hannibal and Napoleon were connected in Freud's mind as fellow crossers of the Alps. It may even be, Freud continues, that "the development of this martial ideal" can be traced back to the age of three, when he had been "in a close relation, sometimes friendly but sometimes warlike, with a boy a year older than myself, and [back] to the wishes which that relation must have stirred up in the weaker of us" (pp. 197–98).

Freud's comments, like much of what we say, are as fascinating for what they leave out as they are for what they include. Or to put it differently, there is so much going on behind the scenes of this passage that it is not even funny. Immediately remarkable in the above statement is the cryptic closing reference to the wishes his sometimes warlike relations with the four year old "*must have* stirred up in the weaker of us," that is, in Freud himself. The three-year-old Freud *might* have wished for someone or something quite like the Hannibal for whom he would wish several years later, but the little boy also might have wished that there were no bullies or warriors in the world, period.

Also fascinating is Freud's reference to the "martial ideal" he had begun to internalize early in life. Although he does not speak of a Jewish ideal or of a Jewish martial ideal, he was on firm ground, if unwittingly so, in eliding the Jewish theme, because from biblical times through his own era martial ideals had *not* been Jewish ideals. Freud was attracted to an ideal that neither Jews (such as his father), nor non-Jews, nor anti-Semites considered Jewish. Surely Freud knew this, but part of him, the tough Jewish part, wanted things to be otherwise; part of him *wanted* Jews, not least himself, to have martial ideals. Desire, then, entered into his scientific commentary as well as into his fantasies. His remarks on the "cap in the mud" story constituted not only a clinical commentary on a dream, but a veritable manifesto of male Jewish toughness. The founder of psychoanalysis is saying to the Jews and to the non-Jewish majority of his day: I am a Jewish man and, as you see, when young I played with toy soldiers. History has known Jewish generals and I, myself, have martial ideals that are, well, very much like your own. We Jews are *men* in your meaning of the term. Accept me, then, as an equal. This is not, however, only an appeal. If you cannot accept me, beware; for now, if you strike me, I will strike back.

Freud ignored what is elided in making assumptions that were actually political but appeared to be factual and neutral, especially his assumption that big and strong refer to male bodies and combat between them. We, however, are less entitled to ignore the elided material. We must acknowledge that what is excluded by such an assumption is not only the prospect of "big, strong" women in the same muscular and fighting sense, but also the prospect that big and strong might have radically different terms of reference. They might refer to the scope and power of one's generosity or to one's dedication to peace. This line of thought points to one of the guiding themes of these reflections: if the dilemmas posed by gentle Jews (victimization) and tough Jews (brutalization) are to be resolved, an important first step will be critically to work through and ultimately beyond the male assumptions of our present thinking. No less important will be the need to move beyond narrowly *Jewish* ways of reflecting on tough Jews, the theme to which I now turn.

Attention should focus for a moment on the Jewish dimensions of the Freud passage. Those dimensions are most pronounced just when they seem not to be, that is, just when

Freud seems to be moving away from the expressly Jewish toward the more general human contexts. After noting that his childhood favorite among Napoleon's marshals had been the Jew, Massena, for example, Freud adds in parentheses what seems to be a more neutral, less Jewish link: "No doubt this preference was also partly to be explained by the fact that my birthday fell on the same day as his, exactly a hundred years earlier" (p. 198). From there, he proceeds to his experience as a three year old, which takes him another step away from the Jewish frame of reference. There is, of course, the Jewish matter, Freud seems to be saying, but then again there are all these other matters, generically boy and man matters, birthday-coincidence matters, and so forth, that make the whole story more typical of the species rather than of Jews alone, a story for everyone, not merely for Jews.

It is easy to miss the Jew's disappearance from these lines. The Nazi genocide is the most recent and massive case of Jewish disappearance, but Jews are not newcomers to vanishing en masse from the ranks of the living. *Disappearance* carries a different sense as well. Freud's remarks remind us that by the time he was at work on *The Interpretation of Dreams*, the very *notion* of *the* Jew was, among Jews if not among anti-Semites, departing from the scene. German or eastern European, religious or Zionist, traditional or modern, tough or gentle, speaking Yiddish, Hebrew, or, say, French—these are some of the choices opened by the de-ghettoization or emancipation of Jews in Europe that had begun a century earlier and had by 1900 replaced the singular Jew with the plural. Beyond this, Freud's comments disclosing his "martial ideal" and identifying with Hannibal actually *cause* one particular sort of Jew to disappear—exactly the centuries-old and normative meek and gentle Jew embodied in Jakob Freud's disappointing conduct. From the standpoint of Jakob Freud or a gentle Jew, Freud's whole analytic strategy in these passages would *itself* seem to be a case of a Jew's disappearance into the non-Jewish martial ideal. Yet at that very moment—when ambivalence, basic to his Jewishness, was most poignantly on display—Freud was at *his most* Jewish. As I may well be in making the point.

Furthermore, in 1930 Freud added a telling note to the passage we have been examining. To the sentence "And at that time my declared favorite was already Massena (or to give the name its Jewish form, Manasseh)," Freud appended the following simple, brief note: "Incidentally, doubts have been thrown on the Marshal's Jewish origin" (p. 197). So much for the marshal as Jew. Freud evidently finds this new information entirely unproblematic: what mattered in context is that the young Freud *believed* Massena was a Jew, and identified with him as such. But this is actually not an insignificant matter, even though Freud leaves it without comment. On the contrary, the brief note suggests one of Freud's, and this study's, main themes: *The power of wish and image, especially bodily image, over fact.*

The cancellation of Massena's Jewish credentials is suggestive in another way as well. Hidden within Freud's apparently simple notation there is a promising vision of a pluralist-cosmopolitan world in which the question of whether one is a Jew (or a Christian, Muslim, Arab, white, or black person) *is* of no consequence. This proposition, central to these reflections, runs against the grain of today's pervasive clannishness, separatism, and nationalism and therefore warrants brief amplification. I have, for example, been examining Freud's "cap in the mud" story as a Jewish, specifically, a tough Jewish, story. Clearly, it is also a story pertaining to dreams per se and a story of fathers and sons and of males, not merely Jewish males. It is, further, a story about racism—not only anti-Semitism—and what might be called the dynamics of persecution. One does not have to be Jewish to relate to the "cap in the mud" story.

I intentionally stress the not-only-Jewish aspects of the story because I want to interrupt and challenge that discourse which sees *only* the Jewish aspects, the discourse of Jewish nationalism (Zionism), the key premise of which is that there is ultimately no place for Jews in the non-Jewish nations. Ergo Jews need their own nation-state. Such a view is already culturally operative—that is, *latent*, to use the psychoanalytic term—in the "cap in the mud" story. Although Freud does not explicitly pursue the political dimension, the discourse of Jewish nationalism is nevertheless decisively present in the story, in the form of yet further absences. For in addition to excluding woman, the tale of the "cap in the mud" also *banishes the figure of the non-Jew who is not anti-Semitic.*

This is a decisive exclusion because the absent non-Jew who rejects anti-Semitism is essential to the story: without that absence, there would not *be* a "cap in the mud" story. Consider what happens when such a character is inserted (as Freud inserted the protector-redeemer Hannibal): the non-Jew who rejects anti-Semitism would have prevented the incident, or picked up the hat, returning to it Herr Freud with apologies and friendly wishes, or punished the perpetrator. The non-Jew who rejects anti-Semitism would have been there for the Jew, to use the language of contemporary therapy.

But that would have rendered Jakob Freud's unheroic conduct less likely, and the figure of the tough Jew would have been unnecessary. In other words, there would be no story. Because there *is* a "cap in the mud" story, however, we are

42

now in a better position to notice not only whom this story—
and the present reflections—is actually about, but to see as
well to whom these apparently intra-Jewish tales are also *addressed*, namely, to the non-Jew who refuses anti-Semitism.
And the message serves to underpin my critique of the tough
Jew: Rewrite the story and help erase the circumstances that
have given us both cringing Jews and their Nat Dickstein
avengers. Move to cancel the necessity of the tough Jew.

Rewriting a story, however, is easier than rewriting reality.
Although the mature Freud might have considered Emile
Zola, the French writer who courageously defended the Drey-
fusard cause in France in the 1890s, to be a genuine non-Jew
who refused anti-Semitism, he might just as well have rejected
the entire proposition as a fiction, arguing that there were
rather few Dreyfusards, let alone Zolas, in either Germany or
his own intensely anti-Semitic Austria. And we could note
that non-Jews who reject anti-Semitism were found in only
limited supply in Europe during the decade following Freud's
death, in 1938, or, at the moment, among Arab peoples in
the Middle East.

Only when one thinks the matter through in nonnationalist
terms of the *connections* between Jews and non-Jews are there
alternatives to the unacceptable choice of being either a Jewish
victim or a tough Jew. Against the backdrop of a broad historical record that is profoundly unpromising, developments
in the United States in the last fifty years present an unprecedentedly hopeful picture of integration and mutuality. So
hopeful a picture, I contend, that it is in many ways threatening
to a great many Jewish Americans who are actually ambivalent
about the entrance into the story of the non-Jew who refuses
anti-Semitism. Jews have sought what has always been in such
horribly short supply: the non-Jews' recognition, support, sol-

idarity, and even friendship; but they have feared, along with resurgent anti-Semitism, the loss of a Jewish identity *as victim* and thus as a people with special claims to what is called the moral high ground.

We arrive now at the moment of bodies. Freud's "cap in the mud" story and my own Nat Dickstein story lead us to it, for both stories are dependent not only on absent women and absent non-Jews who reject anti-Semitism but also on *Jewish ambivalence toward the world of bodies*. Jews have no monopoly on such ambivalence (which, as John Hoberman has shown, is an important dynamic in the modern history of intellectuals as a social group),[17] but they nevertheless have had more than their share of it. This ambivalence is not a function of some Jewish racial or religious essence or inclination toward the mental (spiritual, financial, and so on) rather than the physical domains. It is, instead, a function of Jewish history; in historical terms, the distinction between mind and body is suggestive. Prior to the articulation of tough Jewish imagery in this century, for example, virtually the only operative images of Jewish force, strength, or power involved the Jewish *brain*, which would typically be housed in frail (the Jewish scholar) or fat (the Jewish merchant) male bodies but never in rugged, muscular, or lithe ones.

Between the destruction of the ancient Jewish state and the defeat of the last outposts of Jewish armed resistance to Roman power in the second century and the founding of Israel in 1948, Jews were not merely stateless. They were a people largely, often completely, excluded from landownership, farming, hunting, and war—from much of the world of effective bodily activity. As sociologists and economic historians have long noted, Europe's Jews had been bound to the sphere of circulation and commerce—the sphere of money, cunning, and abstraction. They were denied admission into the worlds of material production and violence, though as victims, they entered the latter world in droves.

Of this historic necessity, Jews made a virtue, by constructing a remarkable culture of meekness, physical frailty, and gentleness, a pale, slouched identity nurtured in the stale air of their exclusion from the worlds of work and war. Jean-Paul Sartre paid fine tribute to that culture and identity in his *Anti-Semite and Jew* (1946):

The Jews are the mildest of men, . . . passionately hostile to violence. That obstinate sweetness which they conserve in the midst of the most atrocious persecution, that sense of justice and of reason which they put up as their sole defense against a hostile, brutal, and unjust society, is perhaps the best part of the message they bring to us and the true mark of their greatness.[18]

In context, the remarks just cited actually constitute an aside, forceful though it is. But Sartre's context, too, is germane here: his laudatory words on Jewish gentleness are an aside from his well-known criticism of certain Jews for denying what is Jewish about themselves by speaking only and always in terms of abstract and ultimately weak, humanistic universals. Sartre terms such persons "inauthentic Jews." He develops a fascinating argument concerning certain inauthentic Jews who tend to "deny the body that betrays them" (p. 119). Sartre contends that the fanatically rational inauthentic Jew responds to racist claims regarding the importance of body types and features by proclaiming the body to be simply an instrument or a machine, and thereby denying it.

I would argue that Sartre's great commentary misses the element of ambivalence in Jewish attitudes toward bodies: even gentle Jews, such as Philip Roth, Sigmund Freud, and myself, have tough Jewish fantasies or primal tough Jew experiences. Further, I find in Freud and Roth, and others may find in my own report, the type of a Jewish male yearning to enter the world of bodies from which we perceive ourselves to have been excluded. Viewed in this light, Freud's Hannibal, or tough Jew fantasy, assumes an additional layer of meaning: to that of the frightened Jew yearning for a tough defender, and that of the boy/son aspiring to a manly manhood, we can add that of the Jewish male (represented by the small body of the boy Freud) finding in Hannibal entrée into the non-Jewish world of bodies, the world occupied, for example, by the anti-Semite.

Psychoanalytic theory itself can be considered part of this yearning, the product of a highly cerebral Jewish man (Freud) trying to enter the sphere of bodies. John Murray Cuddihy has developed an interpretation of these matters. It is not an accident, he proposes, that the three theorists he analyzes, Marx, Freud, and Levi-Strauss, were Jews. Indeed, he sees their respective social theories as exemplifying a brilliantly improper, ill-mannered Jewish revenge on anti-Semitic WASP civility by exposing the latter's dirty foundations—the proletariat (Marx), savage society (Levi-Strauss), and sex (Freud).[19] My own small amendment to this theory is that the proletarian, savage, and sexual spheres evoked and explored by these theorists are also objects of their wishes, representations of desired and variously proscribed worlds of bodies. Freud's deep attraction for his non-Jewish disciple and colleague Carl Gustav Jung can be understood in this framework. Philip Roth, whose novels bespeak extensive Jewish assimilation into the post-1945 United States, can be similarly read, his greatest characters, Alexander Portnoy and Nathan Zuckerman, having announced that the Jew has finally entered the flow of bodies that permits not only survival but also the life of a sex fiend.

In Freud and Roth, both gentle Jews, the Jewish desire to join the world of bodies proceeds along the path of sex. Zionism, like psychoanalysis, took form in Europe in the late 1890s and gave that desire politico-nationalist articulation, pursuing it down the road of land, work, and, war. As part 2 argues in more detail, Zionism was emphatic regarding the Jewish yearning to enter the body politic. In 1898, one year before publication of *The Interpretation of Dreams*, Max Nordau, Herzl's lieutenant, proclaimed that the weak, pale, and frail Jews of previous generations would be supplanted by "muscle Jews"; and these new Jewish bodies—no longer traditionally Jewish, no longer frail, unathletic, effeminate—will in turn embody themselves politically in a state. This is Nordau's tough Jewish fantasy. It resembles Freud's "cap in the mud" story and my own Nat Dickstein experience, but it also differs from them. Nordau, like Herzl, was one of those "specializing in the realization of dreams," in Freud's words.

The Jewish desire to enter the world of bodies is the desire of an excluded, beleaguered minority for what the dominant majority considers *normalcy*. Zionism has been straightforward in its contention that a Jewish state is the key to the normalization of the Jewish situation and that the abnormality of the Jews was a political problem caused by statelessness. And statelessness, according to Zionism, is the cause of meekness, frailty, passivity, humiliation, pogroms, futile appeals to reason and dialogue—in short, Jewish weakness and gentleness. The rejection of physical combat had long been emblematic of the way Jews—typified by Jakob Freud and Philip Roth—differentiated themselves from non-Jews. Zionism boldly redefined that commitment to nonviolence as a chronic Jewish ailment that could be cured only by forging a Jewish state, which would transform the Jews into a nation like the others.

In the political sphere, the sphere of states, however, normalcy involves not only flags, symbols, youth movements, national anthems, patriotic holidays, and the like, but also *conquest and organized killing.* Indeed, waging war and obliterating large numbers of people figure prominently among the things normal nations and their inhabitants do, and that is certainly one of the messages of the events underlying the creation of the actual Jewish state of Israel: the Second World War and the Nazi attempt to exterminate the Jews of Europe. Those events made clear what hope and idealism may have blurred for earlier generations of Zionists: that to enter the world of bodies politically speaking and to be normal there *means* to kill. This is one part of the core of the problem of the tough Jew.

One might counter: The only problem is the one constructed by the gentle Jew. *Getting* killed was normal for Jews *before* the Zionist idea of toughness. Is *that* the normalcy you gentle Jews want to sustain? Several years ago, I would have responded as follows: The final point is moral not practical. It is that Jews have a special mission among peoples and nations, namely, to refuse violence. To opt for the so-called tough Jewish or Zionist solution is to embrace a non-Jewish definition of normalcy and thereby to reject what is essential about being a Jew. I would have agreed with Philip Roth that, as Jews, "our worth as human beings . . . was embodied in the *incapacity* to perpetuate the sort of bloodletting visited upon our ancestors."

I no longer accept this approach for reasons already sug-

48

gested. Like Zionism, the gentle Jewish argument itself pre-supposes what cannot be presupposed, namely, a Jewish es-sence. And again like Zionism, it excludes the non-Jew who not only rejects anti-Semitism but is today as likely as is a Jew to be incapable (or capable) of visiting a bloodletting on any-one. My work on this project has convinced me that if there is such a phenomenon as essentially Jewish behavior, it is not the behavior one would place under the rubrics weak or gentle. Jews, to be sure, generated a vital *historical identity and tra-dition* of gentleness and frailty, which Sartre called "the best part of the message they bring to us," that is, to non-Jews. But there have also always been tough, fighting Jews. Although they have existed largely on the margins of the prevalent, nonviolent Jewish tradition, such figures nevertheless indicate that Jews will do, so to speak, what a man has got to do when faced with the opportunity for toughness; they will be as tough as the proverbial next guy—or tougher. In that sense, it cannot be said that Jews are essentially or "by nature" prone to one or another sort of conduct.

Zionism's position in all of this is the decisive break with the gentle Jewish tradition: the Zionist ethos cancels that tra-dition and identity and liberates Jews from its constraints, to be tough, or more. In doing so, however, Zionism and Israel also liberate the heritage of gentleness from its Jewish con-straints, opening it to *everyone*. By creating a state of their own in the only way a state can be created—through armed conquest—Zionists brought to an end both the history of Jews as unresisting victims of anti-Jewish brutality and the image of the Jew as the defenseless, peace-loving conscience of a violent, non-Jewish world. That in turn generated both the opportunity and the need for anyone and everyone to embody the violent world's defenseless, peace-loving conscience.

Zionism, as in the case of my own Nat Dickstein or tough Jew fantasies, is ambivalent, and the ambivalence is not innocent. Zionism is at once a decisive break with the traditions of Jewish weakness and gentleness and also not so decisive a break: it rejects meekness and gentleness in favor of the normalcy of toughness, while preserving the older tradition of the Jews as a special or chosen people, which *depends on* imagery of Jews as frail victims. Zionism needs its weak and gentle Jewish counterparts to give moral justification to Jewish participation in the world of bodies, specifically, of physical violence, including killing or even sadism. To put the matter most starkly: the image of Jewish victimization vindicates the image of the Jewish victimizer. This is my own fusion of Nat Dickstein and Isaac Bashevis Singer writ large.

It may be that the notion of the primacy of ethics in Jewish life and of the Jew as uniquely ethical or gentle was a function of the history of Jewish exclusion from the world of bodies (material production, conquest, combat). The experience of many Jews in the United States and Israel indicates an erosion of that notion as Jewish participation in the world of bodies increases. With grim irony, Zionism's vision of a normalized Jewry has in part been *realized* in Israeli brutality toward Palestinians, for in the framework of civilized nations, brutality is the very essence of normalcy. It was their statelessness, defenselessness, and gentleness, after all, that had made Jews eccentric. In forsaking that eccentricity for normalcy, Zionist Jews also made a more diverse alliance of eccentrics both possible and vital. In somewhat the same way as developments in the United States gave rise to the advertisement "You don't have to be Jewish to like Levy's rye bread," so developments in the Middle East suggest that you don't have to be Jewish to, in Sartre's words, be "passionately hostile to violence" and to have "a sense of justice and of reason" as your "sole defense against a hostile, brutal, and unjust society." As assimilation in the United States and Zionism in Israel proceeded, Jews (as Jews) could no longer be counted on to uphold so abnormal a banner as that of gentleness. The responsibility has been shifted, so to speak, onto people of all races, religions, and creeds.

The Jewish yearning to enter the world of bodies and some consequences of fulfilling that yearning serve to underscore the social, cultural, and political power of images, fantasies, and desires. When the dimension constituted by layers of fantasy about bodies, manliness and effeminacy, toughness, weakness, gentleness, images of corpses, of fathers and sons, of Dicksteins, golems, Hannibals, is left unexplored (and therefore free to distort), Jews, and non-Jews as well, are generally unable to be temperate when debating such questions as the Palestinian *intifada*, U.S. policies in the Middle East, Jews in the Soviet Union, relations between Jews and blacks in the U.S., or the secular question of who is a Jew. This hidden agenda of discussions of Israeli policies and Jewish identity must be made more accessible. That, indeed, is a goal of these reflections.

Are there actually grounds for my confidence in my ability to make more accessible an agenda that is not only hidden, but dense and difficult as well? Who am I, after all, to be making these claims about tough and gentle Jews: I am a Jewish American man and college professor writing in the United States in the final decade of the twentieth century. It is primarily the American aspect that I want to pursue now.

The Americanization of Tough Jews

The American aspect of the issue of tough Jews—as something Made in the U.S.A.—is central in these reflections. The tough Jew today is to a large extent a peculiarly American product shaped by American circumstances and by the needs, fears, and wishes of Jews in the U.S., even as Israel and events in the Middle East play an inspirational role.

Thus, this is an American Jewish book in no less basic a way than that the author's decisive experiences as a Jew are reading, fantasizing, and writing—and not as one harassed or tormented by anti-Semites or as a member of the Israel Defense Forces. My focus on fantasy and reading could be said to reflect my privileged position as an American Jew, which, in the scale of Jewish history, is unprecedentedly comfortable. I try to remember this as I write about people—Jews and Palestinians—whose situations have been significantly less sheltered.

The focus on fantasy has ironic overtones as well: for many American Jews, precisely the comfortable circumstances are a source of discomfort in matters of identity. The dilemma itself is simple. Being a Jewish American means *not being* in either Auschwitz or Israel: it means being here rather than there, in either of the two, great secular reference points of American Jewish identity. Whether as conviction or unexamined assumption, the notion that *real* Jews either vanished in Nazi crematoria or are soldiers in the Middle East is, I believe, widespread among Jews in the United States. It is as if the more fully Jews are integrated into American society, the more they experience their mediocrity as Jews—and the more they need fantasies of Israel avenging Auschwitz. The need for such fantasies is thus twofold. Not only do these fantasies justify Israeli treatment of Palestinians, but they serve as a reservoir of Jewish anguish and heroism in the context of an assimilation that, comparatively speaking, demands neither.

Especially in the American context, it would be a notable lapse to ignore the social and political centrality of image and fantasy. For one need not accept all the arguments of a critic such as Jean Baudrillard in order to recognize America's remarkable achievements in filling—Baudrillard would say *replacing*—society and history with mass-produced, well-packaged images and fantasies.[20] Regarding images of tough Jews in particular, the matter of prefabrication and mass circulation was recognized three decades ago by Daniel Boorstin in his capsule analysis of American visitors to Israel in *The Image: A Guide to Pseudo-Events in America*:

> Tourist-pilgrims are eager to visit the "actual" scenes where famous novels like *Ben Hur* and *Spartacus* were really photographed. Mount Sinai becomes well-known as the site about which *The Ten Commandments* was filmed. In 1960 a highly successful packaged tour was organized which traced the route of events in Leon Uris' novel *Exodus*; the next year El Al Israel Airlines announced a new sixteen-day tour which promised to cover the very places where Otto Preminger and his film crew had shot scenes for the movie version.[21]

Aside from the passage just cited, Boorstin's book does not deal with Jewish themes. It is, rather, an analysis of the prepackaged, mass-produced character of the American experience; it has important implications for the Jewish themes, however. To what extent, for example, can the visit to Israel, a transfiguring experience for many American Jews, really be understood as a Jewish experience at all? Might it not be that the Jewish element of the experience is actually overwhelmed by the unrelentingly homogenizing circuitry of American mass-cultural images and signs? I will consider this question in more depth in the discussion of the tough Jewish pulp novels in part 3. For the moment, I want only to look briefly at one of the cases cited by Boorstin, namely, that of *Exodus*.

Leon Uris's novel, first published in 1958, is surely among the best-selling of best sellers, having gone through nearly sixty printings in the paperback edition alone. It is a fictional account of the events leading to the founding of Israel, with its dramatic center being the harrowing journey to Palestine of the ship *Exodus*, packed with desperate Jewish survivors of Nazi Europe. The novel's hero, Ari Ben Canaan, is the virtual prototype of the American image of the Israeli tough Jew. Uris himself was straightforward about his wish to create a new and improved model Jew for America. His note on the inside cover of the 1981 Bantam Books paperback edition informs readers that "all the cliché Jewish characters who have cluttered up our American fiction—the clever businessman, the brilliant doctor, the sneaky lawyer, the sulking artist . . . all those good folk who spend their chapters hating themselves, the world, and all their aunts and uncles . . . all those steeped in self-pity . . . all those golden riders of the psychoanalysis couch . . . all these have been left where they rightfully belong, on the cutting-room floor." Uris adds that he has "shown the other side of the coin." "We Jews are not what we have been portrayed to be," he told an interviewer soon after the novel first appeared. "In truth we have been fighters."[22]

Uris has been taken to task on these matters by Philip Roth, who by the late 1950s had himself entered the ranks of those Jewish American writers whose imagery of neurotic, non-violent, ambivalent Jews Uris was seeking to displace. In response to Uris's assertion "In truth, we have been fighters," Roth writes bitterly: "So bald, stupid, and uninformed is the statement that it is not even worth disputing." He then contrasts

Uris's celebration of the tough Jew with Elie Wiesel's short novel *Dawn* (1960), about a Jewish terrorist group in pre-1948 Palestine, one of whose members is to execute a British officer who has been taken hostage. "I should like to tell Uris," Roth writes, "that Wiesel's Jew is not so proud to discover himself in the role of fighter, nor is he able to find justification for himself in some traditional Jewish association with pugnacity or bloodletting."

In further defense of what I call the gentle Jewish position, Roth then cites a fascinating story from *Time* magazine, which focuses on an interview with Captain Yehiel Aranowicz, who had been in command of the blockade-running *Exodus*. Israelis, Aranowicz claimed, "were pretty disappointed in the book, to put it lightly. The types that are described in it never existed in Israel. The novel is neither history nor literature." *Time* then notes Uris's succinct rejoinder: "You may quote me as saying, 'Captain who?' and that's all I have to say. I'm not going to pick on a light weight. Just look at my sales figures."[23]

Uris speaks from a position of strength. What that position lacks morally, it almost compensates for—accidentally—with insight. Uris, after all, is on the firm ground of fantasy, image, desire, and violence. Edward Tivnan writes that prior to the publication of *Exodus*, "most Americans . . . knew virtually nothing about Zionism, and less about events in Israel." That changed, Tivnan continues, with the appearance of Uris's novel, which quickly became "the primary source of knowledge about the Jews and Israel that most Americans had." In his *Mitla Pass* (1988), Uris makes these facts part of his fiction—or is it the other way around? Main character Gideon Zadok, a Jewish American writer in Israel to draft a novel based on the 1956 war with Egypt, evokes the following response from an Israeli official: "This would be the first American novel about Israel. It could be valuable in gaining favorable world opinion."[24] With the release of Otto Preminger's film of the novel in 1960, "Israel's reputation seemed secure in the U.S. Suddenly, Jews were glamorous." Suddenly, one might add, Jews were Paul Newman, who starred as the heroic—and fair-haired, blue-eyed, small-nosed—Ari Ben Canaan. In any case, *Exodus* has sold over twenty million copies since its publication. "The Israel of most Americans, including Jews," Tivnan proposes, "is still the *Exodus* version."[25] This observation should be placed alongside Boorstin's example of American Jewish "tourist-pilgrims" in Israel, retracing the steps of the making of the *film*. To conclude only that the result is a distortion of reality, however, would be to ignore the reality of the distortion.

The Politics of the Tough Jew's Americanization

The story of Uris's *Exodus* exemplifies many of the ways in which the American framework of the tough Jew is shaped by images. The American framework is also shaped by history and politics, though it is worth remembering that we perceive history and politics in large measure *through* the sorts of images discussed here, while those images are themselves historically and politically constituted (by people and their imaginations).

We can begin to get at those domains by raising the obvious question: Why tough Jews in America now? What are the recent circumstances that have generated the imagery examined in these pages, that have generated this study itself? (Part 2 examines the broader or more long-range historical genesis of Jewish toughness, tracing it to the formation of the Zionist movement in Europe at the turn of the last century, then observing its passage through Nazi mass murder, and its consolidation in the founding of Israel in 1948, the event *sine qua non* of the tough Jew.) If the establishment of a Jewish state was the necessary condition in the landscape of contemporary stereotypes for the sprouting of the tough Jew, then Israel's victory in the 1967 Six Day War proved to be the virtually sufficient condition for its full flowering. What interests me is why American Jews in such large numbers and with such sustained passion *chose* to be so profoundly affected by the 1967 war?

Edward Tivnan is on target when he notes that, with the Six Day War, Israel quite suddenly became for American Jewry "the most important thing, perhaps not in their life, but certainly in their Jewishness," adding that polls at the time showed 99 percent of American Jews to be in firm support of the Israeli position. "As Jewish pundits were soon saying," Tivnan concludes, "American Jews had all become 'Zionized.' "[26] But American Jews were not simply passive recipients of Israeli initiatives. On the contrary, they brought initiatives and needs of their own *to* the Six Day War, shaping and constructing its impact accordingly. If American Jews became Zionized, and large numbers certainly did, Zionism was also Americanized in the process.

We have spoken of the decisive place of the 1967 Arab-Israeli War in the development of the tough Jewish stereotype and imagery, and we have commented in a similar vein on the impact of Uris's and Preminger's *Exodus* (which had appeared a decade *earlier*). How does one reconcile claims about the 1967 war as a turning point in the itinerary of Jewish toughness with Tivnan's remarks about *Exodus* (1958) and Philip Roth's observation, presented as early as 1961 in his critique of Uris, that "there does not seem to be any doubt that the image of the Jew as patriot, warrior, and battle-scarred belligerent is rather satisfying to a large segment of the American public"?[27] In fact, the impact of *Exodus* and that of the Six Day War are altogether compatible and not at odds at all. Indeed, they function in tandem. Specifically, the reception of Uris's novel is a significant part of what can be seen in retrospect as the preparatory work for the transformation of the tough Jewish theme in American life that would be wrought by the 1967 war.

Still, contrasts should not simply be erased. Neither the Holocaust, nor the founding of Israel, nor the *Exodus* phenomenon, separately or in combination, exerted an impact on American Jews comparable to that of the Six Day War. That war's influence has been so fundamental that we are now inclined to take it for granted. It is no exaggeration to say that suddenly—literally overnight in numerous cases—many American Jews took genuine delight in being Jewish for the first time in their lives. That they were inspired to do so by a display of Jewish military might and skill makes it the most interesting moment in the entire history of Jewish stereotypes and values.

What occurred in the Middle East in early June 1967 transformed the way American Jews thought not only about Israel but about the Holocaust, politics, their parents, grandparents, children, Jews, non-Jews, and, not least, themselves and their bodies. And that is an understatement. In an editorial uncritically celebrating the twentieth anniversary of the Israeli victory, the editors of the *New Republic* were correct at least on this point: the 1967 war transformed the very idea of the Jew by restoring "Jewish power to the stage of world history."[28] Edward Tivnan, in a more critical context, has expressed similar thoughts. "The Six-Day War changed the American Jewish community forever." Where even the greatest Zionist leaders had failed, the 1967 war succeeded, according to Tivnan. It "turned millions of American Jews into 'Zionists,' . . . distant members of the faith but total supporters of Israel nevertheless."[29]

Yes, the American Jewish community was changed forever. It is true that before the summer of 1967, American Jews, numerous of whom were Zionists, grappled with the Holocaust, read *Exodus*, and, perhaps, imagined a world in which all Jewish males resembled Paul Newman. But one must be cautious not to be misled by the look of things seen in retrospect. A recent note on the activities of the National Jewish Community Relations Advisory Council (NJCRAC), the coordinating body for community relations activities in this country, is instructive. "Since 1967," writes Albert Vorspan, an executive in the Union of American Hebrew Congregations, the organized body of Reform Judaism, "the Israel issue [and, I would add, the issue of tough Jews] has been the highest priority for the NJCRAC. Prior to the Six Day War, Israel was *not even one of the major issues in the field* [emphasis added], eclipsed then by immigration policy, church-state separation, and civil rights."[30]

Sudden and deep, the shift in 1967 is also complex. In her fine study *The Schlemiel as Modern Hero* (1971), Ruth Wisse shrewdly grasps what was then the still-recent American Jewish echo of the Israeli victory in 1967. While a "new Jew" was born in 1948, Wisse writes, "the cliché of the bronzed warrior emerged ready to replace the older cliché of the wizened rabbi" only as a result of the 1967 Arab-Israeli War. Wisse offers, as well, insight into the element of ambivalence in the response of American Jewry. Next to "chest-thumping accounts of victory," she observes, one could make out the nasal voice of the schlemiel, in such material as *Irving of Arabia: An Unorthodox Interpretation of the Arab-Israeli War*, which evidently depicts a Jewish soldier heading to the battlefront with his mother at the door, shouting after him, "Marvin, please. Take your galoshes," or a poster showing a scrawny Hasidic Jew bounding from a telephone booth, his cape emblazoned with the logo Super Jew.

Some American Jews, Wisse proposes, "perhaps as an instinctive reflex of self-protection, continued to trace old outlines under new events. Better to stick to the identification with the schlemiel-loser than to risk believing in newfound strength. Or perhaps from where he sits," Wisse concludes, "the American Jewish humorist perceives the continuing vulnerability of the Jewish position, for all its seeming might. . . . Perhaps the Israeli's proficiency in warfare has only reinforced the American Jew's contrasting perception of himself as a *schlemiel*."[31] Such self-doubt and self-satire was also crystallized in a small book published not long before the Six Day War: *Loxfinger. A Thrilling Adventure of Hebrew Secret Agent Oy-Oy-7: An Israel Bond Thriller* by comedy writer Sol Weinstein.[32]

Weinstein's book and the examples cited by Wisse express more than American Jewish self-doubt and inadequacy in relation to Israeli soldiers or to Ian Fleming's James Bond. Less visibly, they also suggest the alternative values of a world without power or violence. In the tradition of the schlemiel, both Oy-Oy-7 and Marvin, the soldier who forgot his galoshes, are self-satirizing, parodic rejections of both war and the swaggering spy. But even as Ruth Wisse was penning her observations in 1970, the ambiguities she had detected were being washed away by a tide of tough Jewish imagery. Similarly,

Loxfinger could not have been written very long *after* 1967, for by then American Jews were contemplating the notion of a Jewish James Bond with increasing seriousness. Inspired by the Israeli "military miracle" of 1967, Jews in postindustrial, postmodern America were clearly entering their postschlemiel era. The utopian perspective is fragile indeed.

In another study from the early 1970s, Michael Selzer, a Jewish critic of Zionism, gauged the direction of the politico-cultural winds more accurately than did Ruth Wisse. Selzer sees the decade or so prior to 1967 as having been marked, for American Jews, by the creation of a Yiddishkeit, or Yiddishness, an idealized imagery of the late nineteenth and early twentieth century eastern European Jewish culture, and a kind of romance with the shtetl. On the basis of Selzer's work and that of Ruth Wisse, one can conclude that *prior to 1967, American Jews were attracted by and could make connections with imagery of Jewish gentleness and physical weakness.* The Six Day War, in Selzer's view, abruptly terminated the infatuation with Yiddishkeit. He himself had been a vigorous participant in that renaissance, which was reaching its full stride on the very eve of the 1967 war. The passions and issues to which the war gave rise, Selzer argues, "were more than enough to place in abeyance the preoccupations of the Jewish masses in America with their East European past. The nostalgia for the *shtetl* now gave way to the triumph of military conquest; the Lower East Side exhibition was replaced in the Jewish Museum by one depicting the excavations of the fortress of Masada (the Israeli Alamo) on the Dead Sea. A mammoth procession of instant potboilers on the Six Day War," Selzer notes, "caused publishers to rue their stockpiles of books on Yiddishkeit."

For Selzer, moreover, the American Jewish enthusiasm for

the new imagery and ideals flowing from Israel in June 1967 was hardly a sign that they had overcome "the sense of inferiority which many Jews have regarding their alleged lack of physical virtues." On the contrary, that "militaristic enthusiasm" indicates the extent to which the Jewish inferiority complex is "as strong as ever." Indeed, as Selzer sees it, the American Jewish embrace of the Israeli warrior is nothing less than a form of "self-rejection," since the true Jewish self is anchored in eastern European history and resembles the timid and gentle Jewish tradition examined here.[33]

The revival of Yiddishkeit among American Jews prior to 1967 is related to the theme of the tough and gentle Jews. It is a many-layered, sometimes contradictory, and nearly always paradoxical phenomenon. So, for example, in the period between the late 1950s and the Six Day War, American Jews enthused over *both* the Jewish (Israeli/Zionist) imagery of *Exodus* and the gentler (eastern European) imagery of Yiddishkeit. While this was sometimes a matter of different sections of American Jewry embracing apparently polar ideals, as often as not, both models were present within one person's consciousness, at one moment competing for predominance, at others combining in particularly dynamic ways. This should appear neither surprising nor strange. In its basic structure, it is, after all, the same form of consciousness that was operative in my Dickstein-Singer fantasy.

Indeed, Singer's own burgeoning renown as a writer (he would receive the Nobel Prize in literature in 1978) was well along in the mid-1960s and was an integral part of the revival of Yiddishkeit. So was the rediscovery of Sholem Aleichem and the theatrical and film (1971) success of *Fiddler on the Roof*. Bernard Malamud's best-selling novel *The Fixer* (1966), which appeared on the very eve of the Six Day War, belongs to the same current. Based on the anti-Semitic Beiliss trial in tsarist Russia in the early years of this century, *The Fixer* chronicles the persecution of Jews, their vulnerability and dread, and, not least, their gentleness, to which the novel is a kind of hymn. Ruth Wisse's *Schlemiel as Modern Hero* is itself inspired by this pre-1967 development, as are such American neoschlemiels as Woody Allen in his own films and Philip Roth's stories in *Goodbye, Columbus* (1959).

This revival of Yiddishkeit and gentle Jewish imagery from eastern Europe should be glimpsed in its *American* as well as in its Jewish American context. Edward Tivnan, for example, notes that by the mid-1960s it seemed apparent that "American Jews had arrived"—with disproportionately high annual incomes and representation in white-collar jobs and the country's best colleges. Yet, according to Tivnan, many American Jews found that their success as Americans was haunted by their failure as Jews.[34] In this context, the Jewish American turn to eastern Europe (the shtetl, Yiddish, the schlemiel) *and* the post-1967 turn to Israel can both be seen as efforts to find a positive Jewish identity amid an unprecedentedly deep assimilation into America.

That impulse itself is suggestive of how American American Jews had become. For the rediscovery of gentle Yiddishkeit and then the attachment to mighty Israel were both emblematic of a far broader germination of ethnic consciousness in the United States during the 1960s. As signified by the publication of Nathan Glazer and Daniel Patrick Moynihan's *Beyond the Melting Pot* (1963) and by such developments as the emergence (1963–64) of a new black nationalism, the decade was witness to a wide range of quests for personal meaning through ethnic-community roots in an America rushing toward suburban, consumerist, and corporate homogenization.

Such slogans as Black Power, I'm Black and I'm Proud, and Black is Beautiful were soon followed by their Jewish, Italian, Irish, Native American, Polish, Armenian, and numerous other counterparts. This whole development was further nurtured by and reflected in new directions in scholarship, particularly the proliferation of studies of immigrant communities, their roles in the American labor movement, and their struggles to adjust to American ways while preserving their old country traditions.

The American Jewish retrieval of Yiddishkeit in the decade prior to 1967 is a characteristically American phenomenon in another way as well. Although, to borrow H. Rap Brown's phrase from the mid-1960s, violence has always been as American as cherry pie (though it had not yet become as Jewish as kreplach), it is also the case that the late 1950s and the early 1960s saw other significant expressions of what we have been calling gentleness. The most obvious and important was the pacifist message and strategy that Martin Luther King, Jr., and his associates, and the Student Nonviolent Coordinating Committee, brought to the civil rights movement. The spread of nonviolent initiatives to college campuses and to the early phase of the 1960s student rebellion (many participants in which were conversant with political ideals such as those expressed in Albert Camus's *Neither Victim nor Executioner* [1947; French original 1946], was part of this current, as were the beginnings, in 1965–68, of the movement against the war in Vietnam.

In a society that not long before had idealized the soldier, even electing one to two terms as president, these sociopolitical movements, like the revived interest in the peaceful, vulnerable Jewish culture of eastern Europe, expressed a desire among some Americans for more gentle images and relations.

Notably, the retrieval of the gentle imagery of Yiddishkeit was itself not restricted to Jews. Isaac Bashevis Singer won the Nobel Prize in literature in addition to many Jewish awards and found a highly diverse, genuinely national readership in the United States. Similarly, Malamud's *The Fixer*, and *Fiddler on the Roof*, reached very broad audiences. As many non-Jewish as Jewish college students hung posters of Woody Allen, the latter-day schlemiel, and Albert Einstein, the frail, peace-loving absentminded professor.

When one turns this enlarged lens on the other side of 1967, specifically Jewish trends again reflect the broader American ones. For if the late 1950s and early 1960s witnessed some significant expressions of nonviolence and gentleness, the last years of the 1960s, including the June 1967 Arab-Israeli War, were marked by the spread of violence, of apparently revolutionary conditions, and of imagery of tough bodies. In this sense, the many Jewish Americans who developed deep attachments to the ideals and images of Israeli warrior Jews after June 1967 were quite within both the historical American grain and the country's specific dynamics in the late 1960s.

The Six Day War, for example, entered the consciousness of Americans just as the Vietnam War was reaching crisis proportions both in Indochina and at home and only shortly before the assassinations of Martin Luther King, Jr. and Robert Kennedy. The year prior to the 1967 war in the Middle East had witnessed the spread of black ghetto revolts and riots, and the adoption of armed self-defense and sometimes "armed struggle" by the increasingly nationalist and even separatist black movement, crystallized in the Black Panther Party's macho and martial style. As America's role in Vietnam grew more bloodthirsty, important sections of the antiwar movement turned toward tactics of confrontation and violence. At the center of this development was the group calling itself Weatherman (in which notable numbers of young Jews participated); although it caused far less physical damage than is generally thought, it certainly helped to fill the air at the close of the 1960s with high-volume rhetoric of righteous revolutionary violence. Viewed in this context, Meir Kahane's formation of the Jewish Defense League in 1968 is not only striking as a Jewish event; it is also an almost representative American event, not the same as, but surely of a piece with, the formation of Weatherman and the Black Panthers.

The blossoming of tough Jewish imagery, especially of the sort found in the fiction examined in part 3, should also be seen in connection with events such as the publication in 1969 of Mario Puzo's *The Godfather* and the positive reception it was accorded. For all its specifically Italian American elements and stereotypes, the novel and subsequent film offered a marvelously aestheticized version of what was becoming the message of the late 1960s and early 1970s, namely, that life is a battlefield where only the tough, icy-veined, and well armed survive. As the 1980s progressed, *The Godfather* would seem increasingly tame next to the assortment of Avengers, Terminators, Equalizers, Superflies, Dirty Harrys, Robocops, and Rambos who came to fill the fantasies of millions of Americans, including the nation's president and its Jews. Not only did American Jews become Zionized; they—and Zionism—became Ramboized, that is, Americanized, as well.

One might have expected American Jews—with their historic lineage of gentleness and vulnerability (not least, the example of the Nazi Final Solution) and especially their revival of the culture of Yiddishkeit in the early 1960s—to challenge the new toughness and brutality, in fulfillment of what many considered to be an essentially Jewish mission. In fact, American Jews as a group did not emerge as distinctive critics of the new violence and militarism. On the contrary, in large numbers they supported Israeli armed might and thus contributed to the new imagery of toughness in this country. After 1967 Sartre's observation regarding the inherent peacefulness of Jews was rendered increasingly obsolete.

Psychologically, this was a complex business. For the more or less national turn toward violence and tough imagery beginning in the late 1960s was also a turn *away* from a contrasting imagery and conduct that included not only the nonviolent ideals and experiments of the early civil rights and antiwar movements, but also the initial expressions of women's liberation and the new androgynous look in popular culture that was announced by the girlish hairdos of the Beatles and would get fuller expression among the hippies and flower children. The Jewish American retrieval of Yiddishkeit, with its scholars, storytellers, and schlemiels; the stateless vulnerability of the shtetl; the absence of soldiers and military norms; the pale and often delicate look of shtetl children—this, I propose, was part of what could be called an American flirtation with the imagery and practice of gentleness. But it was an imagery that, in a male-dominated society such as ours, was inevitably perceived as being insufficiently manly or simply effeminate.

The increase in violence and toughness in America from the late 1960s on is, then, to be understood in part as a counterattack in the name of manliness and toughness against the threat of gentleness perceived as feminization. Like the gentle threat itself, the tough counterattack was widespread and not confined to a single group. Jews and blacks constituted especially vocal participants in the resurgent toughness of the late

1960s—just as they had assumed disproportionately significant roles in the steps toward gentleness that had blossomed over the previous decade.

Historically, the masculinity of Jewish and black males was challenged and debased by racists. For a variety of good reasons, neither group was willing to stand for such treatment any longer. Although their respective positions were quite different, many blacks and Jews perceived themselves as having real prospects of integration into American society. Both groups were thus especially sensitive to explicit or coded charges of effeminacy and quite ready to embrace a rejuvenated version of the traditional American manly and tough ethos, which was reasserting itself at the decade's close—not in spite of but largely because of what had happened prior to the late 1960s. Blacks and Jews feared that the nonviolence and doctrine of love at the center of the civil rights movement and the physically impotent shtetl would be taken as signs of a lack of manliness among Jewish and black men. What could be called the masculinist bravado of visible currents of black male style from about 1966 onward and American Jewish romanticization of the Israeli soldier could likewise be seen as responses to such fears. Recent tough Jewish fiction quite insistently idealizes a Jewish version of the hard, sharply chiseled, taciturn Aryan masculinity of the "standing tall," "hanging tough" variety that continues to occupy much space in the American imagination.[35]

The emergence of black power and the dissolution of the civil rights movement had additional consequences for the gestation of tough Jewish imagery in this country. Those developments marked, at least temporarily, the end of the longstanding connection, often even the real bond, between progressive black intellectuals and activists and their counterparts among Jews. The pain and bitterness of this separation is the subject of Jonathan Kaufman's recent *Broken Alliance: The Turbulent Times between Blacks and Jews in America*.[36] By the late 1960s black anti-Semitism and Jewish anti-black racism were making themselves felt on the American scene. Jewish fear of blacks had already been voiced, indeed, legitimated as a cultural-political vision by Norman Podhoretz in his essay "My Negro Problem—and Ours," which originally appeared in *Commentary* in 1963.[37] Some blacks and Jews have remained outside the spiral of entwined paranoias, and some have occasionally debunked it, but large numbers have not. Widespread black anti-Semitism and Jewish anti-black racism suggest that each of these two minorities seeks to convince the dominant society that neither one has anything in common with the other—with the other "other," as it were. It is as if some sadomasochistic psychological mechanism were at work, with blacks demonstrating their fitness as Americans by displays of anti-Semitism, and Jews doing the same thing with their racist views of blacks. As Kaufman's study shows (pp. 190ff.), the 1967 Six Day War helped to raise tensions between Jews and blacks beyond the simmering point. Many black political activists expressed solidarity with the Palestine Liberation Organization, which was formed in 1968, while many Jews viewed American blacks as the local arm of Arab anti-Semitism.

The American Jewish desire for toughness had other, more powerful sources as well. That the culture of Yiddishkeit revived by American Jews in the 1960s had been annihilated by the Nazis forty years after it had been shaken by the pogroms of tsarist Russia was a prime factor. The idealized vibrance and richness of the world of shtetl and shul could not entirely hide the fact that American Jews already knew the fate of that culture and already knew that Sholem Aleichem's children would—evidently with little, if any, resistance—be shot, starved, clubbed, and gassed to death by Nazis and their supporters.

Two books published at the start of the 1960s moved this issue to the center of discussions of Jewish identity in America. These were Bruno Bettelheim's *Informed Heart: Autonomy in a Mass Age*[38] and Hannah Arendt's *Eichmann in Jerusalem: A Report on the Banality of Evil*, her analysis of the trial of Adolf Eichmann in Israel in 1961, first published as a series of articles in the *New Yorker*.[39] In different ways, both authors raised similar questions of Jewish passivity and weakness in the face of Nazi brutality, and Arendt raised, in addition, the question of Jewish compliance with the machinery of genocide. In the intense, growing discussion generated by these two works the question was asked again and again: Why had the Jews let themselves be taken to their deaths in the Nazi camps like lambs—soft, gentle, and feminine—to the slaughter?[40]

Neither the renaissance of Yiddishkeit nor Arendt's and Bettelheim's theses, however, exhausted the field of imagery to which American Jews were giving form in the years prior to the 1967 war. Also entering the picture at this time was *Exodus*, both the novel and the film, which offered a radically different view of Jewish conduct in the face of the Nazi extermination attempt. And in 1961 Uris followed his first success with one nearly as great, *Mila 18*, based on the story of the Jewish resistance and uprising in the Warsaw Ghetto and, like *Exodus*, a song of praise to the tough, fighting Jew. It is also worth remembering that by today's standards discussion of the Nazi mass murder of Jews was at best limited between the end of the Second World War and the early 1960s. So often is the term *Holocaust* employed and evoked today, so basic a part of Jewish American identity has it become, that it is bracing to be reminded of the relatively recent vintage of both the term and the discussion. Not until the late 1950s, for example, was the word introduced by the Israeli Yad Vashem memorial institution, only slowly entering the American vocabulary during the next several years. In sketching this shift, Leon Jick has noted that 1959 saw the publication of a much-read book entitled *Holocaust*—which dealt not with the mass murder of Jews but rather with the 1942 Boston nightclub fire that had left hundreds dead.[41]

By 1967 *Holocaust*, with its immense and eventually mind-numbing resonance, was becoming the central term of Jewish American discussion and identity. In retrospect, it seems that by June of 1967 American Jews were ripe for the Six Day War, with one arm extended to their crushed European relatives, reviving the latters' culture and remembering the dead, and the other arm, sleeves rolled up, ready for Israel's injection of tough Jewish serum. The encounter of American Jews with the stunning Israeli victory over a coalition of Arab armies that had threatened to obliterate the Jewish state constituted a fantastic turn in what was becoming the central Jewish American fantasy: the vulnerability of the Jews destroyed by Nazism was easily transferred to Israel's vulnerability on the eve of the Six Day War; the Nazis were easily replaced by Arabs. The Holocaust was about to be replayed in the Middle East. Only this time, and in merely six days, the eradication of Jews *had been averted* by the decisive military action of a wonderfully new sort of Jew. The narrative could and would be rewritten, as Freud had rewritten the "cap in the mud" story and as I rewrote Ken Follett's *Triple*. Images of Jews cowering, running, crying, and dying were replaced by a remarkable Jewish fighting force.

This time, the first in their history, the Jews won; they actually proved to be tougher.

Precisely by restoring Jewish power to the stage of world history, as the *New Republic* put it, the Israeli victory in the Six Day War created a dilemma for American Jews for whom the heritage of powerlessness, gentleness, and physical frailty still held great, if increasingly residual, meaning: How are the tough Jew and Jewish state power—specifically, the actual conquest of land (the West Bank of the Jordan River, the Gaza Strip, and the Sinai desert) and subjugation of people (Palestinians)—to be justified? What are Jews if not, as Jakob Freud, Jean-Paul Sartre, Philip Roth, and countless others might say, gentle, nonviolent, guided by humane ethics, and so forth? The resolution to this dilemma—the link between the Holocaust and the Six Day War—was waiting to be grasped.

It is really only *after* the June 1967 war that we see the proliferation of scholarly studies, films, courses, lectures, conferences, tough Jewish pulp fiction, and intense popular discussion. Among American Jews, Israel's victory in June 1967 expanded and escalated what had previously been a limited relationship to the Holocaust. Since then more than one observer has even spoken of a Holocaust industry (a *shoah* show, some have called it) that desecrates the memory of the murdered by sale, resale, and overuse of their terror and death. In any case, from June 1967 to the present, Jewish Americans have increasingly thought of themselves in relation to both Israel and the Holocaust, that is, in terms of the imagery of tough and gentle/weak Jews.

The two events can be linked according to this formula: The Israeli triumph in the Six Day War provided American Jews with the imagery of Jewish toughness and politico-military self-assertion which enabled them to rethink the Holocaust as something more than simply Jewish passivity and victimization (part 2). At the same time, the Holocaust, precisely because of its imagery of Jewish victimization, enabled Jewish Americans (and Israelis) to embrace the consequences of the Israeli victory: occupying the West Bank and the Gaza Strip, turning the Palestinians there into a subject people, and now suppressing the Palestinian uprising. The Holocaust made this acceptable to large numbers of American (and Israeli) Jews.

I will put the matter more sharply and angrily: as my own Nat Dickstein fantasy of 1982 indicates, the more brutal Israeli policies become, and as more Israelis speak of the country's self-brutalization as well, the more American Jews discuss, indeed, the more they need, the Holocaust.[42] What is critical, then, is not necessarily *how* one interprets Nazism, or whether one sees the Jews as having been inept victims of Hitlerism, as depicted by Bruno Bettelheim, or fighters, as represented by Leon Uris. What vindicates power is *that* the unparalleled genocide against the Jews is being discussed, debated, and reconsidered. For the more the Nazi Final Solution to the Jewish question is discussed, the more the discussants (Jewish and not) can attach a moral sheen to the actions of Israel's tough Jews. This function of the Holocaust discussion is rooted in a deep, historically formed Jewish need: the need to be ethical.

PART TWO

From Masada to Mossad: A Historical Sketch of Tough Jewish Imagery

I

JEWISH TOUGHNESS BEFORE ZIONISM

IN ADDITION to putting the Jewish present and future on a radically new footing, the recent proliferation of tough Jewish imagery has also altered perceptions of the Jewish past. Previously, Jews generally tended to ignore, mute, or repress historical examples of Jewish toughness. Today, one is more likely to see this twig bent in the other direction: Jewish publicists are so fervently in search of progenitors of the new toughness that they are often inclined to deny the very existence of examples of Jewish timidity, gentleness, resignation, or frailty. As part 3 indicates, the post-1967 wave of tough Jewish novels constitutes a vivid example of this sort of overextended historical revisionism. In its own way, so does the present chapter, which offers a historical sketch of pre-1967 tough Jewish imagery, but from a non-Zionist viewpoint.

Most contributors to the larger revisionist effort uphold one of two theses. The first contends that prior to the twentieth-century emergence of the Zionist movement and the establishment of Israel, Jews were trapped in the tragedy of weakness, powerlessness, frailty, and gentleness. The values informing this approach differ radically from those of, for example, Michael Selzer, evoked in part 1. Yet, although they evaluate the elements differently, both the hards and the softs represent history in similar, similarly flawed ways: as millennia of Jewish frailty followed by a new, recent era of Jewish toughness.

The second of the two Zionist-inspired standpoints is historically more differentiated and nuanced. It emphasizes the presence of tough Jews *throughout* history, which is helpful; but then it claims all such examples as forerunners of contemporary Zionism, which is not. My own view is that, given both the long-standing primacy of meek and gentle Jewish imagery and the recent Zionist rupture with it, surveying the Jewish past with an eye on its tough images may enrich one's historical sense of the present. Specifically, I want to indicate the extent to which Jewish toughness and physical self-assertion are not simply moments in the prehistory of Zionism. In understanding them instead as integral dimensions of Jewish history in its broader senses, I am suggesting two things: (1) that Jews have needed neither Zionism nor a Jewish state in order to be tough; and (2) that Zionism has transformed the previously sporadic and self-limiting history of Jewish toughness into a full-blown cultural politics. While my perspective differs from those of the historians and analysts to whose views I have referred anonymously above, I could not have proceeded without their work. My dependence on their research is substantial.

Like Lambs to Slaughter? Jewish Toughness
in the Holocaust

The reappraisal of the Jewish past has been most vigorous in connection with the theme of Jewish responses to Nazi genocide. More than any other historical moment, this one has given the world its starkest and most pervasive images of Jewish powerlessness, timidity, and victimization. Countless are the photographs of Jewish prisoners in the death camps, still alive but resembling the corpses so many would soon become; the stories of hundreds, even thousands, of camp inmates facing a handful of modestly armed guards in traumatized resignation; and the times since 1945 that the question has been raised of why so few Jews sought to escape, to resist, or to fight back.

We cannot reckon fully with these questions here, but several points are nevertheless appropriate. First, millions of Jews caught in the Nazi net behaved and died in exactly the fashion depicted above: in fear and trembling. Many of those who died without resisting, moreover, undoubtedly did so for reasons of the culture of Jewish timidity and gentleness they carried in their hearts. Equal numbers of others must have died in resignation or virtual paralysis brought on, not by their cultural heritage, but by the massive trauma of their situation. Second, although many of the widespread cases of nonresistance, helplessness, and resignation certainly had specifically Jewish sources, such behavior is not accurately classified as simply or typically Jewish: it has also been *characteristic of non-Jews* in less extreme situations of traumatizing confinement. Among American prisoners of war in Korea in the early 1950s, for example, passivity and susceptibility to brainwashing by their North Korean captors were notoriously widespread. Similar patterns characterized Russian troops captured by the Nazis during the Second World War. In both cases those involved had been trained in combat, risk, and bravery; they were not products of a culture of timidity and gentleness. Yet resistance to incarceration still remained minimal at best.

Isaiah Trunk, a major contributor to the reappraisal of Jewish timidity, raises the following questions: "Why isn't there one recorded instance of armed insurrection by Gentile inmates of a concentration camp, when the conditions for such were more favorable than for the Jews . . . ? Why," Trunk proceeds, "were the children and youth of the Warsaw Ghetto, the pathetically armed remnants of a decimated nation, the first to rise against the Nazis anywhere in Europe?"[1] The final point here concerning Jewish behavior in the face of Nazi terror is contained in the ellipsis in the passage cited from Trunk. He writes that conditions for armed insurrection were more favorable for non-Jews than for Jews, who, however, "*rose many times*" (emphasis added), as the sentence concludes. Indeed, historical research published in the past two decades has begun substantially to alter the still-prevalent picture of Jewish behavior and self-images in the Nazi years. It is now becoming clear, as Yehuda Bauer has put it, that Jewish armed resistance to the Nazis and their collaborators "was considerably more widespread than has been subsequently [that is, in the decades following 1945] assumed."[2]

Nor, as these more recent analyses argue, should armed actions be the sole measure of Jewish resistance. Trunk, Bauer, Yisrael Gutman, and other scholars have begun to examine the varied efforts of timid, gentle, and tough Jews alike to sustain Jewish life in the Nazi-controlled ghettos: kindergartens, embroidery classes, religious study circles, book-vending networks, soup kitchens, old-age homes, and so on. These historians have also argued that Jews who martyred themselves or their children, or went to their deaths with Jewish prayers on their lips, may or may not have been gentle Jews, but ought not to be counted among the timid, frail, and weak.

There are new answers, then, to the old question of why Jews fell before the Nazis without a fight. Those answers, however, generate a new question: Why do we have new answers *now*? Trunk provides part of an explanation. In their initial efforts to fathom the Third Reich and its program of mass murder, researchers focused on the Nazis themselves, on the party and state institutions, and on the mechanisms of imprisonment and annihilation. As a result, Trunk suggests, the Jewish and other victims were often viewed as passive objects worked over by the machinery of death, and thus less worthy than their murderers of close study.[3] Investigations such as Trunk's are part of the shift, initiated largely by Jewish historians, toward a focus on the ghettoized and terrorized Jews as subjects rather than as mere objects in the crisis of 1933–45.

Studies by Trunk, Lucy Davidowicz, and others are explicit rejoinders to the arguments Bruno Bettelheim and Hannah Arendt presented in the early 1960s. They are also, I propose, shaped by the shift toward a tough Jewish consciousness that had been set in motion by the Israeli victory in June 1967. Indeed, a brief look at the Holocaust discussion in Israel itself sheds light on developments in this country. In his fascinating, but now nearly forgotten study of Israeli society, *The End of the Jewish People?* (1965)—a text that was pushed into obscurity by the 1967 war—Georges Friedmann, the late French sociologist, reported on the variety (depending on age, experience, and country of origin) of Israeli responses to the 1961 Eichmann trial. Focusing on the sabras, young Israelis born in Mandate Palestine or, after 1948, Israel, Friedmann remarks that "having been brought up in complete liberty as citizens of a state that had established itself by fighting, possessed a strong army and was primarily preoccupied with its own security, they regarded self-defense as an elementary duty and . . . felt themselves to be very different from the Jews who 'had let their throats be cut like sheep.' Their attitude to the victims of the great massacre," Friedmann continues, "was a mixture of pity, incomprehension and remoteness. Some even considered that, apart from the activities of some partisan groups and the Warsaw Ghetto revolt, the whole thing was an inglorious episode in Jewish history."

According to Friedmann, this response was cause for concern among Israeli political, civic, and educational leaders. By 1963 they launched efforts, including the addition of mandatory courses on the history of anti-Semitism and European Jewry into school curricula, aimed at providing young Israelis with a more positive picture of the experiences of pre- and non-Israeli Jews. In this connection, Friedmann observes, the Yad Vashem memorial to those killed by the Nazis describes itself in its pamphlets and bulletins as commemorating, not victims, but heroes and martyrs.[4] And Israeli author and politician Amnon Rubenstein has recently observed in a similar vein that "actually accusing the Jews of going to gas chambers like sheep to the slaughterhouse abounded in *sabra* literature" already from the early days of the state.[5]

Thus, we have a proximity between the young sabras' responses to the story disclosed by the Eichmann trial and the theses presented by Bettelheim and Arendt. Although they took different routes, Israeli youth and the two older, German Jewish intellectuals in the United States reached the common conclusion that the Nazis' Jewish victims, with few exceptions, had been just that—victims: weak, resigned, unable to resist, sometimes even facilitating, if unintentionally, the killing. The rejoinders to this view continue to appear unabated today and parallel this view. Israeli leaders in the aftermath of the Eichmann trial had essentially the same goal as the revisionist historians discussed here: to introduce tougher Jews.

Tough Jews in Ancient Times: The Erosion of a Stereotype

Having evoked examples from the 1933–45 period, the focus now shifts to ancient history, to the beginning of the long tale of tough Jewish imagery from early times to 1948.

For centuries in pagan, polytheistic antiquity, Jews were known, and knew themselves, as great soldiers and tillers of the soil as well as great worshipers of the one almighty God of Israel. Their warrior heritage was sustained until the second century A.D., with the destruction of the Jewish state by Rome. The empire's armies first defeated the resistance struggles of the Zealots, led by Simon ben Eleazar, at the Masada fortress in 73 A.D. (chronicled in Josephus' *The Jewish War*); in the following century they crushed, after three years of bloody battle (132–35), what proved to be the last burst of Jewish armed resistance, the revolt led by Simon Bar Kokhba in Roman-annexed Judea.

This ancient, tough Jewish heritage seems to have come to a close in the aftermath of the Bar Kokhba revolt. It is worth recalling, however, that two of the recent tough Jewish novels examined in part 3 (and an American television special as well) are based on the Zealots' resistance and final collective martyrdom, and that the Masada fortress, rediscovered and excavated in the mid-1960s and then restored, is today a much-

visited national shrine in Israel and the site of numerous ceremonies of the Israel Defense Forces.[6]

Simon Bar Kokhba's second-century revolt has likewise been
elevated to the status of national myth in Israel—so powerful
a myth that it has recently been challenged as a dangerous
force in Israeli political culture. In 1983 Yehoshafat Harkabi,
an Israeli expert in theoretical strategy and former hard-liner,
provoked something of a scandal in his country with the argument that, far from being worthy of emulation, Bar Kokhba's
revolt was politically foolhardy and militarily flawed. So potent
was the warrior heritage, Harkabi argues, that it overshadowed
coherent politics. He adds that the willful failure to take critical
measure of the Bar Kokhba revolt has fueled a cult of audacity
that propels contemporary Israel toward altogether unrealistic
(and, as in the original revolt, self-destructive) policies in the
occupied territories.[7]

Harkabi's study is especially pertinent here because of its
approach to the issue of the *fate* of the ancient tough Jewish
stereotype. The period following the Roman victory over the
Bar Kokhba revolt witnessed a transformation in Jewish stereotypes and self-images as profound as that which has been
unfolding in this century. By the latter part of the second
century the previously solid Jewish warrior ideals began to
erode rapidly. In their place arose something new: images of
timid, resigned, and gentle Jews. The stories of the Jewish taste
for revenge and capacity for violence told in the Old Testament
would increasingly be confined to prayers and daydreams, and
increasingly less a reflection of the Jews' actual social life.
Although Harkabi does not employ these terms regarding the
transformation in stereotypes, he emphasizes that the defeat
of Bar Kokhba's forces "altered the position of the Jewish peo-

ple," pushing them toward the margins of history and transforming a once-active force into a passive object (p. xi).

Harkabi's terminology—active agency and passive object—is the same as that proposed by Isaiah Trunk in his reappraisal of Jewish responses to Nazi persecution. Indeed, such formulations are widespread in post-1967 discussions of Jewish history. For example, the *New Republic* editorial commemorating Israel's 1967 victory describes the June war as having restored the Jewish people to the status of active historical subject.[8] As commonly used, these terms are tightly linked to Jewish statehood (active) and statelessness (passive). By contrast, Trunk's *Jewish Responses to Nazi Persecution* speaks of Jewish victims transforming themselves into active units of resistance that are independent of Jewish statehood, which of course did not exist at the time. To be sure, a variety of Zionists played instrumental roles in the transformation analyzed by Trunk, but so did a variety of non-Zionist Jews. I stress the point because one of the theses of this historical survey is that *neither Jewish toughness nor collective historical activism is dependent on Jewish statehood*. The notion that without statehood or the movement to achieve it, Jews are condemned to passivity and timidity is a pivotal myth of Zionism.

Zionists, including Harkabi, could certainly reply that history provides much fuel for such a myth. His work shows that superior Roman power, though the main factor in the Jewish abandonment of the warrior spirit, was not the only one and that the imperial pacification program was enhanced by what amounted to Jewish self-pacification directed by the community's religious leadership. "Rabbinic expressions," according to Harkabi, "sought to erase the Bar Kokhba Rebellion from the national memory" (p. 92). The revolt, he argues, had been shaped by a double illusion. First, political considerations (prospects of a "negotiated settlement") were dwarfed by the combination of the Jews' prophetic-messianic yearnings and the heritage of armed resistance. Thus on the eve of the revolt the learned Rabbi Akiba blessed Simon Bar Kokhba as the Messiah: "There shall step forth a star out of Jacob, and a scepter shall rise out of Israel, and shall smite through the corners of Moab, and break down the sons of Seth."[9]

Such hopes were dashed. And Rabbi Akiba was evidently one of the Ten Martyrs who took their own lives following the defeat of the revolt. The second part of what Harkabi calls the double illusion came in the postrevolt period, when the rabbis went to the opposite extreme of Bar Kokhba and Rabbi Akiba and forbade discussion of specific events and insisted that matters be pushed "upward to the divine level." This, Harkabi adds, "was of momentous importance to Jewish culture. . . . Jewish destiny in the form of disaster and misfortune was not seen as proceeding from political mistakes but as ordained by the almighty" (pp. 92–93). This premise was given weight by rabbinic oaths proscribing immigration to Israel en masse, and calling for overall accommodation to the conditions of foreign rule. The Romans were said to have been granted dominion by God, and the rabbis encouraged Jews to "pray for the welfare of the ruling power, since, but for fear of it, people would swallow each other alive," and reminded them to "let the dread of the ruling powers always be with you" (p. 94).

While the facts of Jewish dispersion and the defeat of the Bar Kokhba revolt drastically restricted the Jews' options, the emphasis on political passivity and "withdrawal from history" was in Harkabi's view not mandated by circumstances. Nonetheless, such withdrawal proceeded and was then "completed

by an immersion in *Torah*. With *Torah*-study at the very center
of the people's life, history was quasi-neutralized" (p. 95). The
Talmud—with its recommendation that "all who occupy
themselves in the study of *Torah* are saved from oppression by
the ruling powers. . . . The disciples of the wise remove the
yoke of exile from themselves"—was composed during this
period of the Jews' new political powerlessness. The culture
of passivity, resignation, and timidity that came to dominate
Jewish life after 135, Harkabi emphasizes, would continue to
do so through the eighteenth century: Sabbatai Zevi's revival
of the heroic imagery of Simon Bar Kokhba in seventeeth-
century Poland was an exception.

This analysis, though a compelling and persuasive explanation of the historical roots of the stereotype of Jewish weakness and gentleness, suffers from a major lapse: Harkabi's view
that for close to seventeen hundred years timid Jews and a
Jewish "withdrawal from history" constituted the entire picture. On this matter, alternatives to Harkabi are needed. They
are also available, thanks to two historians, Reuben Ainsztein
and David Biale.[10]

Victims Par Excellence? Tough Jews in the Middle Ages

Ainsztein, a Polish leftist with experience in the anti-fascist
resistance movement, served as a fighter pilot in the British
Royal Air Force in the Second World War. He has little
patience for Jewish timidity or gentleness, viewing them as
myths at best, calumnies at worst. At the core of his remarkable
study is a tension between Ainsztein's *historical* approach to
Jewish life and values and his conviction concerning a trans-
historical Jewish essence. For Ainsztein, the spirit and skills

of the soldier, far from being foreign elements, are part of the very fiber of Jewishness; whenever and wherever conditions enabled Jews "to be themselves," they were warriors of merit (p. 33). If eastern European Jews in particular were such fatalists and war-shy weaklings, he asks, how is one to explain the disproportionately large number of Jewish officers in the Soviet Red Army? Because, he responds, when given the chance, Jews prove they are essentially fighters.

David Biale, a young American historian writing in the aftermath of the 1982 Israeli invasion of Lebanon, has sought to show that between ancient times and the establishment of Israel, Jews have not been *politically* powerless. On the contrary, they have been a people who, under uniquely beleaguered and fragmented circumstances, exercised various forms of power and generated far more dense, if often ambiguous, civic and political cultures than most observers have realized. Just as Harkabi criticizes the Israeli "cult of audacity" and its source, the "Bar Kokhba syndrome," so Biale is similarly interested in raising questions about Israel's present-day misuses of power. He argues that both Israeli and American Jews can and should derive salutary lessons from the whole and varied history of Jewish experiences with political power. Biale's work, considered in tandem with Ainsztein's (which Biale does not mention) offers many suggestions for the revision of longstanding and widely held assumptions about the stereotypes of Jewish timidity, gentleness, and toughness.

"The picture of medieval Jews as victims *par excellence* who sought salvation in prayers or flight [as Harkabi and countless others seem to have assumed], as people who knew how to die but not how to defend themselves, is a false one," Ainsztein writes (p. 19), a view with which Biale concurs (p. 72). So effective has this picture been, however, that many Jews themselves ignored or suppressed (and here are shades of the other part of Harkabi's argument) instances of robust, martial action by their coreligionists. Citing the case of the ninth-century Jewish fraternity of daring merchant-adventurers known as the Radanites, a multilingual band whose members journeyed from France through Spain to China and India, Ainsztein deems it "typical of the treatment Jewish men of action have received *until quite recently* that whatever we know about the Radanites, we owe to the Arabs" (p. 9; emphasis added). Although he concedes that Jews may have played a role in the gestation of images of their own weakness, he is inclined to see this stereotype as having been imposed from without. Thus, in the medieval West, "the fighting and soldierly element among the Jews survived all the combined efforts of the Catholic church and its secular allies to turn them into contemptible usurers and old-clothes traders, whose very appearance, in the words of Peter the Venerable, was to be '. . .dependent, miserable and terror-stricken' " (p. 19).

David Biale corroborates Ainsztein's account, noting sporadic instances of armed uprisings in late antiquity and the early Middle Ages among Babylonian and Iraqi Jews. In western and central Europe, Jews retained the right to bear arms and continued to do so even after this right was widely revoked in the thirteenth century, since no penalties were attached to violations. They were also permitted to issue duel challenges. Biale cites rabbinical texts from early thirteenth-century Spain and Germany justifying the carrying and use of weapons by Jews on the Sabbath, in case their towns should fall under siege or face other life-threatening crises. According to Biale, such texts imply that Jews likely bore arms the rest of the week (pp. 72–73).

Earlier, confronted with the Crusades of the eleventh and

twelfth centuries, Jews had used their weapons to defend themselves, often fighting alongside soldiers of the local (non-Jewish) ruler against the crusading forces. Rather than being viewed and viewing themselves as helpless victims, occasionally protected by their patrons, Biale argues, Jews were expected to participate in their own defense (pp. 73–74). During the Middle Ages and even beyond, moreover, Jews gained reputations as arms makers, a trade for which they had achieved renown in ancient Palestine. Spain provides the example of what Biale calls "perhaps the only Jewish general of medieval times," Samuel ha-Nagid, a poet, communal leader, and "Jewish Machiavelli" ("Take risks when you aim for power," Samuel wrote, "and defeat the foe with the sword"), who led the armies of Granada in the early eleventh century.

Summarizing the matter, Biale writes (p. 77), and Ainsztein concurs (p. 11), that "the great Jewish military prowess of antiquity . . . did not disappear with the loss of Jewish sovereignty." This is the revisionist component of both Ainsztein's and Biale's studies, but it, too, needs revising. For while their studies are extremely helpful and persuasive in beginning to disclose the extensive presence of tough Jews in (in this instance) medieval society, they also remind us of the absence of a *stereotype* and image of toughness that Jews might have embraced and made a part of their collective sense of themselves.

Biale observes, for example, that into the sixteenth century Jewish religious and civic leaders commonly represented the sacrilegious or the bad Jew with illustrations of figures armed with sword or pike. "Woe to the wicked son and woe to his neighbor" is the caption over a picture of such a wicked son in a Prague Haggadah—and he is armed. "This evidence confirms that Jews did indeed carry arms, even if those who did so were regarded as somewhat brutal and uneducated; the armed Jew might be religiously indifferent, but he was still a Jew. One even wonders," Biale continues, "whether the Prague *Haggadah* may in fact betray a certain hidden admiration for the armed Jew who could intimidate his enemies" (p. 73)—just as I wondered in part 1, in connection with Jakob Freud, about Jewish longings for toughness beneath the self-imagery of timidity and gentleness. Such projections onto the past may serve to put the dominant meek Jewish imagery into better historical perspective, but they do not thereby make it any the less dominant.

Following the lead of historian Jacob Katz, Biale shows that the European Middle Ages witnessed what can be called only with irony a revival of the ancient practice of martyrdom, which, it was long claimed, had achieved epic proportions in the collective suicide of the Jews at the besieged fortress of Masada. Aside from women and children, several of whom hid, survived, and provided Josephus with an important source for the later pages of *The Jewish War*, the Jews at Masada were themselves tough in the most exact sense. The principles on which they took their own lives flowed directly, if not inevitably, from their experience and ethos as warriors.

As recounted by Josephus, Simon ben Eleazar addressed his roughly one hundred loyal followers in these words:

At such a time we must not disgrace ourselves: hitherto we have never submitted to slavery, even when it brought no danger with it: we must not choose slavery now, and with it penalties that will mean the end of everything if we fall alive into the hands of the Romans. . . . And I think it is God who has given us this privilege, that we can die nobly and as free men, unlike others who were unexpectedly defeated. In our case it is evident that daybreak will end our resistance, but we are free to choose an honorable death with our loved ones. This our enemies cannot prevent, however earnestly they may pray to take us alive; nor can we defeat them in battle.[11]

Jewish martyrdom in the Middle Ages is all the more extraordinary and wrenching precisely because the culture of those who chose it was not that of the original Zealots. Their situations, however, were often as hopeless. During the Crusades of the eleventh and twelfth centuries, the vastly outnumbered Jews often turned passive martyrdom into a form of active resistance. Rather than accept Christianity, they took their own lives instead of allowing themselves to be killed.[12]

Nobody Dared Lift a Hand: From the Middle Ages to the French Revolution

Biale pursues the theme of Jewish *political* power from the Middle Ages to the present, but his remarks on Jewish toughness—physical strength, armed activity, and bravery in battle—include only one example from the postmedieval period. That is the worst calamity that befell the Jews during the early modern era: the assault on Polish Jewry in 1648–50 by Ukrainian Cossacks led by the very tough Bogdan Chmielnitski (p. 74).[13] The wave of destruction and death that swept across Jewish Poland in those years was no less traumatic than the events surrounding the expulsion of the Jews from Spain in 1492 or the outbreak of widespread anti-Jewish actions on the eve of and throughout the Lutheran Reformation.

As in early sixteenth-century Germany, so in mid-seventeenth-century Poland, tensions and crises in the larger society focused hostile attention on the Jewish minority. For

Chmielnitski's movement was not simply anti-Jewish. It was also a revolt against an exploitative Polish landowning elite, whom Jews often served as intermediaries (rent collectors, tavern managers, and so on). The Cossack bands thus roamed the Polish countryside at the end of the 1640s, turning on Poles as well as on Jews. The Jews were especially good targets—guilty of having served the Polish exploiters and obviously vulnerable. The entire episode is invariably seen as emblematic of Jewish helplessness and timidity.

Isaac Bashevis Singer sets his novel *The Slave* (1962) in the aftermath of the Chmielnitski massacres. One especially rich passage concerns Jacob, the main character, who has survived the assault on his town, Josefov. He has lost his wife, his children, and his Jewish world, having been captured and sold as a slave to a small, ostensibly Christian, but primarily pagan, Polish farmer. The remarkable novel revolves around the great but anguished (because forbidden) love between Jacob and the farmer's daughter, Wanda.[14]

Jacob is the very model of gentleness. He sustains his saintly philosophy, which Wanda shares, through ordeals few could survive without becoming radically disillusioned. Realizing that he is above all else a survivor, physically as well as morally, he reflects on the question of strength and toughness toward the novel's end: "What would happen to the might of the wicked if the just were not so craven?" he wonders.

Stories he had heard of how the Jews had behaved during the massacres shamed him. Nobody dared lift a hand against the butchers while they slaughtered entire communities. Though for generations Jewish blacksmiths had forged swords, it had never occurred to the Jews to meet their attackers with weapons. The Jews of Josefov, when Jacob had spoken of this, had shrugged their shoulders. The sword is for Esau, not for Jacob. Nevertheless, must a man agree to his own destruction? Wanda had often asked Jacob: Why did the Jews permit it? The ancient Jews of the Bible stories had been heroic. Jacob never really knew how to answer her. (pp. 248–49)

The Slave, published shortly after Bruno Bettelheim's *Informed Heart* (1960) and just before the publication of Hannah Arendt's *Eichmann in Jerusalem* (1963), poses questions in the passage just cited that are close to the issues raised by Bettelheim and Arendt. Presumably, Singer's line of inquiry was also provoked by the matter of Jewish behavior in the face of Nazi genocide and its prominence in the United States in the early 1960s—although in Singer's case, loyalty to the principles of gentleness is sufficiently deep that *The Slave* probably would not have been written differently after the 1967 Six Day War.

Nor does Singer propose a response; he opts instead to leave the questions open. There are four dimensions to Jacob's reflections. First, they confirm the picture that Jews do not resist—not in the face of the Chmielnitski massacres in particular and not throughout the Jewish experience generally, since the time of "the ancient Jews of the Bible stories" (Jacob seems not to know such later Jewish fighters as the Zealots of Masada and the Bar Kokhba guerrillas, though presumably Singer does). In light of the overall portrayal of Jacob in the novel, *The Slave* should be counted among those American texts of the early 1960s that buttressed the stereotype of Jewish gentleness and goodness. Furthermore, Singer, learned historian of Polish Jewry, believes this stereotype prevailed in the seventeenth century as well.

The second important dimension of Jacob's reflections is the disclosure of the culture of Jewish timidity and gentleness and of some of the ways that it shaped behavior. Third, the passage challenges that culture, in passing but pointedly: "What would happen to the might of the wicked if the just were not so craven?" Or "Must a man agree to his own destruction?" The gentle Singer even permits the gentle Jacob to recall Jewish fighters of biblical times. (To the best of my knowledge, these are singular lines in Singer's extensive oeuvre.)[15] Jacob's reflections offer another example of the doubts and tensions of gentle, powerless Jews, of their occasional but recurrent longings for strength and toughness in a world that relentlessly mocks their own most vital principles.

The fourth and final dimension of the passage leads directly back to the historical sketch of tough Jews. Jacob remarks that "nobody dared lift a hand against the butchers while they slaughtered entire communities." According to Biale (p. 74) and Ainsztein (pp. 57–67), this is an inaccurate and incomplete perception. Both historians suggest that Jewish resistance to the butchers was extensive. Many Jews fought alongside Poles against the attacks of the Cossacks. Many opted for suicide rather than surrender.

Ainsztein also indicates that class was a factor in Jewish responses to the massacres, with lower-class Jews more inclined to armed resistance than those of the upper strata. The latter, however, shaped both the dominant community values and the effective interpretations of events. Not only were lower-class Polish Jews active in armed resistance in 1648–50; in the wake of the massacres, some even joined the Haidamaki, adopting the Greek Orthodox faith of these itinerant, Robin Hood–like fraternities. In a grand outburst of the militant secularism that informs Ainsztein's study, he remarks that the

Haidamaki episode demonstrates "the existence of a fighting and adventurous element that felt stifled in a society which increasingly sought escape from reality in the religious mysticism of Hasidism" (p. 58).

There is yet another example of armed Jews in the seventeenth century. The fact that a handful of Jews became soldiers in New Amsterdam is more significant than its slight dimensions suggest. The first twenty-three of what would much later be known as New York Jews arrived in New Amsterdam in the mid-1650s. They were Sephardic Jews, that is, from Spain and Portugal, whose families had resettled in Amsterdam after being expelled from the Iberian peninsula in 1492. Some moved from Amsterdam to Dutch colonies in Brazil. When the Portuguese reconquered several of these colonies in the mid-seventeenth century, the Jews there, as Dutch subjects, were forced to flee. On their arrival in New Amsterdam, Peter Stuyvesant sought to expel them because of what he termed the Jews' "customary usury and deceitful trading with Christians," but he was overruled by his superiors in the Dutch West India Company, in which Amsterdam Jews were major investors. Although the company's home office concurred with Stuyvesant's decision to deny the Jews in the new world any "free and public exercise of their abominable religion," the two dozen exiles were permitted to remain.[16]

Soon afterward, several members of this small community joined the ranks of New Amsterdam's armed forces. According to Ainsztein, this confirms that Jews became soldiers whenever they were given the opportunity to do so (p. 85). In pursuing this countermyth of Jewish behavior, Ainsztein, a sedulous and invaluable researcher, fails to take note of the strikingly original aspect of the soldier-Jews of New Amsterdam: they had taken up arms—and actual military *careers*—in what was *not* an immediately Jewish cause.

As in Amsterdam itself, so in the New World, Jews were at best a tolerated minority with few civic or religious rights. In contrast to their contemporary coreligionists in Poland, however, they were not targets of massacres. The New Amsterdam Jews who became soldiers (only four or five men, but they constituted a large percentage of the tiny Jewish population in the colony) were not responding to a mortal crisis of their community, though they were indirectly serving a Jewish cause: by enlisting in the armed service of the non-Jewish host nation, they demonstrated their loyalty to it and their sense of civic responsibility, hoping thereby to earn more general acceptance. In this respect, the handful of Jewish soldiers of mid-seventeenth-century New Amsterdam anticipate an important later development.

The French Revolution and Its Aftermath: The Emergence of the Jewish Soldier

Jewish soldiers were a phenomenon of western and central Europe and of the New World. The situation in Russia proved to be quite different. As Ainsztein stresses, the tsarist system used military service to oppress Jews. Only in England, Germany, France, Italy, the United States, and elsewhere in the West was service in the armed forces linked to the civil and political emancipation of the Jews. Despite the Jews' participation in western military and political life from the eighteenth to the twentieth centuries, however, their contributions were never translated into an *image*, or stereotype, of the Jewish soldier. As Mark Twain observed in the postscript ("The Jew as Soldier") to his remarkable 1898 essay *Concerning the Jews*, "I was ignorant—like the rest of the Christian world—of the fact that the Jew had a record as a soldier."[17] These are the words of a man who was generally well informed about Jews and a critic of anti-Semitism. Twain's ignorance of the Jewish military record was typical: the surprisingly substantial Jewish contribution to soldiering was not sufficient to pierce either the prevailing Jewish self-image or the anti-Semitic view of Jews as weaklings.

Turning, then, to the theme of the modern Jewish soldier, the data include the following: Ainsztein reports that in 1776 there were 2,500 Jews in an American colonial population of 3,900,000. Six hundred Jews, including 24 officers, served in the War of Independence (p. 85). American Jewry also provided troops and officers in the War of 1812. Regarding the Civil War, Twain examined War Department figures and notes that Jews were strongly represented in the armies and navies of both the Union and the Confederacy, where they compiled a "record of capacity, for fidelity, and for gallant soldiership in the field . . . as good as anyone's" (pp. 29–30).[18]

Twain concluded that the "Jew's patriotism was not merely level with the Christian's, but overpassed it," stressing that this was not simply a matter of higher percentages. "When the Christian volunteer arrived in camp," Twain emphasized, "he got a welcome and applause, but as a rule, the Jew got a snub" (p. 29). Regarding the Spanish-American War, Ainsztein indicates that Jewish participation was more substantial still, the 5,000 Jewish combatants constituting a remarkably high rate of participation (p. 87).

Such developments were not limited to the United States.

Ainsztein estimates that 2,000 Jews participated on the British side in the Boer War (1899–1902). In France in the mid-1890s, the case of one Jewish soldier became a *cause célèbre*. Captain Alfred Dreyfus was falsely accused by French military intelligence officers, later exposed as anti-Semites, of passing military secrets to Germany. Before he was finally exonerated, the beleaguered captain spent years in prison and became the unheroic center of the storm known as the Dreyfus Affair, which whirled around him and across much of Europe and America well into the first decade of the twentieth century. It is often thought that Dreyfus was targeted because he was the one Jewish officer in the French army. But Ainsztein presents some surprising data: there were in the French armed services 9 Jewish colonels, the same number of lieutenant colonels, 46 majors, 89 captains other than Dreyfus himself, an equal number of lieutenants, and 104 noncommissioned Jewish officers (p. 92). Dreyfus was framed because his handwriting resembled that of the non-Jewish officer who was the real culprit selling military secrets to Germany.

The Jewish French soldiers, like their counterparts in the United States and elsewhere in western and central Europe, were part of a development that had assumed clear form in the American War of Independence and was subsequently defined more sharply during the French Revolution and the Napoleonic era, where Jews began to be granted some of the rights and obligations of citizenship. The story of Jewish emancipation is complex and uneven, but many Jews greeted the new circumstances with enthusiasm. And many became soldiers throughout the nineteenth century, out of a conviction that emancipation could be achieved only at the price of Jewish blood spilled in the struggle for fatherland and liberty.

Such efforts did not fundamentally alter the prevailing image of the Jew as a weak, unmanly parasite on the body of the fatherland. As fear and hatred of the Jews intensified in the later decades of the nineteenth century, that imagery became even more widely disseminated than before. Again, we turn to Twain's *Concerning the Jews*, a calm but lacerating critique of a series of anti-Semitic myths and stereotypes. Yet even Twain concedes in his postscript, "The Jew as Soldier," that when he wrote the essay (1898), he "was not able to endorse the *common reproach* that the Jew is willing to feed upon a country but not to fight for it, because I did not know whether it was true or false. I *supposed it to be true*, but it is not allowable," he inserts, "to endorse wandering maxims upon supposition." Twain concludes that this "slur upon the Jew cannot hold up its head in presence of the figures of the War Department. It has done its work, and done it *long and faithfully, and with high approval*: it ought to be pensioned off now, and retired from active service" (p. 30; emphases added).

Though Twain was speaking of the United States, his remarks have broader reach. Indeed, his essay on the Jews had been occasioned by his earlier account of the constitutional crisis of the Dual Monarchy, based on a trip to Austria late in 1897. He cited some of the numerous anti-Semitic episodes that punctuated the crisis, which in turn had prompted *Harper's* readers to send letters, some of which included prejudiced remarks about Jews. In response, Twain wrote *Concerning the Jews*. His observations relate to the era in Europe around 1900, the era called the *belle époque*. As it passed through a second industrial revolution and massive urbanization, Europe was delivering itself of a barrage of white supremacist violence in its colonies while beginning to mass produce a new anti-Semitism at home.

The shift from religious to racial anti-Semitism was linked to the pseudo-scientific thinking that emerged from the late-eighteenth-century Enlightenment, was enhanced by social Darwinism, and reached its high point in Nazi ideology. This development was grounded in modern nationalism, whose hardy roots in the French Revolution, the Napoleonic Wars, and early-nineteenth-century Romanticism would yield phenomenal harvest by the century's end. That the very terms *anti-Semite* and *anti-Semitism* evidently first appeared in 1879 is symptomatic. They were coined by Wilhelm Marr, who founded the German Anti-semiten Liga (League of Anti-Semites) in that year. Also in that year, Marr's pamphlet *The Victory of Judaism over Germandom: Regarded from a Non-Denominational Point of View* went into its twelfth printing. As Paul Mendes-Flohr and Jehuda Reinharz note, the pamphlet's originality was in its contrast of Jews not with Christians but with Germans, an argument that highlighted the national and racial problems posed by the Jews.[19]

Marr's contemporary countryman Adolf Stoecker, a preacher and indefatigable despiser of Jews, presented his views from his Reichstag seat between the 1880s and the early 1900s and founded the Christian Social Party, one of what would soon be numerous populist-nationalist, antimodern and anti-Semitic movements in *fin de siècle* central Europe. These were the models on which Hitler would later build.[20] In the mid-1890s, however, France, rather than Austria or Germany, was in the vanguard of the anti-Semitic current in Europe proper; this thanks to the Dreyfus Affair. At the same time, between the 1880s and the early 1900s a series of often state-sanctioned and devastating pogroms hit the Jewish Pale of Settlement in tsarist Russia.

The Jewish Gangster

This increasingly widespread and intense anti-Semitism of the decades surrounding the turn of the century radically challenged, though it did not overturn, the often fervent and well-founded Jewish hopes for acceptance and assimilation in the West. One of the Jewish responses to this challenge was something neither the world nor its Jews had experienced tangibly for nearly two thousand years: Jewish nationalism, in this instance in the form of Zionism. And from this, the maelstrom of the new anti-Semitism, the crisis of assimilation, and the rise of Zionism, there emerged the tough Jew.

Until this point, the notion of the tough Jew has assumed two basic forms. Following leads provided by Reuben Ainsztein and David Biale, we have identified instances of Jews defending or martyring themselves, and eighteenth- and nineteenth-century examples of Jews as soldiers in French, American, and other national armed forces. But these cases do not exhaust the picture of pre-Zionist tough Jews. The nineteenth and early twentieth centuries generate several other tributary types, the most important of which is the Jewish gangster. The leftist as tough Jew and the Jewish cowboy are also worthy of note. The gangster as well as the cowboy and leftist emerged in the era of Jewish emancipation and thus, like the Jewish soldier, arose from the experiences of Jews engaged in extensive intercourse with the dominant non-Jewish world.

The notion of tough Jews would surely be too loose were Karl Marx squeezed into it. On the other hand, I do think that his concept of class struggle can be understood as a theoretico-philosophical form of Jewish toughness, especially when seen against the backdrop of the many rabbis in Marx's family tree. And consider the figures from the later Marxist and the broader socialist-anarchist traditions who can more readily be seen as tough Jews. Leon Trotsky is the prototype.[21] Author of countless books (including a defense of revolutionary violence) and organizer of the Red Army in the Russian Revolution and Civil War, he is a Jewish intellectual on horseback.

Once one begins investigating this whole theme, the possibilities appear to be endless, with tough Jews emerging so frequently from the shadows of timidity and gentleness that one is often struck by the impressive power of those shadows themselves. It happens that the early-nineteenth-century British heavyweight boxing champion and the man generally credited with developing scientific boxing was a Jew, Daniel Mendoza (1764–1836).[22] As was the first of the modern "master spies," at least in some small sense. Sidney Reilly may or may not have been working for more than simply the British government, whose agent he was in Soviet Russia in the early 1920s. There appears to be no doubt, however, that he was born Sigmund Georgievich Rosenblum, the illegitimate son of a Jewish doctor. Richard Deacon, who reports this fact in his panegyric, *The Israeli Secret Service* (1977), even speaks in another connection of "the Jewish natural talent for espionage."[23]

The story of the tough Jew as cowboy, a story confined to the United States, is lightly but ably told by Harriet and Fred Rochlin.[24] That phenomenon is restricted in the sense that the cowboy (and in that specific sense, the tough) component vanished with the passing of the Wild West, even though numerous of the business empires established by Jewish cowboy-entrepreneurs in the nineteenth century have endured to this day. In fact, the Rochlins' account belongs as much to the cultural history of American capitalism as it does to Jewish history per se. Like the figure of the gangster, the cowboy can be seen as a point of intersection of two forms of toughness: the immediate, physical form and the economic. The Rochlins' story also implicitly supports Reuben Ainsztein's point that especially when Jews were released from the confines of their ghettos in the modern era and new conditions permitted or required tough Jews, they appeared punctually (which is not to say naturally).

The Jews who not only became successful businessmen but genuine cowboys in the rugged American West were German Jews who had emigrated to this country in the aftermath of the 1848 revolution in their native land. A version of their story is the basis of the most recent novel by Gloria Goldreich. More will be said about her in part 3, because she is an active contributor to the recent tough Jewish fiction. To my knowledge, her *West to Eden* is the first Jewish cowboy-family saga.[25] The Rochlins chronicle the Jewish cowboys' achievements— little is said of the failures—not least in the many illustrations of gun-toting Jews riding high in the saddle. Those achievements included numerous late-nineteenth-century Jewish mayors and sheriffs: between 1896 and 1900 Abraham Emanuel was mayor of no less a town than Tombstone, Arizona. The Rochlins also provide reproductions of the cattle brands used by Jewish ranchers and of frontier synagogues; and they introduce Josephine ("Josie") Sarah Marcus, who became the wife of the notorious gunman Wyatt Earp. Her autobiography, *Why I Married Wyatt Earp*, includes her purported eyewitness account of the infamous gunfight at O.K. Corral (1881), in which the Earp brothers were central figures.

Jewish bandits, rustlers, and hired guns are notably absent from the Rochlins' study. Their Jewish cowboy seems to have been a law-abiding figure—a sheriff or member of the volunteer police or fire department rather than a member of a gang of outlaws. Mark Twain held a similar view of the Jewish people in general. Defending the proposition "the Jew is a well-behaved citizen," Twain noted that in "the statistics of crime, his presence is conspicuously rare—in all countries. With murder and other crimes of violence he has but little to do: he is a stranger to the hangman. In the police court's daily long roll of 'assaults' and 'drunk and disorderlies,' " Twain concludes, "his name seldom appears."[26] In fact, the figure of the Jewish gangster in America really emerges only after the appearance of Twain's *Concerning the Jews*. Jena Weissman Joselit's[27] and Albert Fried's[28] more recent studies of Jewish American gangsters make amply clear that, if the wild West did not generate a Jewish criminal subculture, the city (New York, Chicago, Philadelphia, Boston, Newark) certainly did.

At the turn of the last century, eastern European Jews, along with Irish and Italian immigrants, were filling the tenements of New York (and later of other cities). That oppressive, impoverished, and crime-breeding world was bound to tarnish the seemingly unblemished Jewish record of upstanding citizenship. Jewish gangsters, prostitutes, pimps, youth gangs, ruffians, and even assassins proliferated, as often as not operating in tandem with their subsequently better known Italian and Irish counterparts. Although the emergence of this Jewish criminal element might strike many American Jews as a pathological development, it nevertheless played a significant role in the gradual integration of Jews into American society.

By the late 1940s Jews had by and large escaped the inner-city slums of New York for the more promising terrain of Brooklyn, Queens, and Long Island. Jewish crime and gangsterdom as a *social* phenomenon was virtually finished. The notorious Meyer Lansky in Florida, Moe Dalitz in Cleveland,

and Longy Zwillman of Newark were, to be sure, still in action as prominent syndicate bosses in the 1950s and 1960s, but by then their operations were highly rationalized, ethnically mixed, and no longer rooted in the subculture of the Jewish tenement underworld. They were, nevertheless, heirs to what had once been a distinctively Jewish tradition very distant from the stereotypical tradition of timidity and gentleness: Arnold Rothstein of Murder, Inc., Dutch Schultz, Bugsy Siegel, Waxy Gordon, Abe Reles, Lepke Buchhalter, Gurrah Shapiro, Moses Annenberg, Irving "Knadles" Nitzberg, and others in the 1930s and 1940s, and the likes of Big Jack Zelig, Monk Eastman, Kid Twist, Lefty Louie, Gyp the Blood, and Dopey Benny Fein in the preceding several decades.

The Jewish gangster in America presents an intriguing case. As Jewish crime and gangsterdom began to emerge in the first decades of this century, Twain's perception that "with murder and other crimes of violence" the Jew "has but little to do" was in part sustained. Joselit's *Our Gang*, for example, emphasizes that Jewish criminals in pre–World War I New York turned only rarely to violent crime. On this matter, both Jews and anti-Semites in the early twentieth century agreed that violence was not the Jewish forte, even in crime. Joselit's figures for 1900–1915 indicate the following: Of Jews charged with felonies, 80 percent had been involved in burglary, larceny, arson, horse poisoning, and receiving stolen goods. Only 12 percent of the Jewish felons in those years were convicted of murder or rape. The remaining 8 percent were evidently guilty of gambling and bookmaking.

Joselit cites a 1912 editorial in the German Jewish New York newspaper, *Wahrheit* (Truth), which expresses its concerns with the expanding index of Jewish crime in the city but then notes proudly that at least violent crime "is not in the

Jewish blood." The contemporary anti-Semitic sociologist
E. A. Ross agreed with this perception, but added a gloss on
Jewish venality and cowardice. "Hebrew immigrants," according to Ross, steer away from crimes of violence against
persons and instead "usually commit their crimes for
gain . . . rather than commit the *more daring crimes*" (emphasis added). On this matter Joselit proposes that "the es-
chewal of violence among the Jews seemed to be a conscious
decision, indeed a kind of cultural inheritance, transmitted
from one generation to the next" (p. 43).

Whenever Jews were indicted for violent crimes against
persons in prewar New York, it came as a shock to the Jewish
community, particularly to the established, bourgeois "uptown
Jews" of German descent. The latter were in general unnerved
by the influx of their less respectable eastern European coreligionists. The editorial in *Wahrheit* put it in stark terms:
the association between Jews and violence was "without . . .
precedent in the whole course of Jewish history." Did the
highly educated editors of *Wahrheit* not know of the Jewish
warriors of biblical and early Christian times, or of nineteenth-
century Jewish soldiers in Germany or, for that matter, on
these shores during the Civil War? Do these gaps represent
(conscious) suppression or (unconscious) repression? When the
editors spoke of violence, did they mean only violent crime?
Several years earlier, in 1908, another newspaper, the *American Hebrew*, had offered a succinct physiological and cultural
interpretation of why Jews seemed "less addicted" to violent
crime: it had to do with the Jews' "slighter physique and general tendency to suffer ills without retaliation" (p. 43). This
Jewish anxiety over Jewish violence, as revealing as it is poignant, discloses significant class and intraethnic tensions among
American Jews between the 1890s and the 1920s. Similar

tensions arose in central and western European cities at the same time and for the same reason: the intrusion of lower-class Russian, Polish, and Romanian Jews into the settled, assimilated, respectable world of the *yekkes* (as the German Jews were called by their Yiddish-speaking coreligionists). [29]

Real as this conflict was, however, the matter is not quite reducible to class tensions between lower-class eastern European Jews and bourgeois German American Jews as Joselit's study implies. For both groups—the bourgeois Germans and the lower-class, artisan, small merchant eastern Europeans—*shared* key values concerning toughness, timidity, and gentleness. Joselit confirms this point with apt citations from *Life Is with People: The Culture of the Shtetl* (1952) by Mark Zborowski and Elizabeth Herzog. The authors of this classic study show that the shtetl was "at one in regarding physical violence as 'un-Jewish.' " Like all shtetl children, those who made their way to Manhattan's Lower East Side and other northeastern American cities in the early 1900s had internalized a clear understanding of the purported differences between Jewish and un-Jewish behavior. As Zborowski and Herzog put it, the former emphasized "intellect, a sense of moderation, cherishing of spiritual values, and the cultivation of rational, goal-directed activities," whereas the latter, un-Jewish behavior placed its "emphasis on the body, excess, blind instinct, sexual instinct and ruthless force" (quoted in Joselit, p. 43). In these convictions, the transplanted shtetl Jews were of one mind with the transplanted *yekkes*, for whom violent crimes were "not in the Jewish blood." [30]

Joselit's summary—"For centuries, European Jewry had identified any show of violent behavior with non-Jews and studiously refrained from engaging in it"—is surely based on abundant evidence and undeniably accurate in the main. Jewish gentleness and mildness *had* prevailed for centuries. But it should also be clear from our discussion up to this point that Joselit's valuable work overlooks the significant historical evidence of Jewish toughness and violence. In this respect, *Our Gang* is not unique but typical. [31]

One might argue that Jewish gangsters in New York in the early 1900s, some of whom committed violent crimes against persons, exhibited a form of antisocial behavior that amounted to something quite new under the Jewish sun. This is not persuasive, however, for the New York, Newark, and Chicago Jewish gangsters of the early twentieth century had predecessors. From the late eighteenth century through the first decades of the nineteenth century there arose an active Jewish criminal underworld in a number of German and Dutch cities. Although there are literary clues pointing to the existence of this long-forgotten phenomenon, they have not been pursued. Friedrich Schiller's play *The Robbers* (1781), for example, a major work of both the Enlightenment and the emergent romantic rebellion against it, presents a Jewish gangster, Moritz Spiegelberg, who is engaged in a definite if unusual project of Jewish de-ghettoization and assimilation, namely, crime. [32] But he has always been overshadowed by a more respectable and more impressive late-eighteenth-century central European Jewish type, though both emerged from the same demographic soil.

By the last third of that century, in what amounted to a minor dress rehearsal for the larger drama of population shifts that would occur more than one hundred years later, small numbers of Yiddish-speaking Jews from eastern Europe sought their fortunes in German cities. One of these pioneers was Solomon Maimon (1753–1800), who rejected his eastern European, Orthodox Jewish heritage, and mastered both the German language and German philosophy, as a student of Immanuel Kant. He eventually emerged as an eminent thinker in his own right. Although Maimon's itinerary required immense reservoirs of courage and stamina, I do not count him among the tough Jews. His remarkable achievements represent instead the values of bourgeois culture, humane learning, civility, and rational theism so highly prized by the publicists of the German Enlightenment and so passionately embraced by a generation of newly emancipated Jews in Germany. *The Autobiography of Solomon Maimon* (1793) was in many ways their manifesto.

Even more influential in this regard was Moses Mendelssohn (1729–86), whose forebears had been in Germany for generations. Like Maimon, he embraced the compelling modernity of enlightened German culture. Mendelssohn's friendship with Gotthold Ephraim Lessing, the late-eighteenth-century German dramatist and, next to Kant, the greatest voice of the German Enlightenment, was renowned. According to George L. Mosse, Lessing's play *Nathan the Wise* (1799) "was and remained the Magna Carta of German Jewry, the popularization of *Bildung* [humanistic cultivation] and the Enlightenment. The play," Mosse concludes, "was thought to provide a clear statement of Lessing's love for humanity regardless of religion, a love exemplified by his close friendship with Moses Mendelssohn."[33]

The life stories of Maimon and especially Mendelssohn were known, and in many respects, the two thinkers were important interpreters and transmitters of the Enlightenment values with which the German American Jews in New York would begin to reckon with Jewish crime on the Lower East Side. Furthermore, the achievements of the cultivated Jews of the German Enlightenment obscured the rather different activities of the real-life Moritz Spiegelbergs, the Jewish gangsters in the Age of Enlightenment.

We know about this phenomenon thanks to the impressive labors of Dr. Friedrich Christian Benedict Ave-Lallement, a mid-nineteenth-century scholar of law and language, and a German police official. He provides a rich sketch of the vigor and violence of a Yiddish-speaking criminal underworld in Germany and the Netherlands during the eras of Enlightenment and Romanticism.[34] Ave-Lallement follows some "individual stars" of this underworld and provides extensive lexicons of Yiddish terms and translations of Yiddish texts that demonstrate that the argot of the nineteenth-century German gangster was extensively influenced by Yiddish, or "Jewish German." He also introduces an early Arnold Rothstein or Meyer Lansky type, a man who may have been the first "Jewish Godfather": Jakob Moises, whose operations were based in Antwerp, Ghent, and Brussels but covered more extensive terrain. Ave-Lallement observes that beginning in the middle of the eighteenth century "a disorderly bunch of small Jewish mobs" (*eine wüssten Masse jüdischen Gesindels*) who intimidated, robbed, and sometimes killed their victims moved from Poland to Prussia and then to the western regions of Germany, subsequently opening routes to Holland and France.

The gangs led by Jakob Moises were not composed entirely of Jews, and they regularly worked in tandem with other non-Jewish, German gangs, especially in the Rhine and Mosel regions. In the Trier, Frankfurt, and Mannheim areas around the time of the Seven Years' War (1756–63), for example, Jewish and non-Jewish gangs collaborated in a series of small-scale robberies aimed "especially at Jewish travellers" (p. 101). Ave-Lallement views this sort of cooperation as entirely natural (p. 100). Apparently, he was sufficiently familiar with Jewish gangsters that it simply did not occur to him to see their activities as being in any way at odds with other, presumably dominant Jewish values.

Jewish German underworld cooperation continued into the early nineteenth century, by which time crime in Germany had evidently assumed more violent forms. In 1831 in Berlin, Ave-Lallement reports, authorities carried out their largest crackdown and trial of an underworld operation to date. It resulted in the arrests of some two hundred alleged criminals said to have engaged in more than eight hundred crimes, including many armed robberies that had netted the perpetrators substantial sums of public and private money. The existence of this extensive ring had come to light in the course of police investigations into the activities of a Berlin businessman, Moses Levin Loewenthal, and his consorts (p. 114).

Ave-Lallement does not record the reactions of law-abiding German Jews to the activities of Moses Loewenthal or Jakob Moises. Perhaps their reactions were similar to those of the German Jewish Americans in the early twentieth century, reactions that at least initially were primarily ones of distress and denial. Nor does Ave-Lallement have anything to say about the itinerary of the Yiddish-speaking gangster underworld in Germany and the Netherlands after the mid-nineteenth century. Nevertheless, in bringing to light the existence of these Jewish gangsters, he opens a door to what may be still other chapters in this story.

Thanks to Joselit's research, however, more is known about the complexity of Jewish responses to Jewish crime, especially violent crime in the American case. Her account also provides insights into the conflict of stereotypes and self-images that was unfolding in Jewish consciousness both in this country and in Europe. Thus, among American Jews, increases in

Jewish crime on the eve of the First World War and the increased public attention it was attracting—including anti-Semitism—generated two responses: first denial and then reform. So deeply embedded was the conviction that crime, especially its violent forms, was altogether foreign to Jewish life that New York Jews initially kept all discussion of the subject to themselves. On this matter, Joselit cites Irving Howe's *World of Our Fathers* (1976): "East Side leaders and institutions were steadily worried, more than they allowed themselves to say in public or admit to gentiles. . . . And over the years the Jews had developed a cultural style encouraging prudishness and self-censorship; there were things everyone knew, had no choice but to know, yet only rarely was it deemed proper to speak or write about them. Life was hard enough without indulging in luxuries of revelation" (quoted in Joselit, p. 55).[35]

Two events challenged this approach. In 1908 the New York police commissioner, Theodore Bingham, published a major report disclosing the extensive Jewish presence in the city's criminal underworld. This, Joselit writes, "undid the positive image most Jews held of themselves and that others had held of the Jews" (p. 56). Initially, many Jews refused to accept Bingham's charges and sought to discredit the commissioner and his evidence. In 1912, however, denials of Jewish gangsterdom were decisively put to rest when Herman "Beansy" Rosenthal, a notorious gambler, was murdered by several Lower East Side Jewish youths. The follow-up investigation revealed the involvement of more than a dozen Jews in a series of underworld murders, an episode that "rocked New York Jewry to its very core." Joselit puts the matter succinctly: "As an excited metropolitan press treated the public to continuous discussions of the haunts and personalities of the Lower East Side underworld, New York Jews found they could no longer freely boast of their deep-seated morality; the Rosenthal case made a mockery of such claims" (p. 56). At that point, denial was finally discarded in favor of extensive efforts by Jewish community leaders to curtail and eventually eliminate Jewish crime from the streets of the Lower East Side.

These efforts to stem the tide of crime on the Lower East Side eventually succeeded, largely because Jews in the post–World War I period began departing for Brooklyn, the Bronx, and other more promising areas. With these beginnings of upward mobility, Jewish crime began to fade as a social phenomenon, although it would be a factor again with Jewish bootleggers during Prohibition and with racketeers in the 1930s and after. Whereas the prewar Jewish gangster had been a local community product, the Jewish bootleggers and racketeers from the 1920s through the 1960s were far larger fish and also had less of an impact on the dynamics of Jewish stereotypes. Joselit notes that Jewish crime barely figured in anti-Semitic imagery in America between the wars. That imagery focused instead, as it did in Europe at the same time, on the Jews' allegedly superior economic status (pp. 167–68).

Joselit's conclusions indicate that there emerged, decades later, a delayed, third response (in addition to denial and reform) to crime in their community, namely, affirmation and pride. She reports the results of several interviews held in the late 1970s or very early 1980s with men who had been youths in the Lower East Side at the turn of the century. For them, memory is suffused with tough Jewish fantasy. One recalls puzzling over the question of why other groups had all the criminals; "Jews need their share, too," he remembers having thought. Another recalled being "secretly proud" that Jews were adept at using guns. In his memoirs, cited by Joselit,

Meyer Lansky himself contends that he had entered the world of crime and violence in order to move into the American mainstream—adding that he was fulfilling the injunction a Jewish soldier had communicated to him in Grodno, his Polish hometown. Jews, the soldier had said, should stand up and fight (pp. 169–70).

These views, which had not been representative of Jewish American opinion during the 1900–1940 era, presuppose that Jewish crime and violence in America is a thing of the past. But, according to Joselit, as Jewish assimilation into American life proceeded, one could look back on Jewish gangsters, not as parts of a disease calling for a cure, but as a sign of normalcy in a culture that, as Rupert Wilkinson has recently shown, often holds the "tough guy," including the hardened killer, in high regard.[36]

There is little doubt, then, that the Americanization of the Jews accounts in large measure for their belated affirmation of early-twentieth-century Jewish gangsters. But there is another element to the change as well—its timing. Both Meyer Lansky's memoirs and the comments of Joselit's interviewees are part of the *post-1967* shift in American Jewish attitudes toward toughness and violence; that is, they reflect, paradoxically, the *Zionization* as much as the Americanization of American Jews. Even Lansky unintentionally suggests this with his reference to the Grodno soldier; he has tried to clinch his claim regarding Americanization by evoking precisely the *eastern European seedbed* of Jewish nationalism and armed struggle. Lansky and Joselit's interviewees seem to recall with pride, not Jewish crime itself, but rather its presumably more appealing essence, Jewish toughness—a distillate from which the filter of 1967 has removed the impurities.

Such revisionist retrospectives on early-twentieth-century

New York Jewish gangsters have assumed center stage in one of the post-1967 tough novels. *The Chains* (1980) by Gerald Green is a family saga of three generations, beginning with the founder and patriarch, Big Jake Chain. If the Six Day War and the tough Jewish sensibility it generated in this country made possible a novel such as *The Chains*, so did American popular culture. Green's book, in some respects a distinctively Jewish story, is also a virtual copy of Mario Puzo's *The Godfather*. The marketing of the novel highlighted its American message, billing it on the cover as "the tumultuous epic of a family forged by love and welded by violence to the American dream"—the Puzoesque point being that, alongside their scholars, saints, socialists, and schlemiels, American Jews have contributed their tough cookies, their tickets into the mainstream. [37]

Big Jake Chain is introduced as a young, Lower East Side *shtarker* (a tough, an enforcer, literally a strong one). Alerted by his young son to an assault on a group of Orthodox Jews by anti-Semitic youths, this latter-day golem, outraged by the sight of defenseless Jews crumbling under the attack, wades into the fray, muttering to himself: "I'm dumb and I can't pray . . . but I can fight." And fight he does, inflicting damage on several of the youths and causing the lot of them to flee for their lives. This episode is observed from a distance by Meyer Flugelman, socialist and altruist, who perceives in Jake Chain "shades of Old Testament warriors" and realizes that such an individual could prove vital to the beleaguered union of women garment workers he is helping to organize.

Flugelman "was learning something. This Chain. This stupid man with no fear. None. Fists like cast iron. Was there a lesson? Something not in Marx or The Talmud?" Excited by his find, Flugelman proposes that the union employ Big Jake to protect the picket lines. The comrades, however, are dubious, locked as they are in the heritage of timidity and propriety. Flugelman presses his point. "Why are we always meek? he cries; we need to stand up for ourselves and Chain can help us." "Hmmm," Comrade Brunstein muses in reply, "it's a bit irregular . . . " " 'Brunstein!' Flugelman shouted, recalling his youthful days in Beth Midrash [house of study, an upper-level yeshiva]. 'Brunstein! Was Joshua irregular? The Maccabees? Simon Bar Kochba? Brunstein, Chain is a warrior!' " (pp. 58–62). Brunstein and the others are at last convinced, and Jake begins his career as a union *shtarker*, a career that will culminate, not in the labor movement, but in a successful bootlegging operation in the 1920s, which is then continued into the 1940s by his son, the racketeer. Jake's grandson, a graduate of the Harvard Business School, turns the family business into an international conglomerate. In addition to its American dimension, *The Chains* also incorporates the element of Jewish nationalism, which is suggested by Meyer Flugelman's fervent appeals to Joshua, the Maccabees, and Simon Bar Kokhba.

Gerald Green has no compunctions about portraying Jewish crooks, though, as we have seen, Jewish contemporaries were uncomfortable with their lawless fellow Jews. Albert Fried, in *The Rise and Fall of the Jewish Gangster in America*, confronts the subject directly. Indeed, he takes to task both Irving Howe and the New York Jewish Museum for its 1966 photographic exhibit of life in the Lower East Side, "Portal to America," which was itself a piece of the pre–1967 renaissance of Yiddishkeit in this country. Both instances, Fried contends, evade the reality of early-twentieth-century Jewish crime and gangsterdom. Howe's canvas, "vast and magisterial," relegates Jewish crime to the margins, refers to the major figures only in passing, and generally ignores the "dark" legacy of Jewish underworld culture (pp. xiii–xvii). Fried is not arguing that the Jewish underworld provides a model worthy of emulation, but rather, that the full range of Jewish immigrant experience, including its gangsters, prostitutes, hit men, and racketeers, ought to be told without embarrassment. Presumably, just as they did seventy years ago, so today Jews fear losing their reputation for ethical purity or superiority.

Fried came to his study of the Jewish gangster in America after reading *Jews without Money* (1930), a fictionalized memoir of the miseries of Jewish life in the Lower East Side prior to the First World War. The author, Mike Gold, had grown up there and witnessed many of its sordid products—pimps, thugs, and so forth—which he reconstructs with a candor much admired by Fried. Gold himself had been an active Communist when he wrote *Jews without Money*. His central conviction, expressed in inverted form in the book's title, is that all of New York's Jews were equally trapped in the American cash nexus, from the respectable community leaders and aspiring writers and doctors, across both the middle ranks and the poor, to the gamblers and hit men; indeed, for Gold the Jewish gangster is a product of American capital and culture. Thus, he offers an uncensored view of the range of Jewish life without idealizing Jewish toughness in the manner of, say, Green's *Chains. Jews without Money* is redolent of Marxism, not of Jewish nationalism.[38]

The dual legacy of poverty and capitalist values also figured significantly in three later Jewish American novels. Like *Jews without Money*, they *lack* the nationalism or Zionism of the recent tough Jewish fiction. When Irving Shulman's *The Amboy Dukes* first appeared in 1946 its characters were young Jewish delinquents from the Lower East Side (the novel is set in the early 1940s). In the paperback edition published the following year and widely read through the next decade, they were given new, American names and had become delinquents, plain and simple. According to a recent essay on Shulman's novel by Joan Baum, the original, Jewish dimension will be restored in the forthcoming reissue of *The Amboy Dukes*.[39] Budd Schulberg's *What Makes Sammy Run?* (1941)[40] and Harold Robbins's *Stone for Danny Fisher* (1951)[41] can be more readily situated in the prehistory of the post-1967 tough Jewish genre. Both novels also serve as reminders that not all Lower East Side Jews found hope and fortune elsewhere in the decades after the First World War. The Glick and Fisher families are among those who remained in the tenements. Schulberg's Sammy Glick and Robbins's Danny Fisher follow similar itineraries during the interwar years. Both are Lower East Side street urchins who quickly learn that their parents' uncomprehending timidity and religiosity is worse than useless in the jungle outside, and both leave their families and their Judaism behind.

Sammy becomes a genius of deceit and bravado and claws his way to the top as a Hollywood screenwriter. There he finds non-Jewish women and abundant unhappiness. Danny Fisher is physically tough. He discovers boxing, enters its syndicate-controlled ranks, takes a dive and an Italian American wife, gropes for integrity and love, and is finally killed by a bookmaker he had double-crossed. These are, in other words, reverse coming-of-age stories, tales of manhood not found. Sammy Glick and Danny Fisher are tough Jews, battling their ways through the depression years in America, but they are lost Jews—and lost Americans—as well. As part 3 shows, the characters in the post-1967 tough Jewish novels set in the interwar years (who *might* have been Amboy Dukes, Sammy Glicks, and Danny Fishers) avoid the sad fates of those figures by finding the Jewish cause (and their own souls) in Palestine, a cause they serve as fighters or gunrunners for the Haganah or Irgun.

In reality, however, Jewish Americans did not need Zionism and Palestine to demonstrate toughness in the period before 1948. For Jews in this country, the Second World War opened the door to significant social and civic opportunities. Many Jewish Americans on the political Left joined the anti-Franco International Brigades and fought in the Spanish Civil War in the mid-1930s, and in even greater numbers and from across the political spectrum Jews entered the American armed forces after 1939. [42]

Though anti-Semitism in America certainly did not vanish with the war's end, Jewish involvement in the military proving ground brought Jews further into the mainstream of American life. Norman Mailer's *Naked and the Dead* (1948) and Irwin Shaw's *Young Lions* (1948) are the key literary markers of this important episode. That two of the most highly regarded novels about the Second World War published in this country contained major Jewish characters and were written by Jews who had served in the war—and whose writing generally tended to be tough and manly—is more than an incidental part of the demarginalization of American Jewry. Coincidentally, Mailer's and Shaw's works appeared in the very year Israel was founded. The novels (and their authors), on the one hand, and Israel, on the other, signify the two quite different (major) modalities of Jewish toughness in the era following the war and the Holocaust.

Of the many tough Jewish novels published since 1967 and discussed in part 3, only two are based on the participation of Jews as fighters in the American war effort: Frederic Arnold's *Kohn's War* (1984)[43] and Marge Piercy's *Gone to Soldiers*

(1987).[44] This historical moment has not figured prominently in the recent fiction because as American Jews participated in the war effort, they became more integrally *American* rather than more Zionist. Participation by American Jews in the Zionist struggle in Palestine in 1945 to 1948, actually a less notable phenomenon, would become the event of choice in the post-1967 tough Jewish novels. While the works by Mailer and Shaw and those by Arnold and Piercy are separated by four decades, they nevertheless share the theme of *American* experience as a medium of Jewish self-discovery—though Piercy's *Gone to Soldiers* does have a certain Zionist impulse. In this respect, they distinguish themselves from other examples of the American tough Jewish fiction discussed later in these pages.

II

ZIONIST TOUGH JEWS

Anticipations of Zionism: Tough Jews in Eastern and Western Europe, 1900–1920

The question of the role, or the lack of a role, assumed by tough Jewish *nationalist* imagery among American Jews *prior* to 1948 calls for comment. In the years before the First World War, amid their bookish and gentle self-understanding, Jews in New York not only had access to images of Jewish toughness but, in an unusual episode, actually embraced such images with passion.

To make sense of this important episode, I want to recall the impact on New York Jewish leaders of the 1908 report on crime by Police Commissioner Theodore Bingham and of the 1912 "Beansy" Rosenthal affair. Both Joselit and Fried show how these developments catalyzed a major reform effort by the New York Kehilla (the Jewish community's religious and civic leadership body). Its chairman, Judah Magnes, at the time a young Reform rabbi and head of the American Zionist Federation, led a new Bureau of Social Morals to combat the impact of the gambler and gangster. "Heaven help us," Magnes wrote at the time, "from this kind of Americanization" (quoted in Fried, p. 79). Along with such "uptown Jews" as Louis Marshall and the investment banker Jacob Schiff, Magnes and the Kehilla went to work.

Some years earlier, in 1905–6, Magnes and his associates

had come together in a short-lived but remarkable alliance with Lower East Side radicals, socialists, and labor activists, under the rubric of a newly constituted Jewish Defense Association. According to Jonathan Frankel, the association "became the first political organization to gain the support of Uptown and Downtown, socialist, and non-socialist, nationalist and anti-nationalist."[45] The occasion of its formation was the outbreak, in the fall of 1905, of a new wave of pogroms in Russia. The 1905 pogrom also saw the first efforts at armed self-defense by sections of Russian Jewry. This came on the heels of the particularly bloody Kishinev pogrom, which was itself related to the social crisis that generated the 1905 Revolution in Russia.

In New York, the Jewish Defense Association mourned the victims, many of whom were relatives of Lower East Side Jews, protested the pogroms, and mobilized support for those in Russia who were fighting back. The association's manifesto declared that "the Jewish people is arming itself. We must create the means" (Frankel, p. 488). Amid the grief, fear, and outrage spreading through New York Jewry, the association began raising funds for weapons for Russian Jews. At a late November 1905 mass meeting at Grand Central Palace, the long since demolished midtown Manhattan exhibition center, numerous city dignitaries addressed the crowd. These included corporation counsel John Delaney, who announced that, as an Irishman, he understood the meaning of self-defense and endorsed the Jews' efforts (Frankel, p. 488).

Judah Magnes delivered the main address, articulating the shift in Jewish stereotypes and self-images that was unfolding at that very moment: "We are weak," he reminded his audience of some six thousand, many of whom were survivors of earlier pogroms, "and fawn and bend the back. We of all the Europeans have . . . turned the cheek when smitten. That we have bent to the whip of the Cossacks is as much a reproach to you and to me as is the self-defense of our brethren in Russia an honor to them. Is not the lesson to be learned," he asked, in a powerful blend of American and Jewish nationalism, "from the founders of this great country? Are we not too inclined to look patronizingly upon those of our race in Russia and call them slaves while we congratulate ourselves that we are free?" (quoted in Frankel, pp. 488–89).

The main theme of the Grand Central Palace rally, of the December 1906 protest march from the Lower East Side up Broadway to Union Square, and of the subsequent efforts of the Jewish Defense Association was, as Jonathan Frankel points out, self-defense. Yet six years later, at the time of the Rosenthal affair, Jewish publicists proclaimed that violence—not merely violent crime—"is not in the Jewish blood." Since the situation and thus the agendas of American Jews differed radically from those in Russia and Europe, it is not altogether surprising that the tough Jewish episode of 1905–6 quickly slipped back into the more remote recesses of the American Jewish imagination.

While developments among American Jews at the turn of the century constitute a substantial part of the story of the emergence of the tough Jew, the story's main thread nevertheless originated in Europe and Russia. Even the formation of the Jewish Defense Association in New York was a response to events and initiatives in the Russian Pale of Settlement. The crux of the Magnes keynote address at the Grand Central Palace rally, shorn of its American references, had in effect already been delivered in Russia several years earlier. America, after all, offered its Jewish population greater opportunities for assimilation and upward mobility than did Russia, and to that extent, the need for guns and muscle among Jews in this country was less pressing—circumstances that, at the time, also weakened Zionism's chances here. But Paris, Berlin, and Vienna were at once centers of Jewish emancipation and assimilation and major sites of the virulent new anti-Semitic movements bent on turning back Jewish advances. The Dreyfus Affair highlighted the European situation. Its tremors helped give birth to the organized Zionist movement.

In approaching the Russian and European developments, Frankel is certainly on target in identifying self-defense as the main motif in both Russian and American Jewish responses to the 1903 and 1905 pogroms. But his point needs enlargement. For one glimpses in the Magnes speech not only new forms of political and civic action among Jews but the idea of a new Jewish *type* as well: a Jew who with national, indeed, racial pride would be a warrior on behalf of Jewish communal rights and interests. Conversely—and this, too, is in the Magnes speech—the older imagery of Jewish timidity, frailty, and gentleness was subjected to novel and vigorous criticism by Jews themselves.

The emergence of a tough Jewish imagery at the turn of the century was an extension of the Jewish nationalist awakening of the period as well. Viewed from one angle, Zionism was a logical outcome of the larger nationalist dynamic. As the greater and lesser powers of Europe, not to mention the many ethnic and linguistic groups seeking national recognition, consolidated themselves under banners of nationalism, the idea of a Jewish nation and state would seem to follow naturally. It is equally plausible to argue, however, that for European Jews the logic of nationalism pointed not to Zionism but to assimilation. Indeed, into the late nineteenth century and well beyond there is abundant evidence that nationalism for many Jews meant American, French, German, or Italian nationalism.

In any event, logic is not the decisive element. The intensity and the specific forms of the impact of nationalism on the Jews stemmed from the fact that anti-Semitism loomed so large in many of the nationalist currents. More precisely, *the racial and bodily dimension of much of turn-of-the-century nationalist anti-Semitism was a decisive factor in the emergence of Jewish ideals of toughness, courage, and physicality*. Modern, postreligious, racial anti-Semitism presented a double image of the Jew: first, as the wielder of immense economic power and, through it, of secret but extensive control of the world's political systems, and second, as physically weak, repulsive, and cowardly. Through the anti-Semitic lens, Jewish males were perceived as scrawny, obese, or effeminate, but in any case weak-bodied, with kinky hair, large lips, a foul odor, and lecherous tendencies.[46]

The Dreyfus Affair as a whole was a distinctly modern spectacle involving not merely a battle of ideas, but a battle fought by means of the mass production and consumption of visual images, signs, and symbols. About 1900, millions of Europeans (a good percentage of whom had never seen or did not know they had ever seen a Jew) were exposed in word and picture to anti-Semitic caricatures. And in the process many Jews themselves discovered just what sorts of images appeared in the eyes of anti-Semites when they focused on Jewish bodies.[47]

A related event was the publication in 1895 of Gustave le Bon's *The Crowd: A Study of the Popular Mind*.[48] In focusing on the emergent mass politics of the streets and public squares and on the role of charismatic leaders, the press, and advertising, *The Crowd* signaled the transformation of politics into theater; it would later count Mussolini and Hitler among its most avid readers. Le Bon himself, a conservative distressed by the rise of movements for popular democracy and socialism, is very insightful about the new nationalist, antimodern, and anti-Semitic mass movements on the right that were then spreading across the Continent.

The Crowd is in many respects a guide to a politics of mass manipulation. Le Bon writes that reason, rational dialogue, and utilitarian calculation of interests play rather minimal roles in civilization: "It is seen that, in reality, it is the marvellous and the legendary that are its true supports" (pp. 67–68). Long before Orwell, Le Bon proposed that the art of ruling and directing crowds "consists above all in the science of employing words" (p. 107). Along with the mass press, the new politics of crowds was increasing the flow of anti-Semitic images of Jews and their bodies.

The ideal of the tough Jew that emerges in response to those anti-Semitic images is their inversion. The imaginary Jewish body despised by the anti-Semite is rejected by the *fin de siècle* tough Jews as well. The tough Jews go so far as to create an ideal Jewish body imagery that closely resembles the classical Greek and Roman bodily ideals of the anti-Semites themselves. Jewish toughness, like the anti-Semitism it abhors, is literally a body politics, a politics of ideal bodily images and the moral virtues that supposedly inhere in them: courage, dedication to the national-racial cause, loyalty, self-discipline, readiness for self-sacrifice, robustness, manliness, and so on.

These were not the only sources from which Zionism drew its new tough Jewish ideal. Socialism, particularly in eastern Europe, was an equally viable wellspring. The various socialist currents—labor Zionists (Poale Zion), Bundists (the Bund being short for the General Jewish Labor Union in Lithuania,

Poland, and Russia), and Marxists as well—made major contributions to the gestation of the tough Jew. Immersed in both the theories and the actual exigencies of the class struggle, Jewish socialist and labor militants were especially well prepared to engage in armed self-defense initiatives when Jewish settlements were hit by pogroms.

Thus, no less than the bourgeois Zionist leadership in central and western Europe, the Jewish socialists in eastern Europe were responsible for the articulation of a new Jewish stereotype. Though divided by geography, class, political conviction, style, language, and culture, the eastern European socialists and left-wing Zionists on the one hand and western European bourgeois Zionist groups on the other also shared the impulse to transform Jewish destiny by breaking with its ghetto traditions and harnessing Jewish needs to modern, secular ideologies of socialism, liberalism, and nationalism. The conflict-filled collaboration of these two segments of Zionism—a collaboration that has been on the verge of collapse from the outset—has only the modern and still-lively forms of traditional Jew hatred to thank for its longevity.

Turning now to the Russian seedbed of the tough Jew: the generalized crisis that would culminate in the collapse of tsarism in 1917 had begun to assume clear form in the early 1880s. Symptomatic of this was the disarray that followed the 1881 assassination of Tsar Alexander II by members of the revolutionary group People's Will. The disarray included what proved to be the first of several waves (the early 1880s, early 1900s, and 1917–21) of violent assaults on Jewish towns by embittered and disaffected bands of pogromists who held Jews responsible for the tsar's death and Russia's woes. The attackers' ranks were a social mix, often including railway workers, shopkeepers, and a few industrial workers, with peasants generally active as looters.

The pogroms, which were either incited or tolerated by tsarist officials, typically involved killings, rapes, beatings, and other humiliations, along with destructions of homes, shops, and synagogues. The peak of destruction was reached in the 1903–6 wave, which left hundreds of Odessa Jews dead and thousands injured. The bloodied soil of the previous wave of assaults produced the movement for Jewish "self-emancipation," as announced in Lev Pinsker's *Auto-Emancipation* (1882). That year also saw the enactment of restrictive laws establishing Jewish quotas in secondary schools and universities. Repercussions of these developments were soon felt in London, New York, and elsewhere, as the first large groups of Jewish refugees began arriving in the West. Between the expulsion of Jews from Moscow in 1891–92 and the pogroms of 1903–6, Jewish emigration from Russia reached mass proportions, with significant numbers heading for Palestine as well as the East End and the Lower East Side.

With reference to the pogroms of the early 1880s, David Roskies has recently drawn a contrast between the European writers who had virtually no cultural equipment with which to reckon with the horrors of the First World War and the Jewish poets of the Russian Pale of Settlement who "were overprepared for catastrophe, and nothing could really take them by surprise."[49] By this Roskies intends more than the Jews' knowledge that a general crisis in society invariably confronted them with special troubles; rather he has in mind an entire "liturgy of destruction" that was a central part of Jewish culture, especially in eastern Europe. The liturgical imagery, metaphor, and tone of what Roskies calls the "pogrom poem," with which Jews sought to comprehend and find solace from the assaults of the early 1880s, all stem from the heritage of Jewish weakness and gentleness.

The pogroms of 1903–6, which were connected to the larger crisis that provoked the 1905 Revolution in Russia, signaled a decisive shift in the Jewish response: to one of armed self-defense, with Chaim Nachman Bialik, already emerging as the poet laureate of the Jewish national awakening in Russia, a central player. He and other intellectuals of the "Odessa group" rushed to Kishinev following the terrible assault on that town in April 1903. In what was a radical rupture with tradition, they issued, in Hebrew, a call for documentation of the destruction and for mobilization of defense against the next attack. The Kishinev rabbinate, by contrast, advocated greater cooperation with Russian authorities and interpreted the assaults as an expression of God's will and thus something to be endured. According to Shlomo Lambroza, one rabbi had advised the Jews to "be as quiet as water and lower than the grass," echoing distant forebears among the cautious rabbis from the time of Bar Kokhba's revolt.[50] Recalling a more heroic ancient past, Bialik denounced the timidity and gentleness and the entire "liturgy of destruction" of his own times and cried out for something new. "Great is the sorrow," he wrote, but just as great "is the shame. . . . And which of the two is greater, answer thou, O son of Man. The grandsons of the Maccabeans—they ran like mice, they hid themselves like bedbugs and died the death of dogs wherever found."[51] As Roskies indicates, the poetry of protest voiced by Bialik and others such as Moyshe Leib Halperin was directed not only at the Jewish heritage of meekness and passivity, but at the God of that heritage. In 1903 and after, Roskies writes, the pogrom poem "was freed from its theological foundations" (p. 91), a development that opened new possibilities, above all that of "retribution in a world devoid of God" (p. 88). The pogrom, in Roskies' excellent formulation, "was gradually becoming emancipated from Jewish history" (p. 97).

The new poetry of resistance was accompanied by the practical efforts of leftist Jewish activists, who made decisive contributions to the emerging imagery of Jewish toughness. As both Lambroza and Frankel have shown, the Bund, in forging the major self-defense efforts during the Kishinev pogrom, was keenly aware that a new type of Jew was being born. Into the besieged and frightened Jewish towns of the Pale of Settlement, the Bund brought the spirit of struggle and resistance of the European workers' movement—with a nationalist twist. "For centuries the Jew had lived as a slave," one Bundist remarked. "He considered suffering and silence his highest virtues. When his blood was shed, he fell like a dumb animal under the hand of the slaughterer, without a struggle, without resistance." But as Jews gained experience in self-defense—barricading homes and towns, supporting neighbors, finding, making, and using weapons—the idea arose that, as another Bundist put it, "there are no longer the former, downtrodden, timid Jews. A *new-born unprecedented type appeared on the scene*—a man who defends his dignity" (emphasis added).[52]

In spite of the elementary forms of organization and the inferior weaponry, Jewish self-defense was often successful in repelling attacks. During the Bialystok pogrom of June 1906, for example, several hundred armed residents of the Jewish quarter managed to defend numerous side streets. A participant wrote that "when the *pogromshchik* is met by death at every door, at every window . . . then he knows that the *pogrom* is a war in which you cannot only kill but also be killed. That frightens the hooligans; it frightens the police; it delays . . . the soldiers."[53] "At stake are our lives," the Bundist, Chaim Helfand, concluded, "and still more our honor and human dignity. We must not let ourselves be slaughtered like oxen" (quoted in Frankel, p. 155).

This refusal and the new national consciousness and self-imagery of toughness did not arise simply. On the contrary, as Frankel's lush analysis shows, it passed through a dense web of contending currents and factions—Zionists, Labor Zionists, socialists, secular and religious anti-Zionists, and others—all of whom often drew radically divergent conclusions from the crises, fears, and hopes that were coursing floodlike through Russian Jewry. But from those complex developments in Russia between 1903 and 1906 the tough Jew emerged.

Roskies amplifies this point: Russian Jewish writers at the turn of the century searched not only the Jewish past but the present as well for "models of bravery and physical prowess." One important model was found on the margins of shtetl society, where Jewish resistance writers discovered the *ba'al-guf*, "an inarticulate boor who lived by his passions and responded not to the dictates of Law but to the varied calls of nature. He and his fellows were a motley group of thieves and roughnecks, but when Jews were in danger they fought back, and when the draft-board called them up—they went" (p. 141).

Irving Howe and Eliezer Greenberg have also noted the Yiddish writers' fascination with "the humorous and promiscuous energy of these little-noted Jews, the butchers and porters and teamsters, with their physical prowess and passions, so striking in their contrast to the pale little heroes" who had previously prevailed in shtetl tales and stories.[54] Roskies goes further. The appearance of the *ba'al-guf* in Yiddish literature, he contends, "marked a radical departure from anything ever called a Jewish hero before" (p. 142). Although the *ba'al-guf* is a shtetl rather than an urban figure and although he is not primarily a criminal, he is certainly a relative of both the early-nineteenth-century Yiddish-speaking gangster in Germany and the latter's counterpart on New York's Lower East Side a century later. But in the context of the pogroms, which threatened the Jewish quarters in their entirety, the *ba'al-guf* emerged into Jewish literature and political culture as a *positive type*.

The early-twentieth-century literature of the *ba'al-guf* is altogether lucid about the shift in the stereotype. In Sholem Asch's "Kola Street" (1904), one of the greatest of the *ba'al-guf* stories, for example, "the street of the scholars," where the Rabbi and teachers live and where one finds the ritual bath and poultry-slaughtering yard, felt "very much ashamed of Kola Street: 'They're illiterates, butchers, fishmongers,' " proclaimed the educated. " 'Not at all like Jews,' " the respectable folk would say to one another, while the "upper-class people of Broad Street, such as Reb Achiah," had nothing but contempt for the lack of manners on Kola Street. Yet the proper Jews were well aware that they were dependent on Kola Street if ever a shepherd set his dog on a Jew, or a peasant started a row, or army recruits began smashing windows on the Jewish streets. In such cases, "Jews young and old would run to Kola Street for help." The Kola Street toughs in turn considered the village gentry "limp rags—'Jews soaked in water,' " yet they were dependent on the scholars for appeals to heaven.[55]

In similar fashion, Fishel Bimko's story "The Draft" (1916) presents themes of class consciousness and contrasting Jewish types. "In those days, the younger generation split in two: One half, the soft pantywaists, who could be kneaded like clay figures—they went to the synagogue to pray. And the other half, with Berel the Lout at their head, the roustabouts, they went to Leyzer's tavern. The crowd was made up of tough tailor lads, apprentices who couldn't read or write, and who had always regarded the military as 'bullshit.' "

The story involves an issue that for most Jews of the Russian Pale of Settlement, though not for the *ba'al-guf*, was second only to the pogrom in the terror it invoked: the recruitment of Jews into the tsarist army. One evening outside Leyzer's tavern, several days after the arrival in town of the recruitment board, Berel the Lout and his friends are discussing the brighter side of the draft, when a tipsy policeman arrives and is invited to join the group. Quite drunk, the policeman forgets he is among Jewish recruits in a Jewish tavern, pulls his sword, and hollers, " 'Hey, Jews . . . we're gonna slaughter all of you!' "

Pandemonium is unleashed and Berel the Lout yanks the sword from the officer's hand and drops him with a mighty punch to the stomach. " 'You goddamn pig,' " Berel mutters, " 'you shouldn't show yourself among human beings; go fuck yourself.' " Besotted and in pain, the policeman pleads for mercy. Berel finally calms his angry mates, reminding them that " 'it ain't him, it's the liquor talkin'. He's got a good heart, the goy. Leave him be. He's got an old lady at home and seven brats.' " Berel and his associates then go out carousing, knocking on the windows of "the wealthy [Jewish] boys," teasing them about their religiosity and sheltered lives. The next morning would bring the draft, so the gang resumed its drinking "and . . . stayed up all night, as though watching over a newborn baby during the ritual night before its circumcision."[56]

David Roskies notices a radically new phenomenon in "Kola Street," "The Draft," and the vignettes collected in Isaac Babel's *Benya Krik, the Gangster* (1921?). The streets in these stories had been part of the shtetl for some time, but "not until the transvaluation of values, when a new generation of Jews took history into their own hands, organizing strikes, self-defense units, and revolutionary cells, did the Kola Streets of Eastern Europe present a model to be emulated. Before he could become a striker, fighter or collective farmer, the new Jew was expected to shed the inhibitions of shtetl propriety, bourgeois respectability, and arid intellectualism."[57]

Isaac Babel's *Red Cavalry* stories belong to a slightly later period—that of the Russian Revolution of 1917 and its immediate aftermath. But their accounts of Jewish bodies, weakness, and toughness reflect the thinking of the turn of the century—Babel was born in 1894—and are perhaps the most sensitive and interesting to have come from the Russian milieu that generated the tough Jew.[58] The author is probably speaking of himself when his narrator in "The Story of My Dovecot" announces, "Like all Jews I was short, weakly, and had headaches from studying" (p. 255). Babel's attention to Jewish bodies in the Pale of Settlement is striking; he focuses on "narrow-chested Jews," on the "bitter scorn inherent in these long backs, these tragic yellow beards," on "these anguish-chiseled features" on which there is no fat, "no warm pulsing of blood," and on the "uncontrolled and uncouth" manner of the jerky gait of the Jews of Volhynia and Galicia.

"First Love," based on one of the 1905 pogroms, can be read in connection with Freud's "cap in the mud" tale, although in Babel's telling of it, there is no redemptive Hannibal fantasy. The young narrator describes the Cossacks' assault on the neighborhood and then depicts his father, on bended knees, appealing mournfully and altogether without effect to a courteously sadistic army captain who smartly salutes the poor man and trots off on horseback as thugs destroy the Jew's store. The story ends with the father fully aware that the boy has witnessed everything. " 'My little son,' he stuttered with immeasurable tenderness" (p. 269).

Babel's Jews seem severed from nature. "But swimming proved beyond me," says the narrative voice of "Awakening." "The hydrophobia of my ancestors—Spanish rabbis and Frankfurt money-changers—dragged me to the bottom" (pp. 309–10). The *Red Cavalry* stories also represent Jewish self-transformations: the hydrophobic youth learns to swim; another young Jew reckons with the attraction and horrors of toughness, which Babel himself experienced in a Red Army cavalry unit during the Civil War. In "After the Battle" a Bolshevik soldier teases a young Jewish comrade who is prepared to go into battle but does not put cartridges into his rifle. As the story closes, the young man walks off "imploring fate to grant me the simplest of proficiencies—the ability to kill my fellow men" (p. 187). A shtetl joke may illuminate the matter. Several *yeshiva bucherim* (Torah students) have been inducted into the tsarist army and given basic training on the rifle range. To everyone's surprise, the young scholars-to-be quickly emerge as crack shots and are soon deemed combat-ready. In the trenches, they face their first enemy onslaught. At the command to fire, not a trigger is pulled. Their commanding officer repeats himself, then again at the top of his lungs, but to no avail. "What's wrong with you?" he bellows in despair. "I said *fire!*" "Wait," says one of the students in reply, "those are men out there. If we shoot, someone might get hurt."

Common lore among American Jews of eastern European descent, this tale has more recently been recounted by Leo Rosten in a way that reflects the pre-1967 sensibility of Jewish gentleness, particularly its schlemiel-like mockery of the warrior ethos.[59] The same joke is retold and reinterpreted in Primo

Levi's *If Not Now, When?* (1985), a fine work of fiction based on anti-Nazi Jewish partisans in eastern Europe during the last year of the Second World War. As the late Italian novelist presents it, members of the partisan band are discussing the political and moral ramifications of their activities stalking retreating Nazi troops. Pavel, one of the partisans, recounts the tale of the *yeshiva bucherim*, to which, however, one of his comrades adds a new gloss:

Pavel broke off: Ulybin had come in and set down at the table, and at once the excited murmuring of the listeners had stopped. Ulybin was about thirty, of medium height, muscular and dark: he had an oval face, impassive, always freshly shaven.

"Well, why don't you go on? Let's hear the ending," Ulybin said.

Pavel resumed, with less confidence and less gusto, "then one of the students says, 'Can't you see Captain, sir? They aren't cardboard outlines, they're men, like us. If we shoot, we might hurt them.' "

The partisans around the table ventured some hesitant little laughs, looking from Pavel to Ulybin. Ulybin said, "I didn't hear the beginning. Who were those men who didn't want to shoot?"

Pavel gave him a fairly sketchy summary of the beginning of the joke, and Ulybin asked, in an icy voice, "And you here, what would all of you do?"

There was a brief silence, then Mendel's soft voice was heard: "We're not *yeshiva bucherim*."[60]

This addition to the old joke serves as a vivid marker of the shift in Jewish stereotypes that took place in this century, even though both Levi's Mendel and Leo Rosten share some common ground: neither one actually challenges the joke; both accept its documentary character. For Rosten, the tale expresses something essential and laudable about Jewish values, whereas for Levi's partisan fighter it crystallizes a Jewish self-image to be transcended. Nevertheless, for all the joke's documentary significance as a statement of Jewish community values in both turn-of-the-century Russia and pre-1967 America, it is an incomplete document. It forgets the fighting Bundist of the pogroms and the *ba'al-guf*, a forgetting that the joke is meant to induce. Clive Irving's *Promise the Earth* (1982), one of the recent tough Jewish novels, actually presents a historically more nuanced picture of this matter (although it is otherwise simply not in the same class as *If Not Now, When?*).

Irving's novel is explicit about what the *yeshiva bucherim* joke obscures, namely, that Jews were not only learning to shoot—they were shooting. The novel's hero, Asa Koblensky, had witnessed the Russian Jewish resistance to the pogroms as a child. Having been recruited into the tsarist army during the First World War, he manages to desert and make his way to Palestine, where he puts his toughness and militance to work in the Zionist cause. Soon after his arrival, he joins Sarah and Aaron Aronson, actual historical figures who had formed a Jewish spy ring, NILI, which had worked for the British against the Germans, Turks, and Arabs during the war. Koblensky and two comrades-in-arms visit a small Arab village and are moved by the pathetic state of the inhabitants: " 'They're so abject,' said Feinberg, more in pity than in contempt. . . . Laski turned to Koblensky. 'You haven't much to say.' " Koblensky, recalling his Russian experiences as one of a small corps of fighters from a timorous and passive community, remarks in terse reply: " 'I've seen that kind of abjection before—in Jews.' "[61]

Asa Koblensky's itinerary from the Russian Pale to the Middle East was part of what is known as the second wave of European and Russian Jewish emigration to Palestine, the first having been the far less politicized migration of the early 1880s, and the third coming later, in response to Nazism. The post-1903 migration played a formative role in the genesis of tough Jewish imagery, although, strictly speaking, Jewish self-defense efforts and the gestation of a tough Jewish stereotype in Palestine predate the 1903–6 Russian turning point. On a small scale, bands of "watchmen" (Shomrim), formed in the 1870s and 1880s, protected the earliest Jewish agricultural settlements from attacks by Bedouins, who often viewed the settlers as brazen intruders. According to Arthur Koestler, a gifted observer of the dynamics of Jewish stereotypes, these early circumstances gave rise to "a kind of Hebrew cowboy" who traveled on horseback, wore Arab headgear, spoke fluent Arabic, and defended the settlements. David Ben-Gurion began his political career in the Shomrim. "These Jewish Buffalo Bills," Koestler writes, "'were the forerunners of the *Haganah.*"[62]

Zionism and Jewish Toughness

The wave of refugees from the pogroms of 1903–6 decisively altered the story. Among them were veterans of the self-defense units in Kishinev, Cholon, and elsewhere in the Russian Pale, who in 1909 organized Hashomer (the watchman), the first Jewish paramilitary organization in Palestine. As its members were Zionists and revolutionary socialists, Hashomer eclipsed the earlier Shomrim not only in organizational scope but, as Koestler indicates (p. 69), in bringing a new and highly political cast to the self-defense efforts. In 1920, after Palestine had been placed under the British Mandate (and the "land of the Philistines" actually assumed the name Palestine), Hashomer was in turn supplanted by the Haganah (defense), an illegal, underground paramilitary organization under the aegis of the executive of the World Zionist Organization in Palestine, the Jewish Agency, as it was commonly known. With the creation of the state of Israel in 1948, the Haganah became the Israel Defense Force.[63]

To make better sense of the role of those developments in the formation of tough Jewish imagery, attention must shift from their Russian to their European origins. In addition to the *ba'al-guf*, the Bundists, and the *bucherim*, there were central European figures and currents whose contributions to the imagery of Jewish toughness were equally decisive. We shift, then, to Vienna, in the early 1880s. Sigmund Freud (b. 1856) was a medical student; Arnold Schoenberg (b. 1874) was not yet a teenager; Adolf Hitler (b. 1889) was not yet born. Theodor Herzl (b. 1860) was a cultivated and ambitious college student, and a member of a dueling fraternity at the University of Vienna. Known as Albia, the fraternity accepted a limited number of Jewish members who were considered to display "pronounced Aryan sentiments." Herzl would eventually leave Albia as it became more openly anti-Semitic, but in joining in the first place, he clearly hoped to shed images of Jewish frailty and gentleness. Although not a military man, Herzl was in important respects heir to the nineteenth-century tradition of the Jewish soldier. As his outstanding biographer Amos Elon has shown, when Herzl joined Albia in the 1880s he perceived himself not as a Jew, but as an authentic Austrian and a pan-German patriot.[64]

That Herzl would later turn from the Austrian to the Jewish national cause and exert an impact on world history is of course well known. Aspects of his involvement with Albia and of his Austrian patriotism would carry over to his Zionist commitments: his preoccupation with style and image in general, and with the style and imagery of manliness in particular. As Elon underlines, Herzl "enjoyed the glamorous swords, the colored caps and ribbons worn by [fraternity] members at official functions" and "relished the test and adventure of the duel, the so-called *Mensur,* which was considered manly and edifying." Not passing fancies, these were tastes and impulses conditioned by Herzl's enthusiastic immersion in the pageantry and heraldry of late-nineteenth-century European nationalism. They are central to his impact not only on Zionism generally but on the key place within it of images, symbols, and regalia of Jewish toughness.[65] As a Zionist, for example, Herzl oversaw the founding of the first Jewish *Burschenschaft,* or fraternity, at the University of Vienna in 1897, its purpose, writes Arthur Koestler, later a member, being to demonstrate that "Jews could hold their own in dueling, brawling, drinking, and singing just like other people. According to the laws of inferiority and over-compensation," Koestler adds, "they were soon out-Heroding Herod once more"—practicing dueling for hours each day, eventually becoming the "most feared and aggressive swordsmen at the University."[66]

As to his Austrian patriotism, Herzl resembled Alfred Dreyfus, who throughout his ordeal as a victim of French anti-Semitism continued to think of himself as a Frenchman and as a loyal soldier in the nation's army. Eventually, though, the two men came to embody different possibilities: Dreyfus that of assimilation at virtually any price; Herzl that of Zionism. While the two men did not meet, their trajectories in fact crossed in the mid-1890s, when Herzl, as a journalist for the Viennese paper *Neue Freie Presse,* attended sessions of the Dreyfus trial and was thus on the scene as the trial turned into "The Affair." The experience, combined with the simultaneous upsurge of populist anti-Semitic movements in Vienna, completed Herzl's growing disenchantment with assimilationist strategies and propelled him to found the World Zionist Organization in 1897. Fueled by anti-Semitism, Herzl's initiatives would join (often with extreme friction) those emerging from eastern Europe during the same period, in the process turning Jewish soldiers into *Jewish* soldiers and Jewish toughs into tough *Jews*.

From turn-of-the-century Vienna come two other voices that contributed substantially to the formation of the imagery of Jewish toughness. The first of these was Max Nordau (1849–1923), a widely read literary critic, novelist, and polemicist, who was the most renowned of Herzl's recruits to the newborn Zionist movement. Nordau promptly emerged as a theorist of the tough Jew in a most precise sense. At the Second Zionist Congress, held in Basel, Switzerland, in 1898, Nordau and an associate proposed a physical culture program for Jewish youth, its goal being nothing less than to nurture hardy, athletic Jewish bodies in which to house the new Jewish national spirit. In response to this summons, the Bar Kokhba Gymnastic Club was opened in Berlin, with others soon following elsewhere in Europe.

While the club's name revived and honored the ancient Jewish warrior, its prototype was not Jewish at all. In 1810, Friedrich Jahn, patriot and poet, established a network of gymnastic clubs for German students in the wake of Prussia's defeat at the hands of Napoleon's troops. Since then, youth-centered sports and physical culture programs had become a common and important component of nationalist movements in much of Europe, undergoing a definite growth spurt at the end of the nineteenth century.[67] As with Theodor Herzl's interest in duels, flags, and uniforms, so with Nordau's focus on physical culture for Jewish youth, a key ingredient of the Zionist project is borrowed from the warehouse of Gentile political culture.

When the speech summoning young Jews to the Bar Kokhba Gymnastic Clubs was published (1903), it appeared under the title of "Muskeljudentum" (muscular Jewry, or simply muscle Jews).[68] We must once again create a muscular Jewry, Nordau proclaims—"Once again! For history is our witness that such a Jewry had once existed." After decrying the historic Jewish tendency to accept punishment as a kind of mortification of the flesh, Nordau turns to the Jewish body in its more recent development. Although he concedes that "unlike other people" Jews do not value physical life as their most cherished possession, he insists that it is not true that Jews are oblivious to their bodies. Rather, they have been *prevented* from developing them. "All the elements of Aristotelian physics," he continues in a poignant formulation—light, air, water, and earth—"were measured out to us very sparingly." In the small streets, poorly lit homes, and intimidating atmosphere of the Jewish ghetto, Jewish limbs, eyes, and voices weakened and shriveled. This can now be reversed, Nordau announces: We are today "allowed space enough for our bodies to live again. Let us take up our oldest traditions; let us once again become deep-chested, sturdy, sharp-eyed men."

Although the new muscle Jews "have not yet regained the heroism of our forefathers who in large numbers eagerly entered the sport arenas in order to take part in competition and to pit themselves against the highly trained Hellenistic athletes and the powerful Nordic barbarians," they nevertheless have surpassed their ancestors in moral terms. Citing the example of Hellenistic Jews who wrestled in the nude and had their circumcised penises surgically disguised, Nordau stresses that "members of the 'Bar Kochba' club loudly and proudly affirm

TOUGH JEWS

their national loyalty." All that is needed now is a new "confidence in our physical prowess."⁶⁹

Here, then, is a manifesto of Jewish toughness, at once a singular statement and an articulation of deep feelings percolating within and around the new Zionist movement. Although Nordau himself did not link the muscle Jews to the idea of a Jewish fighting force, his call can be read in connection with that of the Bundist who had announced after the self-defense efforts of the Kishinev pogrom that "there are no longer the former, downtrodden, timid Jews. A new-born unprecedented type appeared on the scene—a man who defends his dignity." In subsequent decades, Nordau's summons to "deep-chested, sturdy, sharp-eyed" Jews and the Bundist's call to armed self-defense would together reverberate through the Zionist movement, especially in Palestine. Yet these two statements of Jewish toughness are not entirely harmonious. The "new-born unprecedented type" of Jew evoked by the Bundist takes up arms, but only to *defend* the dignity of the Jews. Nordau's appeal is superficially more pacific in that it is limited to physical culture; but it also suggests a *cult* or metaphysics of "Jewish physical prowess" and in that sense it is less pacific and less self-limiting. Both aspects of the tough Jew would find expression in Palestine.

A shift from turn-of-the-century Vienna to Palestine in the mid-1920s will amplify the point. In the first kibbutz settlements in Palestine, for example, we find their Labor Zionist founders incorporating a muscle Jew motif into their communitarian, back-to-the-land projects. The new Jewish physique assumed a central place in kibbutz ideology—but in agricultural labor and armed defense of the farms, not in gymnastics clubs. Thanks in part to Israeli public relations efforts

144

since 1948, in part to tourism, and in part to the tough Jewish novels, American Jews are familiar with the kibbutz imagery of tough Jews.

Palestine in the mid-1920s offers another echo of the ideal of the muscle Jews, one that gives a religious twist to what was originally a secular articulation and at the same time unleashes the aggressive potential of the muscle Jew ideal. The voice belongs to David Raziel, a pious and charismatic student leader who arrived in Palestine from Poland in 1923. (At the end of the 1930s Raziel emerged as a major figure in the Irgun Zvai Leumi [national military organization, known simply as the Irgun], authoring the pamphlets that would serve as the guiding texts of the Irgun's anti-British and anti-Arab terrorist missions during and after World War II.) In 1924 Raziel wrote an essay in anticipation of the arrival in Palestine of the Jewish soccer team from Vienna, Ha-Koach (strength), which had recently won the European championship match in England. The essay is an important marker in the itinerary of the theme of the muscle Jew.

Raziel's thoughts suggest that he was fully conversant with Nordau's muscle Jews essay and that he was pressing toward new horizons, not least, that of geopolitical conquest. "From afar comes the voice. The Koach is coming to Israel," he writes. And the message is: "Strengthen the bones of the nation weary for 2,000 years, since exile from its land. Straighten the bent backs—the inheritance of the Diaspora. . . . Show them the new Jew; a Jew who has placed his hand upon the neck of the enemy." Perhaps recalling Nordau's remarks on the ancient Hellenistic Jewish wrestlers, Raziel implores his readers not to be ashamed of their Jewishness. "Do not be athletic Jews, but Jewish athletes. Display your Jewishness proudly," for only thus can a "nation of peddlers, merchants, and scholars" be converted into one that "will refuse to allow any force to trample upon it."

Again evoking Nordau's theme, Raziel warns against replicating the ethos of the "Hellenistic and Herodian eras of assimilation," when Jewish sportsmen knew only sports. Countering this image with the alternative of religious militarism, he encourages his generation to "grasp both sides of the coin—be like the Hasmonean who lifted the sword to drive the enemy out and conversely cleansed the temple of its impurities." Thus, it is not only legitimate, but imperative to interrupt the game to offer the afternoon prayer. For it will make everyone understand, writes Raziel in a striking anticipation of the ideology of today's Jewish settlers in the West Bank, that "a Jew can be loyal to G-d and His law while, at the same time, remaining powerful and strong enough to wield his might against the enemy."

Striking, too, is Raziel's demagogy: an opponent in a soccer match has been transformed into a metaphor of "the enemy" of the Jews—exactly the sort of abstraction into which Jews have been transformed through so much of their history. To be sure, the political backdrop of Raziel's essay must be acknowledged: the bloody 1920–21 Arab riots against Jewish settlers and the threat of their recurrence. That the riots were responses to what Palestinian Arabs perceived as intrusions and conquests is evidently of little or no interest to Raziel. He takes for granted that Palestine belongs to the Jews. "Play and win with the imprint of your phylacteries still impressed upon your arms," Raziel concludes. "Now the picture is complete—you have revitalized the nation!"[70]

The general cast of Raziel's ideas bears the imprint of Rabbi Abraham Isaac Kook (1865–1935), the first Ashkenazic chief rabbi in Palestine during the British Mandate and the most influential synthesizer of what had previously been the antagonistic currents of Zionism and the orthodox religious tradition. The (Nordau-inspired) athleticist and, subsequently, the terrorist ingredients that David Raziel brought to this brew are very much his own contribution.[71] Indeed, Raziel was moving ahead toward nothing less than a political culture of redemptive violence. In 1933, for example, amid his underground gun-running operations in Palestine, he fell in love with a young woman comrade-in-arms. On her sixteenth birthday, he offered her "a most precious gift—a pistol," writes Raziel's biographer, David Levine, who observes further that "the importance of the pistol and its symbolization of the holy act of self-defense can be seen in the dedication which David wrote to Shoshana upon presenting her with a copy of his book *The Pistol*. This is something of which we must 'learn and teach, hold and use'—taken from the morning prayer preceding the *Shema*. His book dealing with military exercises bears the following dedication," Levine reports, " 'Pore over it and over it; learn it and learn it again'—taken from the 'Ethics of Our Fathers.' The authority and pricelessness of the pistol was something which Raziel could express only in religious terms."[72]

I want briefly to return to *fin de siècle* Vienna for a final note on Max Nordau's vision of muscle Jews. His call for a new Jewish physique was voiced against the background of the regnant imagery of Jewish frailty, timidity, and gentleness. That historical context, and the intense debate it generated over Jewish stereotypes and self-images, is illuminated by a remarkable document authored by another turn-of-the-century Viennese Jew, whose views appear at first glance to be the extreme counterpoint to Nordau's. The work in question is

Sex and Character (Geschlecht und Charakter). It was published in Vienna in 1903. Its author, twenty-three at the time, was Otto Weininger (1880–1903).

A brilliant and tormented younger contemporary of Nordau (and of Freud), Weininger committed suicide shortly after his book appeared. Generally considered the classical case of what is commonly called Jewish self-hatred, this precocious figure had converted to Protestantism; *Sex and Character* was part of his desperate effort to overcome what he experienced as the taint of his Jewishness.[73] Not surprisingly, in a Viennese culture rife with anti-Semitism and generally preoccupied with questions of identity, images, and symbols, his book found an enormous audience. Adolf Hitler would soon be among its most avid readers. Freud already was.[74]

Thus, Nordau had sought to end Jewish bodily and moral inferiority by means of a program of physical culture within Zionism, whereas Weininger actually raised that inferiority to the level of a principle, proclaiming it to be the unalterable essence of Jewishness. According to his theory, sex and character traits are connected, and every person is a mix of male and female components. Some human types, such as the Aryan, are predominantly male: assertive, productive, analytical, capable of culture and combat. Others, such as Jews, are predominantly female. Judaism, according to Weininger, "is saturated with femininity," which in his terms means being restricted to procreation or prostitution.

Plagued by sexual ambivalence as well as by anxiety over his Jewishness, Weininger claimed that "as there is no real dignity in women, so what is meant by the word gentleman does not exist among the Jews." In an instance of astute but unintended self-analysis, he wrote that "hatred, like love, is a projected phenomenon; that person alone is hated who reminds one unpleasantly of oneself"—as in his own hatred of women and Jews. Weininger was not unique in feeling these fears and ambivalences. Surely, many young Jewish men in central Europe who knew of Nordau's call for muscle Jews had also read or knew something about *Sex and Character*. It is likely that some of them (and some of their present-day heirs as well) were driven by the impulse to achieve a Jewish manliness which, like Weininger, they feared was not their natural legacy.

Jabotinsky: Grey Eminence of Jewish Toughness

In the genesis of the twentieth-century tough Jew, the destructive, self-hating *Sex and Character* is the great countertext to Nordau's muscle Jews, with its strategy of national-racial renewal and pride. But Weininger and Nordau both believed that alternatives to the old, weak Jew had to be found. And neither can be understood apart from the broader context, which included *fin de siècle* nationalism, anti-Semitism, Herzl, bourgeois Zionism, the Bundists, left-wing Zionists, and the Russian poets of resistance. Indeed, the gestation of tough Jewish imagery was neither a simple process—Alfred Dreyfus's silences and Otto Weininger's anguished reflections also belong to it—nor the work of a single person or group.

Were I forced, however, to grant the title of éminence grise to one figure in the formation of the tough Jew, my choice would be Vladimir (Ze'ev) Jabotinsky, a man highly sensitive to physical stereotypes, images, and symbols. The historical record supports such a choice. The way to Jabotinsky is also pointed by the recent American tough Jewish novels themselves, many of which explicitly evoke him as a sort of *capo di tutti capi* of Jewish toughness. The political direction of much of this fiction amounts to a kind of neo-Jabotinskyism. And developments in Israel testify to Jabotinsky's enduring impact. The 1977 electoral victory of the Likud bloc in Israel brought to power one disciple, Menachem Begin, and more recently another disciple, Yitzhak Shamir, has become prime minister. Meir Kahane also counts himself among Jabotinsky's heirs.

This most controversial leader in the history of organized Zionism is still not widely known in the United States, even among Jews. As the nineteenth century came to a close, Jabotinsky, the precocious son of a middle-class, assimilated family from cosmopolitan Odessa, left his native city for Bern, Switzerland, and then continued on to Rome to pursue legal studies. It was in Rome that he learned of the Kishinev pogrom, the event that ignited his Jewish consciousness. Until then his outlook had resembled the young Herzl's. As a law student in Rome before 1903, for example, Jabotinsky was captivated by the Italian national awakening, the Risorgimento, especially its romantic, nineteenth-century hero Giuseppe Garibaldi. Just as Herzl had brought the spirit of the Albia dueling fraternity and pan-German nationalism to his Zionism, so, as Bernard Avishai has recently put it, would Jabotinsky's new Jewish feeling, awakened by events in Kishinev, be "fused to an admiration for Garibaldian militarism."[75]

Returning to Odessa, Jabotinsky organized a Jewish self-defense group and plunged himself into the young Zionist movement. During the First World War, he helped launch the Zion Mule Corps (1915) and, when the British permitted an armed Jewish unit, Jabotinsky and Josef Trumpeldor, a fighting veteran of the pogroms, organized the Judean Regiment, or Jewish Legion (1917), the first independent Jewish army. In the early 1920s, not long after he had mobilized a defense force in Jerusalem (for which he was jailed by the British), Jabotinsky became a member of the World Zionist Organization's executive body. And in 1925 he founded Revisionist Zionism, or political Zionism, its centerpiece being the call for a majority Jewish state in Palestine on both sides of the Jordan River. As Jabotinsky and his Revisionist followers saw matters, the World Zionist Organization's call for a "Jewish homeland" in Palestine was typical of its vague, soft, and hesitant approach to the crisis of Jewry. In 1935, after breaking with Chaim Weizmann, Jabotinsky established the Revisionist Zionist World Organization, proclaiming it to be the true heir to Herzl and Nordau.

By the late 1930s he was nominally the head of the Irgun though he was not, as some believe, its founder. The Irgun had been launched in 1931 by former Haganah commanders who had joined the Revisionists—Haganah being the military branch of the World Zionist Organization (only subsequently did the Irgun become a terrorist organization). Nevertheless, Jabotinsky, an accomplished poet, essayist, novelist, linguist, and Hebrew translator of Dante, is aptly characterized by Avishai as "the theoretician of Jewish militarism."[76]

He died in 1940, while on an American tour that included visits to camps of the Revisionist youth movement, Betar (the name of Bar Kokhba's last fortress).[77] After the founding of Israel, the fiery controversy that had adhered to Jabotinsky during his life continued in a dispute over his reburial and commemoration in the Jerusalem memorial park for heroes of Zionism. Many of his Zionist critics considered Jabotinsky and his legacy, the Irgun and its offspring, the Stern Gang, to be fascists. His tomb is now in the memorial park. Jabotinsky streets and avenues can be found in Israel's cities; his portrait adorns the Israeli hundred-shekel note. In fact, he casts a larger shadow over the Jewish state than even these signs suggest.

The Jewish Defense League's slogan Every Jew a .22 is typical of Rabbi Meir Kahane's provocative, Jewish populist style. This contrasts sharply with Jabotinsky's aristocratic bearing and broad culture, but style aside, the line from Jabotinsky to the Jewish Defense League slogan is a straight one. For a major segment of Jabotinsky's message to Jews, put forward in the wake of the anti-Jewish Arab riots in Palestine in 1929 and reiterated after the Nazi seizure of power in Germany in 1933 was "Learn to shoot!"

In an important essay from the mid-1930s, "Oifn Pripitchek" (At the Hearth), Jabotinsky gave a radical twist to the popular Yiddish song of that title. In the original, a teacher, seated by the fireside in a Jewish home, encourages the children in diligent study of the Hebrew ABC's, the *alef-bet*, emphasizing the sorrow and suffering embedded in the letters. Building on this touching scene, Jabotinsky introduces Jewish parents to a new curriculum. "I have spoiled your children," he writes, "taught them to break discipline (and sometimes even windows), tried to persuade them that the true translation of *komatz alef-o* is not 'learn to read' but 'learn to shoot!' "[78]

As was noted above, a number of the recent tough Jewish novels have sought to rescue Jabotinsky from the obscurity in which he has remained for many American Jews. Some examples are in order. "Do you know Jabotinsky, Heather?" asks Elena Cohen Strauss, the elderly millionaire matriarch of the Strauss family in James Patterson's novel, *The Jericho Commandment* (1979).[79] Heather is Heather Duff Strauss, the Gentile wife of David Strauss. She will soon be one of the victims of a massacre at the family home in suburban Scarsdale, New York—a massacre that appears to have been carried out by neo-Nazis, but is actually the work of a secret Jewish anti-Nazi organization as the first step in the unfolding of "Dachau Two," the shadowy organization's plan to avenge the Holocaust. Elena Strauss, the grandmother, lurks in the background of "Dachau Two."

"I know Jabotinsky," David Strauss nods. "Zev Jabotinsky. Great guy. The Jewish Garibaldi." Elena Strauss continues, ignoring her grandson's light remark:

"You should read Jabotinsky, Heather. Zev J-A-B-O-T-I-N-S-K-Y. That Jabotinsky understands the enemies of Jews like nobody has."

David placed his hand over Elena's on the arm of the chair.

"All right, we'll both read Jabotinsky. Now tell us how you're feeling, Nana. Seriously."

The old woman shrugged her narrow shoulders. She sagged back into the ottoman chair.

Elena stopped being playful and gave David one of her wise-old-woman looks. For the moment, his grandmother was clearly being the head of the family.

"Read Jabotinsky," she said. "Seriously."(p. 34)

As *The Jericho Commandment* unfolds, neither Heather, who is murdered, nor David, who gets swept away by events and a new love-interest, this time a Jewish one, has a chance to read and reflect on Jabotinsky. But the reference to the founder of Revisionist Zionism and the nominal leader of the Irgun is not merely incidental. Rather, author Patterson seems to invoke Jabotinsky's name precisely as the demiurge of the spirit of retaliation and revenge that runs through his novel.

Jabotinsky appears in a similar light in Gay Courter's *Code Ezra* (1986), a novel set in the Middle East of the 1970s. Alex Naor is described as having broken with his politically moderate parents to join Betar as a youth. There he learns that he and his fellows in the movement are "directly descended from a great line of Kings and Prophets, . . . the heirs of great warriors and judges." Alex "enthusiastically embraced the parades and rituals" and worked his way up the ranks of the Irgun and eventually to his present position in Israeli intelligence.[80] And in several of the novels based on events leading to the founding of the Jewish state, the Revisionist leader appears as an actual character. Gloria Goldreich's *This Promised Land* (1982)[81] and Fred Lawrence's *Israel* (1984),[82] for example, survey some of the political disputes in the early history of Zionism, and they reconstruct Jabotinsky's work with Josef Trumpeldor during the First World War, when the two men led the way to the formation of a Jewish armed force in Palestine.

Such invocations of Jabotinsky actually involve more than mere tough Jewish reinterpretations of recent Jewish history. For they have offered, in addition to that, a more specific revision of Zionist history by highlighting the role of Revisionism. Thus, Jabotinsky and his antisocialist, antilabor, procapitalist followers—though these salient features of Revisionism are not discussed by Patterson, Courter, and the others—supplant Chaim Weizmann and David Ben-Gurion as the main architects of Israel after Herzl. To the extent that these fictional accounts correct the Labor Zionist tendency to diminish Jabotinsky's role, they are helpful. To the extent, however, that they present a selective picture of Jabotinsky and tend to read Menachem Begin, Yitzhak Shamir, and the Likud bloc back into the 1920s, 1930s, and 1940s, they, too, substitute political ideology for critical historical reappraisal.

At the risk of de-emphasizing the importance of these representations of Jabotinsky, it should be said that none of them compares in intensity and subtlety with Arthur Koestler's

Thieves in the Night (1946), which is dedicated to the leader of Revisionist Zionism and is an open endorsement of the strategy and tactics of the Irgun.[83] The prolific Koestler (1905–1983), probably best known in this country for *Darkness at Noon* (1941), his novel about the Stalinist purges of the 1930s, was converted to Zionism when, as a student at the University of Vienna, he learned of the Arab riots against Jews in Palestine in 1920–21. Although he joined the movement in his adopted city (he was born in Budapest), Koestler found official Zionism in the 1920s to be "a depressing affair," in which the vision of Herzl and Nordau had been reduced to a "dreary bureaucratized charity" justifying the joke that "Zionism means one man persuading another man to give money to a third man to go to Palestine." He records in his autobiography that he was "saved from disillusionment by a personality whose decisive part in the establishment of the Jewish State has not been sufficiently recognized. His name was Vladimir Jabotinsky, and he became the first political shaman in my life."[84] After several years in Palestine in the mid-1920s, Koestler returned to Europe and journalism, leaving Jewish matters behind as he immersed himself in the Communist movement during much of the next decade. With his faith in Communism shattered, his Jewish preoccupations were rekindled at the end of the 1930s by both the increasing brutality of Nazi actions against Jews in Germany and the actions of the Irgun in Palestine.

Thieves in the Night, set in Palestine in the late 1930s, involves the evolution of a Jewish terrorist. The hero, Joseph, is an apolitical English intellectual. Although his father is a Jew, he has no Jewish identity—that is, until the night he is tossed from bed by his proto-Nazi lover-to-be who discovers to her horror "the mark of the Covenant" on her partner's penis. This characteristically Koestlerian fusion of sex and politics is the starting point of Joseph's journey through the ideological maelstrom of the 1930s as it is played out within Zionism in Palestine.

At once enchanted and distressed by the new breed of Jew he meets there, Joseph ruminates on these "Jewish tarzans" who have "ceased to be Jews and become Hebrew peasants" (pp. 126–28). With Nazi violence in the background and increasingly ugly confrontations with Arabs in the foreground, Joseph is slowly, arduously drawn to the extreme wing of the Irgun. In his reconstruction of the sensibilities of Jewish terrorism and the Zionist opposition to it, Koestler remains the unmatched political sociologist: of the unbearable pressure of events; the initiation ceremonies; the fascination with stereotypes, images, and signs so characteristic of Herzl, Nordau, and Jabotinsky; the Raziel-inspired cult of the redemptive power of the gun; the leather-jacketed machismo of the unit leaders; the preparations for withstanding torture; the anguished but passionate personal relations within the underground; and the perpetual presence of death.

Amid the recent proliferation of largely mediocre tough Jewish novels, *Thieves in the Night*, this prototype and classic, has not been reissued. Why? My surmise would be that Koestler is at once too extreme and too balanced. His attachment to the terrorist cause of the Irgun is too deep; his presentation of the genesis of Jewish brutality from its Arab counterpart too unflinching; and his depiction of the argument regarding Irgun's fascist aspects too fair-minded for *Thieves in the Night* to fit with the more simplistic Zionism one finds in the recent texts.

Koestler, the journalist and essayist, is also an expert guide through the terrain of Jabotinsky's legacy in particular and Jewish toughness in pre-1948 Palestine in general. But *Promise and Fulfillment* (1949), his account of the events leading to the founding of Israel, is as forgotten as is *Thieves in the Night*. In *Promise and Fulfillment*, too, Koestler focuses on the issue of Jewish terrorism. There were periodic episodes in the late 1930s and during the war, but Jewish terrorism against the British got underway in earnest only after 1945, Koestler argues, with the experience of "The Little Death Ships" (the title of the book's most remarkable chapter), the vessels carrying refugees from Nazi Europe to Palestine. These were being stopped, turned back, and in some cases sunk by the British. The most infamous sinking was the case of the *Struma* in 1947. The *Exodus* was one of those that arrived.

The fate of the refugee ships ignited terrorist attacks against British soldiers and constables, which in turn outraged the British public. Koestler himself sought to explain the crisis in his "Open Letter to a Parent of a British Soldier in Palestine," which appeared in the *New Statesman and Nation* in August 1947, and is reprinted in *Promise and Fulfillment*. Here is the key passage:

Try to put yourself in the place of a Jew of your own age on the jetty of Haifa, shouting and waving to a relative—your son, for instance—on the deck of one of those ships. He is not permitted to land; the ship lifts anchor to take its doomed hysterical load back to where it came from. The figure of your boy grows smaller; a few years later you hear that he has been gassed in Oswiecim [Auschwitz]. If, instead of Smith, your name were Schmulewitz, it might have happened to you. Something on the same lines happened, among others, to a man whom I met in Palestine two years ago [1945]; he told me that his mother and three brothers had been killed "by

German sadism and the British White Paper" [of 1939 curtailing Jewish immigration to Palestine]. His name is David Friedman-Yellin, and he is the head of the so-called Stern Gang. (p. 59)

The Stern Gang (or Lehi, acronym of the Hebrew for fighters for the freedom of Israel), named for its commander, Avraham Stern, had its roots in the Irgun. Stern and his followers broke away during the war, when the Irgun curtailed actions against the British. Like David Raziel, Stern had come to Palestine from Poland in the early 1920s and was also a pious Jew for whom violent actions were a sublime duty. He was arrested by the British police and executed in 1944. In the immediate postwar years the Stern Gang and the Irgun collaborated on numerous actions. Jewish terrorism, then, had in Koestler's words "grown out of the terror of the sea, the gaping mouths of the drowning, the deaf-mute gesture of their splashing hands. The drifting corpses gave blood-poisoning to the nation. The measured utterances of officialdom were answered by the rattle of the automatics of fanatic gunmen. Lawlessness had become the supreme law of the Holy Land" (p. 65).

As if in terrible confirmation of Koestler's insight, the last major Irgun offensive was by far the worst. In April 1948, amid atrocity-ridden combat between Jews and Arabs and the United Nations efforts to negotiate a cease-fire, Irgun and Stern Gang commandos massacred an estimated two hundred fifty Arab civilians, including children, in the town of Deir Yassin, out-side Jerusalem. Menachem Begin, Irgun commander at the time, insisted that Deir Yassin was an Arab military stronghold, although the townspeople had maintained peaceful relations with the Jews. Begin also argued that the Haganah had agreed with the plan to subdue the town, and that the civilian population was given ample warning to flee.

Neither the Ben-Gurion leadership nor much of Jewish opinion in Palestine agreed: the Deir Yassin killings were denounced as Irgun butchery by a majority of the Yishuv, as Jewry in Palestine was collectively known. In none of the numerous tough Jewish novels dealing with the story of the founding of Israel is Deir Yassin mentioned. In the minds of many Arabs, however, the image of the Jew as mass murderer, as pogromist, was indelibly imprinted; indeed, in the widespread fear that flooded Arab Palestine following Deir Yassin, roughly one-half million people fled, seeking temporary refuge in neighboring countries. They would not return. Instigating such a mass exodus from the land may well have been the immediate motive for the massacre. Arab fighters, meanwhile, remained. Some of them took revenge for Deir Yassin, ambushing a medical convoy near Jerusalem and killing seventy Jewish civilians under the impassive eye of a British military post, whose personnel did nothing to stop the killing.[85]

While the legacy of Irgun and the Stern Gang has endured, their days as active organizations were numbered. Numbered, too, until its recent revival by some Israelis, was their shared goal of a "greater Israel," a Jewish state on both sides of the Jordan River. Their demise came in June 1948, soon after the declaration of Israeli statehood and during the invasion of the new country by combined Arab forces. In an extraordinary episode that could have ignited open civil war within the Zionist camp, Haganah forces sank the Irgun-controlled ship, the *Altalena* (Jabotinsky's pen name), which was bringing arms to the organization in Palestine. Sixteen Irgunists were killed in the fighting in an area just north of Tel Aviv. Many were arrested, and the ship's cargo was lost. The future prime minister of Israel, Menachem Begin, was himself one of the last to leave the *Altalena*, swimming ashore amid heavy Haganah gunfire.[86]

Koestler concludes his assessment of Jewish terrorism in Palestine: "Incidents less tragic than the drowning of the *Struma* refugees, and regimes less overtly hostile than Mr. [British Foreign Secretary Ernest] Bevin's in Palestine," Koestler argues, "have generated violent revolutions in history; had the Jews in Palestine not reacted in the same violent and ugly way as other nations have in their hour of destiny, history would have passed them by with a shrug, leaving it to the Mufti and the Arab League to complete Hitler's work." If, he continues, in their general aspect

as resistance movements, Irgun and Stern Group were legitimate children of history, in their specific ideology they were illegitimate offspring of Jabotinsky's national liberalism. They treated him as their patron saint, as the Russians treat Karl Marx, and with about as much justification. They have inherited the Revisionists' maximalist program, their contempt for the official Zionist leadership, their sense of grievance and hatred of the parties of the Left; but nothing of Jabotinsky's liberalism, Western orientation, European spirit. Their ideology was primitive chauvinism, their language a stream of emotional bombast accompanied by Biblical thunderings. They were not Fascists, however, unless we call the Maccabeans and the prophet Samuel Fascists, too. After all, it was this gentle prophet who ordered King Saul to go out and smite Amalek, and not to spare the women and aged ones nor the suckling at its mother's breast. The Old Testament, taken as a practical guide to twentieth-century politics, is a more pernicious influence than Hitler's *Mein Kampf.* (p. 307)

Against the backdrop of Jewish history, it is an extraordinary register of the speed and depth of the tough Jew's development in this century that the very question of Jewish fascism has even arisen. It is equally striking to recall that, in Paris at roughly this time (1946), Jean-Paul Sartre was speaking of Jews as "the mildest of men, passionately hostile to violence." These two elements, Koestler and Sartre, together constitute a vivid indicator of both the staying power of the historic Jewish stereotypes and the burgeoning momentum of their tough Jewish alternatives.

Koestler's distinction between Jabotinsky and his offspring is worth pursuing. Jabotinsky was indeed hostile to "Biblical thunderings" and often ran afoul of Orthodox religious groups. He had also openly disavowed Avraham Stern, whose outlook combined a strange variant of socialism with a mystical philosophy of *action directe*, and an unrelenting hatred of the British. He viewed England as the chief obstacle to the formation of a Jewish state and prior to 1942 sought political agreements with the Nazis and the Italian fascists.[87] Jabotinsky, hardly an admirer of their policies in Palestine, nevertheless insisted on cooperation with the British against fascism. But only by comparison with his former disciple Stern can Jabotinsky be cast as a European liberal, as Koestler calls him. For while in his early formation Jabotinsky stood in the nineteenth-century liberal tradition, his Zionism represented not only the continuity of that tradition, but its dissolution as well.

Avraham Stern's flirtation with Zionist-fascist alliances could, for example, be said to have its model in Jabotinsky's call in 1921 for Zionist cooperation with the anti-Communist and anti-Semitic regime of Simon Petlyura in the Ukraine. Petlyura and his legions were infamous pogromists, and the proposal was poorly received even among Jabotinsky's followers, not to mention his critics. As Shlomo Avineri rightly emphasizes, however, the core of Jabotinsky's proposal is his "historical and aesthetical admiration for what he considered to be the vitalistic authenticity of Ukrainian nationalism and culture."[88] The crux of the matter here is not Ukrainian nationalism—Jabotinsky's essential model was in any case Garibaldi and the Italian Risorgimento—but the affective, aesthetic, and dramaturgical cast of his politico-military vision.

In the spirit of Herzl, Jabotinsky fixed his attention on the task of creating a new Jewish type and was a "convinced partisan of all the elaborate ritual of the corporations [*Burschenschaften*, or fraternities], including the highly controversial custom of dueling." And in the late 1920s a proposal put forward by a representative of one of Vienna's Jewish fraternities to do away with all practices borrowed from the German movement met with the following response, typical of Jabotinsky: "You can abolish everything—the caps, the ribbons, the colors, heavy drinking, the songs, everything. But not the sword. You are going to keep the sword. Swordfighting is not a German invention, it belonged to our forefathers. The Torah and the sword were both handed down to us from Heaven."[89] Actually, Jabotinsky, this chief of obstetrics in the delivery room of the tough Jew, was only rhetorically willing to relinquish all the other rituals, for he deemed them no less vital than the sword, as he wrote in 1933: "Is is a pity that we, the Jews, do not value massed choirs. Among the Baltic people, especially the Estonians, the roots of their national movement go back to choir singing. It is an enormously effective means for the development of unity and discipline."[90]

As has been noted several times in these pages, political rituals, mass choirs in particular, were widespread in nearly all nationalist movements well prior to the 1920s and 1930s (and were integral to the Nazi movement, which came to power in Germany in 1933 and which outdid all competitors in the political implementation of group and mass rituals).

This is precisely Jabotinsky's point: like Herzl, he wanted Zionism to be a nationalist movement just like the others—a normal nationalism. Such political rituals, moreover, were also significant components of movements on the left, communism in particular.

These principles and techniques were tested in the laboratory of Betar, the Revisionist youth movement Jabotinsky had founded in 1923. Central here is the notion of *hadar*, a Hebrew word variously translated as "knightliness," "shine," "pride," and "dignity," which summarizes the idea Jabotinsky sought to instill in young members of the movement. It is a matter of "outward polish reflecting inner warmth," Joseph Schechtman notes, "a concept aimed at the creation of a new type of Jew, outwardly as well as inwardly, and of a new way of life based on what is true and beautiful."[91] It is also, however, a matter of corporatism and political choreography. Betar, Jabotinsky wrote in 1934,

is structured around the principle of discipline. Its aim is to turn Betar into . . . a world organism that would be able, at a command from the center, to carry out at the same moment, through the scores of its limbs, the same action in every city and every state. The opponents of Betar maintain that this does not accord with the dignity of free men and it entails becoming a machine. I suggest not to be ashamed and respond with pride: Yes, a machine.

Because it is the highest achievement of a multitude of free human beings to be able to act together with the absolute precision of a machine.[92]

This explicitly totalitarian passage discloses the limits of Jabotinsky's nineteenth-century liberalism.

Earlier expressions of the same motif had appeared in Jabotinsky's *Samson* (1927), the grandfather of the recent tough

Jewish novels. In one episode, Samson is depicted as being moved to a peak of political ecstasy while witnessing a Philistine mass festival with "thousands obeying a single will." Here Samson believed he had glimpsed "the great secrets of the builders of nations."[93] Like his hero, Jabotinsky, too, believed he had imbibed great truths, in his case, the nationalist movements of the nineteenth and twentieth centuries, and with those truths sought to instill in weak and scattered Jewry the craving for "iron and a King."[94] Employing these ideals and techniques, Jabotinsky strove to awaken, even in "the worst assimilationist," feelings of Jewish national enthusiasm.[95]

On the one hand, the worst assimilationist; on the other, feelings of Jewish national enthusiasm: coming from the pen of this ultra-Zionist, the meaning of these phrases seems self-evident. Yet even Jabotinsky, the final and dominant figure in the larger sketch of tough Jewish history to 1948, however, reveals elusive and ironic aspects of his basic notions of assimilation, which he clearly dislikes, and Jewish national pride, which he clearly embraces. This shifting, often reversal, of the meaning of these terms is not confined to Jabotinsky's thought alone. Rather they are operative in Zionism as a whole and thus in the formation of tough Jewish imagery in this century.

It is often forgotten that the distance between Zionism and Jewish assimilation—between, for example, Theodor Herzl and Alfred Dreyfus—is not as great as it first appears. These seemingly polarized strategies of grappling with the historical question of Jewish marginality, victimization, and "otherness" share with one another the impulse to *normalize* the Jewish situation, to actualize what might be called a positive solution to the Jewish question. Assimilationism proceeds individual-istically to cancel Jewish otherness by transforming Jews into

Germans, Italians, French, Canadians, Brazilians, and so on; Zionism proceeds collectively and politically to the same end—that of canceling Jewish difference—by transforming Jews into Hebrews or Israelis, members of a nation-state like any other.

Both assimilationism and Zionism have sought (without complete success) to transcend the other as well as one or another type of traditional Jew and Jewishness: ghetto and shtetl Jews, the religiously Orthodox, Yiddish (or Ladino) and Yiddish accents, and timid, frail, or gentle Jews. The discussion of the Jewish question in this century has been dominated by these two strategies, although they are not the only way of being a Jew. But one of the functions of the dominant discussion between Zionism and assimilationism is to exclude and marginalize the alternatives.

Within this context, the matter of Jewish self-hatred or anti-Semitism reverberates as an important and volatile subtheme. Almost invariably, the charge is leveled at assimilationists. Their very impulse to integrate themselves into the dominant non-Jewish world is seen by their critics, primarily the Zionists, as being rooted in discomfort or disgust with the Jew within oneself. Thus, the accusation continues, assimilationists seek to cancel, escape from, or hide their own Jewishness. The German expression *mies Assimilant* (disgusting assimilationist or assimilationist wretch) from the early years of the Zionist movement is a succinct summary of the argument.

Zionism, too, has its Jew-hating dimensions, as the following passage from an early (1905) essay by Jabotinsky reveals:

Our starting point is to take the typical Yid of today and to imagine his diametrical opposite. . . . Because the Yid is ugly, sickly, and lacks decorum, we shall endow the ideal image of the Hebrew with masculine beauty. The Yid is trodden upon and easily frightened and, therefore, the Hebrew ought to be proud and independent. The Yid is despised by all and, therefore, the Hebrew ought to charm all. The Yid has accepted submission and, therefore, the Hebrew ought to learn to command. The Yid wants to conceal his identity from strangers and, therefore, the Hebrew should look the world straight in the eye and declare: "I am a Hebrew."[96]

This astonishing passage must be read in context. In 1905 the Dreyfus Affair had not yet run its course, and the terrible pogroms of Kishinev and other towns in the Russian Pale had only recently struck. Far from diminishing with the progress of bourgeois Christian civilization, the degradation, humiliation, and murder of Jews was on the rise. These developments resonate in every one of Jabotinsky's words, as does the energy of the Zionist movement, then less than a decade old. Contained in the passage is the very nucleus of Jabotinsky's thought and career, the cornerstone of his strategies and options. And the words are anti-Semitic or self-hating in the same sense that assimilationism is said to be so. More than Max Nordau's call for "muscle Jews," Jabotinsky's announcement resembles its apparent opposite, Otto Weininger's *Sex and Character* (1903), with its tormented denigration of Jewish effeminacy and weakness. Like Weininger, the classic self-hating Jew, Jabotinsky, the militant Zionist, yearns to replace the pale and frail "Yid" with a new "ideal image of . . . masculine beauty." As in Weininger, so in Nordau and Jabotinsky, the bodily ideal, for all the rhetorical appeals to ancient Jewish warrior roots, is decisively shaped by Gentile, indeed, often anti-Semitic, bodily aesthetics. As Amnon Rubenstein has argued, Jabotinsky's impulses are characteristic rather than exceptional. Within Zionism in its formative period, he writes, "there grew a non-Jewish, even anti-Jewish sentiment, stunning in its strength and in its longings for the pagan and the Gentile."[97]

With Jabotinsky as its apogee, this historical sketch of the tough Jew to 1948 comes to a close. It may serve as an extended preface and link to what follows, namely, a thematic examination of the post-1967 tough Jewish novels. The founding of the Jewish state marks a turning point in the story because once the scattered imagery of tough Jews became connected to the ideological needs and instruments of state power, the foundations were laid for the emergence of a tough Jewish stereotype. Jabotinsky, meanwhile, serves as an especially appropriate transition to the fiction: the anti-Jewish dynamic in his apparently ultra-Jewish cult of the Hebrew is very much at work in the post-1967 literary imagery of the tough Jew. For in the new novels, as in Jabotinsky's thought, the cult of the tough Jew as an alternative to Jewish timidity and gentleness rests on ideals of "masculine beauty," health, and normalcy that are conceived and articulated *as if their validity were obvious and natural.* They have, in other words, internalized unquestioningly the physical and psychological ideals of their respective dominant cultures. In doing so they forget that, far from being self-evident cultural universals, those ideals are predicated on a series of exclusions and erasures—of effeminate men, pacifism, Arabs, gentleness, women, homosexuals, and, far from least, Jews.

PART THREE

The "Rambowitz" Novels

"What Sort of a Man and a Jew Was He?" The Question of the Tough Jewish Novels

IN A FINE ESSAY on the Jewish "Renaissance" in American literature after 1945, Kurt Dittmar observes that "the Jew as a morally sensitive outsider and exemplary victim in a world that had become inhuman is the topos to which Jewish American literature essentially owes its victory in the period following the Second World War."[1] Dittmar proceeds to challenge this topos by disclosing the radical—indeed, unresolvable—tension between its conceptual foundation in the destruction of eastern European Jewry in the Holocaust and its social foundation in the well-being of American Jews. "Here an American Jewry of prosperity, there six million dead," he notes provocatively, adding that "the notion that the literary-cultural reputation enjoyed by American Jews since the Second World War could have in some form morally reckoned with the Holocaust is at best groundlessly naïve and at worst blasphemous" (p. 376). For this reason Dittmar places the term *renaissance* in quotation marks in the title of his essay and recommends discontinuing its use.

In the two decades since the 1967 Six Day War, American literature witnessed what could be called a Jewish literary counterrenaissance, although it emphatically did not flow from the sort of critical perspective proposed by Dittmar. Rather, a veritable wave of mostly pulp fiction has aggressively advanced an alternative topos: the Jew as muscular Israeli and exemplary fighter, that is, the Jew as tough Jew. While the social background of this newer literature—the well-being of American Jews—remains basically the same as that of its predecessor, its conceptual foundation has expanded to include Israel and Jewish power in addition to the Holocaust and its Jewish victims. As I have been emphasizing, the tough Jew of the new fiction should not be seen as a reversal or inversion of the Jew as "exemplary victim" but as a fusion of the old victim and the new avenger.

By way of introduction to these novels, I cite the remark of a friend to whom I had just shown the cover of one of them, *The Wolf of Masada* (1978) by John Fredman. "Hah!" my friend remarked, after glancing at the massive body, heavy armor, and ruggedly chiseled face of the book's hero, Simon ben Eleazar, the commander of the Jewish resistance fighters who had martyred themselves at Masada. "It's Rambowitz!"[2] This astute remark reminds us of the extent to which the new tough Jew is a child of Jewish fantasy and desire, but no less a child of Rambo, that is, of the contemporary American cult of violent masculinity.

As a sample of the atmosphere and substance typical of works in this recent subgenre, I introduce David Laker, hero of *The Aswan Solution* (1979) by John Rowe, an Australian who turned to writing after serving with Australian and U.S. troops in Vietnam and then with the United States Defense Intelligence Service in Washington. Like many of its type,

The Aswan Solution is a tough Jewish bildungsroman or novel of Jewish self-realization: David Laker, an American Jew, goes to Israel in the early 1970s and becomes a tough Jew. Laker is a representative American Jew. He has a minimal Jewish identity, is neither a warrior, nor a schlemiel. An engineer, he is unknowingly recruited for service to Israel by a tough Jewish woman, Miriam Heller, a Mossad agent of beauty and charm who is also the widow of an Israel Defense Forces martyr.

The Israeli government seeks Laker's expertise in connection with an extraordinary attempt to blow up the Aswan Dam in the event of an Egyptian invasion of Israel. His transformation from assimilated Jew into fervent Zionist begins on the flight to Tel Aviv, during which Laker reflects on some of the other Jewish American passengers, one Sammy Bergman in particular. "Were they members of the new Jewish warrior race?" Laker wonders. "Horseshit," he thinks to himself in response. "American Jews are fat asses with soft families rooting for a new kind of football team—the Israeli Defense Forces—and supporting these Jewish Green Bay Packers with cash contributions and a new chauvinism. . . . And Sammy Bergman, he felt scornfully, you say it all. Then he chastised himself. What sort of a man and a Jew was he?" Initially, we are informed, David Laker is not much of either.

Two transformations are at work here. The first, less obvious one is the transformation of an American Jewish theme into an American mass-cultural one. Thus, the American Jew's self-doubt, self-rejection, and envious admiration of Israeli strength find their parallels in the language of beer commercials and Mickey Spillane novels. The second and simpler transformation is the one within the plot itself, namely, David Laker's change as masterminded by the Mossad. Laker falls in love with Miriam Heller; the couple is taken on a jeep tour of the Golan Heights, where an Arab terrorist attack is staged, the driver apparently killed, and Miriam apparently tortured. (They are in fact unhurt.) The plan works perfectly, as David is consumed with thirst for revenge. "But don't you see?" he cries out to the Mossad commander. "I want to get those bastards. An eye for a fucking eye. I want to pay those Neanderthals back. What they did to Miri, Miri and me. I loved that woman."

This increasingly muscular monologue conveys a message about Arabs in particular and anti-Semitism in general that can be found in many if not all of the tough Jewish novels. "They," Laker screams, meaning Arabs, "want to do it to all Jews. Even in America, the Jew hate's just buried. And I want to fight as a Jew—save the Jews. America," bellows this American Jew on discovering his new, true loyalty, "can get fucked." With the novel's climax, Laker's conversion is complete. In the final confrontation with Egyptian forces at the Aswan Dam, he huddles with Miriam (who will soon be killed in combat). She has come to love David—Israel coming to love the newly toughened, Israelized American Jew—not least because "he was brave with the painful courage of the nonfighter who conquers his cowardice." Laker reflects: "He'd almost escaped his Jewish heritage, but here he was, a soldier-martyr at a new Massada."[3]

A few words on the chronology of these books is in order. I have, of course, been emphasizing the pivotal position of the 1967 Six Day War in generating the new tough Jewish imagery. And, indeed, in the case of the Rambowitz novels, only such progenitors as Leon Uris's *Exodus* and *Mila 18* were available prior to the late 1960s. But although several tough Jewish novels appeared at the end of the decade and in the early years of the 1970s, most were published after the mid-1970s.[4] How can we explain the gap between 1967 and the appearance of these books? It would be hard to argue in regard to these pulp novels that aesthetic demands delayed publication.

I propose the following hypothesis: As decisive as the 1967 Arab-Israeli War was in generating the Jewish American cult of both Israel and tough Jewish imagery, it left a small but significant gap, a gap then filled by the 1973 Arab-Israeli or Yom Kippur War. The Six Day War had placed Jewish power on the stage of world history, in the words of the *New Republic*; the 1973 war, in which Israel was nearly defeated, reasserted Jewish vulnerability. Jewish toughness appears to be all the more necessary and all the more ethically grounded. And it is in the years following the Yom Kippur War that the Rambowitz novels begin to proliferate.

Dimensions of a Subgenre

I want to develop a general characterization and typology of the novels, turning then to commentary on specific texts and themes. To begin with, the tough Jewish fiction is a highly concentrated subgenre: the many works appear in a brief period of time, and the great majority of their authors and publishers are American.[5] And most of the authors are men, as are most of their tough Jewish characters. The prolific Gloria Goldreich presents a bevy of such characters, including some tough women, but on the whole she takes them through rather fewer gruesome scenes or flights of Jewish machismo than do her male counterparts. The older stereotypes, meanwhile, of timid, frail, and gentle Jews are also represented almost entirely by—

often effeminate—male characters. To retrieve a theme raised in part 1, we can see in these novels, as in Zionism itself, that the emergent tough Jewish stereotype is linked to a quest, against the backdrop of a castrating anti-Semitism, for Jewish manliness. It is also part of a quest for a tougher self-imagery for all Jews; in this respect there is room for Jewish women. That also means, however, that one does not find here any alternatives to an essentially muscular and martial masculinity.

Some of the authors are widely known. Atop this list is, of course, Leon Uris, a virtual one-man factory of tough Jewish characters. In addition to *Exodus* and *Mila 18*, the classic prototypes, *The Haj* (1984) and *Mitla Pass* (1988) are Uris's most recent contributions to the subgenre. Although Ken Follett is not known primarily as the author of tough Jewish novels, his *Triple* (1979), which provoked these reflections, is one of the most vivid and revealing. Next to John le Carré and Len Deighton, Follett is probably today's most renowned creator of spy thrillers. John le Carré himself presents a special case. *The Little Drummer Girl* (1983), which was made into a film starring Diane Keaton, is linked to the tough Jewish fiction, yet distances itself from it at the same time. Le Carré, the most distinguished writer cited here, is also the only one to go on record as a critic of Israeli policies, particularly since the invasion of Lebanon in 1982, and a supporter of the Palestinian cause.[6] Gerald Green, two of whose novels will be examined here, is probably most familiar as the author of both *The Last Angry Man* (1956) and the book and film script for *Holocaust* (1978), the television special on Jewish victimization. E. Howard Hunt of Watergate fame is the author of *The Gaza Intercept* (1981), a tale of international espionage set in the Sadat-Begin years and one of the more grisly examples of the subgenre.

Most of the novels, however, are the work of less familiar authors such as Gloria Goldreich, who has given us the four-volume saga of the Maimon and Goldfeder families (*Leah's Journey*, 1978; *This Promised Land*, 1982; *This Burning Harvest*, 1983; and *Leah's Children*, 1985). These present a galaxy of timid and tough Jews reaching from late-nineteenth-century tsarist Russia through Manhattan's Lower East Side and Tel Aviv in Mandate Palestine to the manicured landscapes of the New York suburb of Scarsdale. Other authors include Peter Abrahams, whose futuristic thriller *Tongues of Fire* (1982) presents the astonishing Paul Rehv, the son of Israeli and American parents, who, as a note on the cover announces, "was bred to destroy the Arab world"; or John Fredman, author of *The Wolf of Masada* (1978), the cover of which inspired the name Rambowitz. This historical novel is based on the anti-Roman Jewish resistance and martyrdom at the desert fortress of Masada in A.D. 73. Its hero, Simon ben Eleazar, "shepherd boy, galley slave, gladiator, proud centurion, and finally, guerrilla leader—never forgets the dying words of his father, victim of Roman barbarism: 'You must avenge us all.' "

Thus, the tough Jewish novels are placed in a variety of settings, not only the contemporary Middle East. Certain basic characters tend to reappear, however. Like *The Wolf of Masada*, Ernest K. Gann's *Masada* (1970), on which the eight-hour ABC-TV special was based, turns to Jewish warriors from ancient history. I know of no tough Jewish novels set in the long period between antiquity and the late nineteenth century, which is not surprising, since, as was discussed in part 2, major collective examples of tough Jewish activity during that large swath of time are sporadic and local.

A number of the novels take as their reference point the

armed Jewish resistance to the anti-Semitic pogroms in late-nineteenth- and early-twentieth-century Russia, while another substantial cluster of books traces the itineraries of tough (and timid) Jews from the beleaguered Pale of Settlement to Palestine and New York City in the early decades of this century. Still others are essentially variations on *Exodus*, that is, sagas revolving around the battles leading to the founding of Israel in 1948. Uris's *Mila 18* is one of the very few actually set in the context of the Nazi mass murder. Several are situated in post-1948 Israel and focus, by way of love affairs between Arabs and Jews, on relations between the two peoples. Most of the remainder have contemporary settings: international espionage novels generally involving encounters among Mossad agents, Arab terrorists, and the latter's Soviet allies, or thrillers dealing with Nazis who emerge from hiding to complete Hitler's work. Although the settings of these novels are diverse, their authors, in at least two sociological senses, are not. First, Ken Follett, who is Welsh, is among the few authors who are not American. Second, nearly all the authors are also Jewish.

Follett is again an exception, as are E. Howard Hunt and William Caunitz. The latter's best-selling *One Police Plaza* (1984), a New York City cop thriller, is thickly populated with tough Jewish characters. As regards the non-Jewish authors, Follett and Hunt, like many writers and readers immersed in the milieu of espionage, are unstinting admirers of the Mossad; and their tough Jewish spy heroes, Nat Dickstein and Jay Black, are created with obvious affection. And neither the Jewish nor the non-Jewish authors are particularly inclined to raise moral questions about violence applied by Jews to their enemies.

One ought not to make too much of this. Such writers, after all, do not raise many questions about violence, period. If they seem altogether comfortable in the atmosphere of Jewish toughness, this is at least in part because they are evidently at home with toughness and its mass cultural representations per se. And that a number of their many tough characters are Jews is not remarkable, either, because of the political dimension of the alliance between Israel and the United States and its implications for American interests, not only in the Middle East, but in connection with the U.S.-Soviet conflict as well. What we see in the novels by Follett, Hunt, and Caunitz is a picture which has had a decided appeal to many *Americans*, not only to Jewish Americans: tough Jews foiling the nefarious plots of the Soviets and the evil Arabs, killing a good number of them along the way. Pulling for the underdog is after all a matter of general, not only Jewish, interest. Typically in the spy thriller the Mossad emerges bathed in the glow of re-markable proficiency and genuine integrity. The Soviet KGB is, of course, the enemy, and both the American CIA and the British MI5 are depicted as corrupt and bumbling.

The fact that non-Jews are among the authors of tough Jewish novels suggests the breadth of the appeal of the tough Jewish stereotype in contemporary America—and the lack of appeal of Arab images. Novelists such as Follett, Hunt, and Caunitz—along with non-Jewish authors of recent, highly sympathetic, nonfiction studies of Jewish experience such as Conor Cruise O'Brien (*The Siege: The Saga of Israel and Zion-ism*, 1986) and Paul Johnson (*History of the Jews*, 1987)—are latter-day counterparts in the literary field of the historical figure of Orde Wingate, the British army officer, guerrilla strategist, and Christian fundamentalist who dedicated and sacri-ficed his life to what he believed was the messianic cause of Zionist armed struggle against the Arabs in Palestine during the mid-1930s. The parallel needs qualification—Wingate was in al-most all respects a unique figure in his day and was playing for stakes higher than those of today's authors—but otherwise the main point stands: what Wingate was to the Zionist fighters in Palestine, Ken Follett, Conor Cruise O'Brien, and the others are to the emerging tough Jewish stereotype: its Gentile friends.

Moral Ambivalence and the Normalization of Violence

In turning now to particular themes and texts, I introduce an unusually reflective tough Jewish hero, Amos Shomron, an investigator for the Israeli police, who appears in the novel by British writer Emanuel Litvinoff. *Falls the Shadow* (1983) is set in Tel Aviv in the 1970s.[7] In contrast to the ideologically shrill and simple American tough-Jew-in-the-making, David Laker, discussed above, Litvinoff's Shomron is politically torn, a dimension of *Falls the Shadow* that may be a reflection of the 1982 Israeli invasion of Lebanon. Shomron reads Hannah Arendt's *Eichmann in Jerusalem* and George Steiner's *Language and Silence*, for example. In the course of investigating what looks like a routine murder case, he is drawn into the anguish of modern Jewish history as it relates to Israel and the Holocaust.

This unusual detective, a member of a "generation imbued with a spirit of self-reliance," cannot comprehend Jewish passivity during the Nazi mass murder. He acknowledges the Warsaw Ghetto uprising, the doomed break from Treblinka, and the partisans in the Lithuanian forests, but "it was not enough"; he and his peers are still filled with "pity and shame." In a succinct passage, Shomron reconstructs the emergence of the tough Jew, the latter's rejection of the historic imagery of Jewish gentleness and timidity, and the place in this whole development of the 1967 Six Day War:

Many saw only meekness and timidity in the two-thousand-year history of the Diaspora and rejected it, looking to the example of their biblical Hebrew ancestors for inspiration instead. The days before the Six Day War turned them into Jews again. Suddenly enemy armies were massed along their borders and the threat of annihilation revived. Standing crowded on their narrow strip of land, backs to the sea, outnumbered and alone, they heard the barking of guard dogs, the suffocating cries of men, women and children choking on the fumes of Zyklon B, saw again the heaps of wasted cadavers, the queues of naked victims shivering on the edge of blood-soaked ditches awaiting their turn to be machine-gunned. But they were a generation of post-Auschwitz Jews. It must never, never happen again. So they primed their ammunition and fought as Jews had not fought since they were scattered throughout the world by Babylonian cohorts and Roman legions. (pp. 340–41)

Unlike George Steiner and Hannah Arendt, Detective Shomron is not a Jewish critic of Zionism. He is, however, a Zionist and a tough Jew with doubts. He fears, for example, the consequences for Israel of "decades of military struggle, harshness in the occupied territories, the arrest of stone-throwing Arab schoolchildren, long detention without trial, the punitive destruction of people's homes, the stupidities of army censorship: there were times after a bombing raid on PLO targets," Shomron continues to brood, "in which innocent civilians were killed or maimed, or a general strutted like a warlord, or religious bully boys planted a banner of Jehova on Arab land, when the fearful question arose: have we won our wars at the cost of moral defeat?" These were strikingly critical words for 1983. Read seven years later in the context of the *intifada*, they incline one to reply to the closing question in the affirmative.

As for Shomron, near the novel's end, he reflects on the Jewish state which "proved more proficient in the terrible skills of war than in the area of peace." After too many funerals and obituaries, "the mood of many turned sour, their ideals crumbled, they worked as little as possible, for profit instead of joy." Shomron and his generation had somehow lost their way, and he remains uncertain about their ability to "find their way back"—the assumption being that there had once been Zionist ideals that were untainted by displacement, conquest, and war (p. 436).

But Amos Shomron is an exceptional figure in the tough Jewish novels. More representative are those works that make token gestures toward the corrupting logic of state power and violence and then forget them. The operative assumption seems to be that even when Jews are violent, they are still essentially gentle. Moral certitude—not ambivalence—reigns. Consider in this regard a moment in Fred Lawrence's fictional saga *Israel* (1984).[8] Its heroes are a father and son, Chaim and Herschel Kol. The former is a fighter against tsarist anti-Semitism who makes his way to Palestine early in this century; the latter, a sabra who joins the Irgun. In the late 1930s, Herschel Kol is working closely with David Raziel, one of several historical figures who appear in the novel. The two men share an intense exchange on the subject of their terrorist mission and its implications. Raziel reflects:

"I've come to believe that the very qualities that make the Arabs weak will ultimately allow them to prevail. They do not brood the way we Jews do. They somehow remain lighthearted and pure while we grow bitter and spiritually stunted as we apply ourselves to the art of killing as we once pursued careers. I think about the combat manuals [Avraham] Stern and I wrote. I have seen former Yeshiva boys memorize every word the way they once might have studied the Talmud—"

"Well, they—we—have to," Herschel argued. "Guns are what we need these days."

"Of course you are right."

"You don't sound so happy about it."

"That's because I've seen Jews take delight in killing. We have always excelled as students. Now we shall advance to the head of the class in violence, and we shall see what God will have to say on the matter." (pp. 539–40)

It is striking that Raziel's apparently weighty concerns appear nowhere else in the eight hundred forty pages of this novel. One is left awaiting God's judgment while Raziel and Herschel Kol simply proceed with the business of advancing to the head of the class in violence. In Gloria Goldreich's *This Promised Land* (1982), one volume of her quartet of twentieth-century Jewish family sagas, the issue is disposed of with even greater dispatch. Ezra Maimon is in New York City during the First World War raising funds for the Jewish military cause in Palestine. Following an impassioned lecture ("Like Jabotinsky, he had the zealot's impatience with those who could not believe as he did"), Ezra is confronted by a critic:

"Lieutenant Maimon. I have a question about Jews using force." A pale, bespectacled boy wearing the red-and-white button of the Young People's Socialist League stopped him. "Isn't force contrary to Jewish principle? Don't Jews believe that all people should work together for peace and equality?"

"We would, of course, rather not use force," he replied. "But history has denied us the luxury of that choice. We must defend ourselves and fight for what is right." (p. 311)

And the matter of Jewish violence ends.

Joel Gross's *This Year in Jerusalem* (1983) offers a final example of the erosion of the complexity of moral and political issues.[9] In this love story set in the tumult of Palestine on the eve of the founding of Israel, Diana Mann, a young, rich, and pretty Californian, is transformed into a tough Jew and a Zionist by her love for David Stern, a commando in the Haganah. In the pertinent scene—it is 1947 and Diana is already actively involved in the Jewish cause—she explains why Arab gunmen had murdered Charles Rudd, a British constable. " 'Charley Rudd,' she explains, 'was an Englishman who favored the Jews and had some influence, therefore he was killed, murdered in cold blood. That is the way this country works. You don't find Jews doing that.' " Her argument is answered: " 'What's that lady?' said a previously calm constable, his face puffing up with anger. 'What about the Irgun? What about that [Menachem] Begin boy that nobody can catch? What about the [British] soldiers still wet behind the ears that get shot behind their backs? That's not Arabs shooting, that's Jews' " (p. 105). What might have developed into a significant debate ends with this opening exchange, which, moreover, includes praise for Menachem Begin's skill as a terrorist.

The most striking aspect of characters such as Diana Mann, Herschel Kol, and David Laker is paradoxically that there is *nothing* distinctive about them. Neither they nor their milieus are tainted by the old Jewish ethos of gentleness, its hesitations and self-criticisms. These characters—these models—no longer embody the Jew as other. Rather, they are simply very tough and as such *very much a part of the political and cultural scenery of the close of the twentieth century*. In this respect, they may be the first Jews in modern literature who are altogether normal.

Meet, for example, Yachov Anderman in William Caunitz's best-selling *One Police Plaza* (1985), a book that is of interest here precisely because it is neither about tough Jews nor Jewish issues as such.[10] It deals, rather, with violence, sex, corruption, intrigue, and lonely heroism in the New York City Police Department. The novel portrays a galaxy of ethnic types, all of whom are tough and violent in their own presumably special—ethnically appropriate—ways. Like their Arab, Italian, Irish, black and Hispanic counterparts, the several Jewish characters, including Yachov Anderman, are simply there and simply tough: they have arrived. The murder of Sara Eisenger, another of the Jewish characters, opens the story and anchors the plot. Sara, whose parents are concentration camp survivors, seeks revenge by taking anti-Semitic lovers and then rejecting them. One of these rebuffed lovers, a former cop, kills her, out of pique but also because she knows too much about his involvement in a major weapons conspiracy.

Yachov Anderman is less complex. This Ariel Sharon look-alike is an Israeli operative who heads a network of warehouses across the United States, in which, with the American government's permission, vital Israeli military equipment is stored. In return for this privilege, Israel performs intelligence services for the United States, specifically, in assisting the government of South Africa. (Though little is made of this in the novel, the inclusion of Israel's South African connection is presumably meant as a criticism of both the United States and Israel.) Anderman, meanwhile, is very much a man, unlike a younger associate who is portrayed along the lines of an older Jewish physical stereotype—slight of build, Arazi has a shrill, nasal voice that irritates the hero-cop, Dan Malone. In contrast, Anderman is a man with thick forearms, his sleeves always rolled up, his collar always open. He is gruff and direct in conversation, highly skilled at his work, fearless, and well beyond the sphere of moral considerations. His is an unproblematic presence.

"Dr. Shein will be in charge," announces Eli Pomerantz, Mossad agent, in E. Howard Hunt's *Gaza Intercept* (1981)—E. Howard Hunt of Watergate fame.[11] The minor character of Dr. Hadani Shein is a Buchenwald survivor who teaches medicine at Tel Aviv University, has lost relatives to PLO terrorist attacks, and occasionally serves the Mossad as a specialist in torture, in this instance of a female Arab agent who possesses information much needed by the Israelis. This elderly healer from eastern Europe may be getting on in years, but he is no old Jew. He is, rather, a new, tough one who does his work without a moment's doubt or hesitation.

Similarly untroubled is Motti Barak in Douglas Muir's *American Reich* (1985).[12] The novel's hero, Kirk Stewart, is not a Jew; but his lover, Shira Bernstein, a reporter, is. She is murdered while investigating American neo-Nazi groups. Stewart pursues her killers, initially to a swamp in the Florida Everglades, where he and an FBI agent make their way through a deadly bog. Shots ring out and the agent is killed. Shots from another direction follow. Then silence. Then a voice, referring to the dead agent: " *'Olev Shalom*—may he go in peace.' " Stewart now faces what can be called the new Jew: "a short, medium-set man in his thirties. He had a weathered face, receding curly brown hair, a neatly trimmed mustache, and piercing blue eyes. The interloper wore a thin silver chain under an open khaki shirt, bush shorts, and lug-soled hiking boots. In his hand was a smoking Uzi automatic carbine. 'My name is Motti Barak,' the man says. 'I should like to assist you, Mr. Stewart. But I will expect you to help me in return. Can we strike a bargain? I come from the Middle East where bargaining is often a way of life' " (pp. 95–96). Together they save the United States from a neo-Nazi coup and a planned "American Reich."

Toughness and violence also come naturally to young Josef Ascher in Wayne Karlin's *Crossover* (1984), another novel that raises questions about Israel's relations with the racist regime in South Africa, albeit in a muted way.[13] Ascher's father had been an anti-Nazi partisan in the Second World War and the son continues the mission as a Mossad agent. Unlike Yachov Anderman, Dr. Hadani Shein, and Motti Barak, however, Josef Ascher has moments of remorse and self-analysis. In a Belgrade café, for instance, Ascher wonders: " 'Why are these people looking at me? Do they know I'm one of the chosen? Honed and ready. On the edge. A killer. But a killer with compunction. A killer who cared. Whom you could talk to. Interesting, selective. That was the key word. I demanded a certain level of evil in my victims. I was, after all, a moral man. What else? A man of my background. With my father. Enough' " (p. 76).

Perhaps the obvious cynicism of these reflections stands as a sort of critique of Ascher's role and of the new type he represents. On the whole, though, the moments of introspection are few. On more prominent display is his capacity to fuse sex, violence, and the Jewish cause as if he were the Jewish James Bond.[14] Here, for example, Ascher describes his associate and lover, Hanita Kahan:

She examined her leg, completely absorbed. She'd thrust it into the pale dawn light; the rest of her body was shadowed and brown, her long black hair startling against the white of the bed linen. Dark skin and grey eyes; high strong cheekbones and finely drawn, sensual lips. Her mother was from Syria and her father from Russia; I'd once heard Malachi, our Athens control, describe her as a combination of absolutes that wouldn't quite blend. She was a strikingly beautiful woman who regarded beauty as a mask. We'd worked together for almost a year now. The first time we made love was after I'd killed a man she'd brought to a Vienna hotel room. It wasn't my first hit and he was a man who needed killing, but afterwards I hadn't been able to stop shaking and neither had she and we performed the act of love shivering as if we could feel [the dead man's] hands stroking our backs. (p. 10)

In fact, such fictional characters as Josef Ascher, Motti Barak, and Yachov Anderman may not be at all remote from some Israeli realities. *Vengeance: The True Story of an Israeli Counter-Terrorist Team* is George Jonas's recent, nonfictional account of the Israeli hit squad assigned by Ariel Sharon and Golda Meir to carry out reprisals against the PLO operatives responsible for the 1972 Munich Olympics massacre.[15] Jonas writes that the leader, Avner (a pseudonym), liked "the absence of useless bellyaching about all the pros and cons that fertile minds could conjure up, especially if fuelled by the kind of caution that really amounted to cowardice. They were not like that, any of them. They could see the odds at a glance, and if they seemed right—time to act! Perhaps it was not the attitude people in the Diaspora, the old Holocaust Jews, would have called 'Jewish,' but it was the attitude without which Israel would never have come into being. At least not as far as Avner was concerned" (p. 150).

Jonas suggests further that a figure such as Avner was not a representative Israeli. While Israel had engaged in acts of "counter-terror, deception and destabilization" prior to the formation of the 1972 hit squad, "such operations have always been more controversial for Israel than for other powers." The agent who is "licensed to kill," Jonas remarks, "would not have found ready acceptance in Israeli (or Jewish) folklore" (p. 76). This may once have been true, but it is not so any longer. For Jewish folklore now includes the novels examined here as well as such works of nonfiction as Jonas's own; substantially transformed, it can sanction precisely the Jew licensed to kill.

Despite this, the tough Jewish fiction is not devoid of characters who speak out on behalf of peace, gentleness, and, in the case of those novels set in the Middle East, harmony between Arabs and Jews. Notably, however, such voices are invariably doomed. Thus, for example, in Gloria Goldreich's *Leah's Journey* (1978), young, sensitive Aaron Goldfeder leaves the comforts of his suburban Scarsdale home during World War II (a minor anachronism: thanks to anti-Semitism, Scarsdale had not yet become the stereotypical suburban Jewish community) to join a Palestinian Jewish company fighting together with the British in Ethiopia.[16] There Aaron meets his sabra cousin, Yaakov, for the first time. The two are soon immersed in deep talk about their dreams for after the war. " 'When this is over, I never want to see killing again,' Aaron said. 'Not anywhere in the world.' Yaakov remembered the heavy sadness that permeated those words and he was glad, afterward, that he had suddenly taken his cousin's hand in his own and felt Aaron's fingers unclench and respond to his touch." The following day, Aaron is killed in a skirmish with the Italian enemy (pp. 238–39).

So, too, in the numerous novels set in Palestine, the voices of peace are silenced by Arab violence, especially when the peaceful voices are themselves Arab—a horribly common phenomenon in present-day Middle Eastern politics. Mahmoud Malek in Chaim Zeldis's *Forbidden Love* (1983) is typical in this regard.[17] A nonviolent intellectual who favors Arab-Jewish harmony, Mahmoud is portrayed as a solitary figure amid a seething mass of bestial Arabs, incarnated in the person of his lecherous thug of a brother-in-law, Fawzi. Mahmoud launches a new journal to nurture the cause of peace. His wife responds: "It's a beautiful idea, Mahmoud—one that only a man like you could have."

"But there are so many dark forces among the Arabs, my husband; so many forces against peace—surely you know that as well as I do, Mahmoud." He is undeterred. And soon he is dead—his own life and that of his daughter, who had fallen in love with a Jewish boy, having been snuffed out by the Arab "dark forces." A virtually identical scene unfolds in Joel Gross's *This Year in Jerusalem*, in which a young Arab philosophy student and violinist, who often played chamber music with Jews and spoke out for peace among Arabs, Jews, and British, is killed by the mufti of Jerusalem, Haj Amin al-Husseini (pp. 120–21).

"You must forget retaliation and strike first," says Orde Wingate, the British commander and pious Christian who had fought and died with Jewish forces in Palestine in the 1940s, and who appears in Gloria Goldreich's *This Burning Harvest* (1983).[18] "Not so quickly," replies the fictional character, Chaim Shturman, a kibbutz leader. "You know the Bible, Wingate. Doesn't the Bible tell us that we must treat the stranger who dwells among us as we would treat ourselves? The Arab is that stranger." In the tough Jewish novels, such statements are virtual death warrants. Indeed, from the young heroine, Balfouria Maimon, the reader quickly learns how Wingate "had sat at their table and wept openly when Chaim Shturman, who had counseled love and moderation, stepped on an Arab mine and was killed instantly" (pp. 239–40).

A final instance of this pattern is from Lewis Orde's *Munich 10* (1982), which is notable for its violence even in a violent genre.[19] The novel's heroine is Samantha Sutcliffe, a Vanessa Redgrave with a twist. A former Olympic swimmer and now a British actress, Samantha poses as a friend of sectarian leftist groups and the PLO but in fact works for the Mossad. Though not a Jew, Samantha is driven by desire to avenge the death of her lover, an Israeli athlete who had been among the victims of the 1972 Olympic massacre. She works closely with Alan Tayfield, the nom de guerre of a Mossad commander who poses as Samantha's theatrical agent.

At one point, Tayfield sees fit to remind Samantha of the need for restraint and selectivity in their work. "Don't make the mistake of hating all Arabs," he tells her. "My wife died when a terrorist bomb exploded in a Tel Aviv marketplace shortly after the 1967 war. I only hate the men who planted that bomb and the men who were responsible for its manufacture . . . the men whose fingers were on the trigger. To arouse hatred among Israelis for all Arabs is what the terrorists want. Once they do that they will have succeeded in their quest" (p. 44). This advice, which comes early in the novel, is a sure sign that Alan Tayfield will not survive to the end, and he does not—which leads one to ponder the dead man's advice not to hate all Arabs. That one should hate all Arabs seems the obvious conclusion.

Jewish Men Reborn

" 'Any resistance?' " Andrei Borisovitch Karpov, a KGB chief, asks his assistant, Comrade Malik, after the latter and his staff have ransacked the Moscow apartments of several Soviet Jewish refuseniks. " 'From Yids?' " replies this minor figure in Gerald Green's *Karpov's Brain* (1982).[20] " 'Are you joking, Comrade Major? They whimpered like drowning puppies' " (p. 147). Major Karpov's nemesis, however, is a gentle Jew who does not whimper. Apparently modeled on Natan Sharansky, this saintly refusenik, Abram Levitch, carries great courage in the stereotypically frail body of a schlemiel. " 'We are non-violent,' Levitch said. He smiled. 'Who can we hurt? How many guns do we have? I don't even own a cigarette lighter. I can't fight. If somebody punched me, I'd fall down' " (p. 12). As in much of the tough Jewish fiction, so in *Karpov's Brain*, the counterpoint to the situation of Jewish weakness is, of course, Israel, for which Levitch longs. His beloved wife, Sarah, awaits him there, as does "the beach, the hot dry hills, where a man could hike, brown his skin, harden his muscles" (p. 31). In other words, where a schlemiel can become a man.

The quest for Jewish manliness may well be the dominant motif of the tough Jewish novels. In this respect, they echo the impulses of Herzl, Nordau, Jabotinsky, and other founding Zionists. The covers of the tough Jewish paperbacks portray neither schlemiels nor any of the purportedly effeminate Jews who had populated Otto Weininger's—and Adolf Hitler's—nightmares. Instead, one sees a squadron of muscle Jews, the "deep-chested, sturdy, sharp-eyed" Jews for whom Max Nordau had called. Indeed, after perusing these images, one is apt to think: Funny, they don't look Jewish. In the America of the 1990s the prudery and puritanism of early Zionism has faded. Today's muscle Jews are not only politically correct; they are also attractive to women and, of course, satisfy them.

Consider first Chaim Kol, the father of the father-son heroes in Fred Lawrence's *Israel*. Chaim is a reminder to readers that while, as Gerald Green's Abram Levitch believed, the physical attributes of Jews are greatly enhanced by exposure to sun and struggle in the Middle East, tough Jewish bodies can in fact be found anywhere. After battling tsarist pogroms, Chaim makes his way to Palestine around 1910. He is promptly swept off his feet by Rosie Glaser, the sabra daughter of Tel Aviv artist Erich Glaser. Chaim in turn becomes a topic of conversation in the Glaser household. Talk commences between Rosie, her father, and the family friend, Meir Dizengoff, the actual master builder of Tel Aviv, whose main thoroughfare bears his name. " 'He certainly doesn't look like most halutzim [Jews who settle in Palestine, in contrast to sabras, who are born there],' Rosie began. 'He's—.' 'That's right, he doesn't.' Erich Glaser's deep baritone filled the room. 'With his muscles, golden hair and blue eyes he looks goyish, right Meir? I shall put you in my paintings, Chaim. I'm sick of dark hair and brown eyes except for my darling Rosie's' "(p. 114).

One can be direct here: This is Jewish self-hatred masquerading as robust Zionism. By and large, for tough Jews to have maximum appeal in the Rambowitz novels, blond hair and blue eyes are recommended though not required. The broader range of tough Jewish physical types is displayed, for example, in Chaim Zeldis's *Forbidden Love*. The hero, Arie Arnon, whose outlook and rugged good looks replicate those of his namesake and literary prototype, Ari Ben Canaan of Leon Uris's *Exodus*, is himself one of the new types. But the several comrades he selects for a dangerous reconnaissance mission in the Mount Scopus area of Jerusalem during the 1948 war are a more varied lot.

Arnon turns decisively to his task, picking four men from the platoon:

Amnon Peled, a tousle-haired young sabra with piercing blue eyes and a ready, infectious smile that belied his seriousness and competence; Musa—or Moshe—Zaritsky, a squat, powerfully built fellow who had come from Yugoslavia in his teens; Micha Zalmanovich, a reticent, taut-faced man in his mid-forties who had seen combat in the Warsaw Ghetto and with the partisans in the forests of Poland; and Ovadiah Malachi, a plucky, sharp-tongued

Yemenite who was the best marksman in the Mount Scopus unit. Swiftly [Arie] led them out of the machine gun emplacement westward along the deep trench that ran along the northern flank of the mountain. (p. 44)

It may be recalled that when Arthur Koestler journeyed to Palestine in the 1920s, he was an assimilated, cosmopolitan Jewish intellectual who was both impressed and perplexed by the husky Jewish warriors he encountered there. Jewish Tarzans, he called them in *Thieves in the Night*, an expression that blended his affection for and doubts about the type. Such doubts and perplexity have all but vanished from today's tough Jewish fiction. Only the affection remains, often with strange results. As in the case of the worship of Chaim Kol's Aryan features, so with one Abraham, a Mossad agent who flashes briefly across the pages of J. C. Winters's spy thriller *Berlin Fugue* (1985), we are presented with the sorts of male bodies idealized in Nazi propaganda.[21] " 'I am Abraham,' said the tall blond man standing by the closed news agent's stall." This particular specimen is then sized up by one of the novel's major characters, the British intelligence chief, Joshua Davies: "Strong build, suntan, broad jaw, arrogant nose. The blond hair was too long for most military services. The man looked a positive Adonis. The Director wanted to dislike him on principle, but Abraham had a disarming smile" (p. 175).

In the tough Jewish novels, the spiritual and political contrast between the new Jew and the old Jew is occasionally anchored in explicitly counterposed physical types, but generally the contrast is simply implied. J. C. Winters, for example, need not remind his readers that the Adonis-like Abraham bears no resemblance to an absent-minded Jewish professor or a wizened Hasid. And Gloria Goldreich, apparently concerned that the point might be lost, highlights it in a brief but pregnant passage: in *This Promised Land*, the tanned, handsome, and sturdy Ezra Maimon visits New York, where he presents fund-raising lectures for the Jewish cause in Palestine in the mid-1940s and is confronted by a "small, bespectacled" young socialist who questions Maimon in the name of "Jewish principle." This passage is a reminder that the tendency to link moral and ideological values to physical-racial stereotypes may have been typical of the Nazis, but is not confined to them.

More important, the passage indicates a satellite motif in the tough Jewish fiction, one that is particularly prevalent in the novels set in Palestine and culminating in the founding of Israel: the denigration of what is called the Jewish Diaspora. Goldreich's "pale, bespectacled boy" and his pesky question— "Isn't force contrary to Jewish principle?"—are embodiments of the non-Zionist, non-Israeli situation. In the form of the young socialist, the Diaspora comes out poorly in contrast to the manly and martial Ezra Maimon, bearer of the new Zionist Jewish spirit and body. One thinks here of those positive Jewish American characters we have met so far: David Laker in John Rowe's *Aswan Solution* or young Aaron Goldfeder, the Scarsdale boy in Goldreich's *Leah's Journey*. Their virtue stems entirely from their commitment to struggle in the service of Zionism or Israel. Jacob Chain, the Lower East Side *shtarker* in Gerald Green's *Chains*, earns high grades as a self-affirming Jew (since most of his life predates the opening of armed conflict in Palestine, he is not faulted for not having joined that cause).

In stark contrast is the portrayal of the assimilated German Jews, the *yekkes* as they are often derogatorily called. They rarely appear in the tough Jewish fiction, but when they do,

it is in an altogether negative or even pathetic light. Ruth
Niemoller in Goldreich's *This Burning Harvest* is typical. Ruth
is the daughter of what is customarily termed a mixed marriage.
Her mother is not a Jew, and her Jewish father is assimilated,
bourgeois, and proud of his German citizenship and culture.
In the mid-1930s Amos, another member of the Maimon
family, arrives in Germany as a representative of the Jewish
Agency in Palestine, whose mission is to arrange the evacu-
ation of Jewish children in Ruth's care. The romance of Amos
and Ruth unfolds against a backdrop of impending doom for
the Jews of Europe, in the face of which Ruth's elderly parents
naïvely uphold the conviction that Hitler is a temporary problem, sure to pass. Ruth must choose between leaving with
Amos and the children and remaining behind with her beloved
parents. She makes the anguished decision to depart, leaving
her parents clinging to their false hopes and eventually to be
caught in the gears of the extermination machine.

Life in Palestine provides little relief for Ruth, but it does
offer a significant change. Following an Arab attack on a Jewish
movie theater in Jerusalem, Ruth weeps in Amos's arms. " 'It's
just like Germany. They hate us. They would kill us without
cause, without reason.' 'No, it's different,' he replied sooth-
ingly. His large hands stroked her long silver-blond hair. 'Here
we are not afraid to fight back' " (p. 223). At this moment the
new, tough Jew transcends historic Jewish weakness and its
suicidal faith in non-Jewish civilization, as typified by Ruth's
hapless father, Hugo Niemoller. Here, too, the bodily dimension catches the eye. Where the hands of the schlemiel
are typically small, chubby, or effeminate, and those of the
assimilated, cultivated German Jew typically delicate, fighting
Palestinian Jews such as Amos Maimon stroke their women's
hair and pull the triggers of their guns with more substantial

hands, hands befitting the pioneer. In this case, moreover, they stroke "long silver-blond hair," the mark of Gentile-Aryan womanhood Ruth had inherited from her mother. Its purity, far from being polluted, as Nazi ideology claimed it would have been, is protected and preserved by the muscular touch of the new, tough Jew.

That Arab militants perpetrated many brutal assaults on Jews in Jerusalem and throughout Palestine in this period is a matter of historical record. But that does not vindicate Ruth Niemoller's assumption that the assaults are entirely without political grounds. The belief that such assaults stem from an Arab penchant for violence and a universal hatred of Jews rather than from the conviction, for example, that Jerusalem and Palestine as a whole belonged to its Arab residents—and that the Jews are European interlopers—is a characteristic of nearly all the tough Jewish novels set in the Middle East.

Gloria Goldreich's portrayal of Hugo and Frau Niemoller is virtually duplicated in Joel Gross's *This Year in Jerusalem*, where the characters of Dr. and Mrs. Mann are Jewish Americans of German or *yekke* stock. Residents of Beverly Hills, California, the Manns are prosperous, assimilated, and altogether aloof from the crisis in Palestine in 1947—a crisis that has captivated and transformed their beautiful adopted daughter, Diana. This comely, privileged journalist falls in love with David Stern, the curly blond, blue-eyed fighter in the Haganah—yet another replication of Ari Ben Canaan.

As in Goldreich's *This Burning Harvest*, so in Gross's *This Promised Land*, the German Jewish heritage is depicted not merely as a political failure, but as a morally repellent position. Initially, Diana, like Ruth Niemoller, is torn between loyalty to parents and loyalty to the heroic man. Diana, again like Ruth, manages to extricate herself from the grip of the *yekke* tradition, and in both instances, the vehicle of that emancipation is a handsome, tough Jewish man. Thanks to both David Stern's love and the Arab brutality Diana witnesses in Palestine, however, she herself emerges as a tough Jew. By the novel's end, she has shed the debutante sensibility and Beverly Hills values of her home, adopting in their stead those summarized in the following dialogue: " 'Look, is there anything I can get you before I go? I'm carrying a lot of cash,' " says Diana Mann's brother as he departs Jerusalem after a brief visit. " 'You're not carrying a gun by any chance?' said Diana. Joey [a non-Jewish tough from New York who has joined the Jewish cause] smiled at her. She was talking his language now. 'Or maybe a switchblade?' " (p. 232).

Diana Mann's pedigree is a particularly interesting instance of intra-Jewish stereotyping. She is the Manns' adopted daughter. Only later in the novel does it emerge that Diana is not only not of *yekke* stock, but is, indeed, the daughter of Louis "The King" Bernstein, a Jewish gangster, long dead, whose roots were in eastern Europe. Having embraced her adoptive parents' values, Diana, who knows of her natural parents, avoids contact with her father's brother, Marty Bernstein, who is also connected to the gangster underworld. Unable to raise funds for the Haganah in Dr. and Mrs. Mann's genteel *yekke* circle, however, Diana turns at last to Uncle Marty. Crude and raucous, Marty Bernstein is also a proud Jew, who promptly offers his assistance. In working together for the cause of Jewish armed struggle in Palestine, Diana and Marty bring about a reunion of the true family, while the adoptive parents, and with them the Diaspora, sink into the moral backwater. Here is the key exchange in which the non-*yekke* Jewish hearts of the young debutante turned gunrunner and the squat, thick-fingered toughness of Uncle Marty begin to beat as one:

"I was trying to explain why I'm so involved—"

"Hey, you're Jewish. They're killing Jews, right?" said Marty Bernstein.

"Right," said Diana.

"So what else do you got to say, sweetheart?" Marty smiled. "The Jews are going to get a fighting chance to get their part of Palestine when the British walk out, and you want my help to get some guns."

"Yes. Until they're a state, it's not legal—."

"It's not legal, but it's right," said Marty Bernstein."(p. 51)

Marty Bernstein lacks the Aryan good looks of David Stern but he, too, is also physically different from the pale and ultimately empty assimilated attractiveness of the Manns and Niemollers. The robust if simple Jewishness of his soul imparts a certain glow, even a certain sensuality, to his stocky, sixty-year-old body. Tough Jews are sexy Jews. Not to be found as leading men in the texts examined here are the notoriously insurmountable neuroses concerning sex on the part of such schlemiels as Woody Allen's film characters or Philip Roth's *shiksa*-starved Alexander Portnoy. An earlier tough Jewish novel, Leon Uris's *Mila 18* (1961), offers a significant negative example in the area of sexuality. Dr. Paul Bronski is the representative of the Jewish community in its negotiations with the Nazi rulers of the Warsaw Ghetto. Desperate to protect his family and to maintain the bourgeois norms he has internalized, this young doctor takes on the task of coordinating the Nazis' distribution of ghetto Jews to slave labor or extermination. As Bronski sinks more deeply into the quagmire of complicity, his opposition to the emerging Jewish resistance movement grows increasingly shrill. It is no coincidence, then, that his lovely and chaste wife, Deborah, falls in love with another man, a young journalist, Christopher de Monti; although not a Jew, he is sympathetic to the resistance. The unsubtle point here is that Paul Bronski's political and moral spinelessness erodes his romantic and sexual appeal.

Men who move in the opposite direction, however, arouse their women with displays of their new manliness. These are men who, from inauspicious beginnings, manage eventually to articulate their Jewishness in tougher and more courageous ways. The transformation of the gentle, ethereal Nadav Langerfeld in Gloria Goldreich's *This Burning Harvest* exemplifies this lesson. The patriarch of the Maimon clan, Ezra Maimon, had long noticed with distress the arid quality of the relations between his daughter, Elana, and her husband, Nadav, a singularly academic political scientist. But as the conflict with the Arabs in the mid-1930s was changing "gentle dreamers into daring partisans," even Nadav Langerfeld finally abandoned "the lecture hall and excavation site for the dangers of strange forests and mysterious mountain passes" to emerge as a "daring ambassador of intrigue" (p. 382). The impact of his transformation on both father-in-law and wife is literally potent: "Ezra noticed a new spontaneity between his oldest daughter and her husband. The war had altered Nadav. He had become a man of action, and a new confidence distinguished him, an assertiveness to which Elana responded with loving softness. She had missed Nadav during his absences, and her heart beat faster when he returned" (p. 393).

An exemplary link between Jewish toughness and sexual prowess is forged by the remarkable Simon ben Eleazar, the heroic Jewish gladiator and guerrilla leader in John Fredman's *Wolf of Masada*. He is a source of great pleasure for Messalina, the sexually voracious wife of the Roman emperor Claudius. Following what both Messalina and Simon know is their final night together (the time is roughly A.D. 40), she is going to denounce the Jews but promises to give Claudius false information about Simon. "If I were to give proper advice," Messalina remarks, "I would tell the Emperor to kill you." The massive Simon responds:

"Then why not do so?"
    "Because although it will be your destiny to fight Rome, it will not be my destiny to see it." She smiled roguishly, drawing her cat's tongue over her soft lips. "Besides, there is another reason."
    "What is that, my Empress?"
    "You make love superbly. I could not kill such a man." (p. 94)

Tough Women

Israel's triumph in the Six Day War generated not only Jewish hunks of this type but their female counterparts as well. In one of the few pre-1967 tough Jewish novels—Lionel Davidson's *Menorah Men* (1966)—Shoshana Almogi is a young Israeli woman who serves as a guide to Caspar Laing, a British and non-Jewish Semitic scholar-adventurer. Almogi is cut from a mold that the Six Day War rendered obsolete: she is *zaftig* (full-bodied, literally juicy), down-to-earth, and pure. Her prototype is Naomi in Roth's *Portnoy's Complaint*—a member of the Israel Defense Forces who repels her suitor (Portnoy) with several well-aimed punches with her plump but powerful sabra arms. Davidson's Caspar Laing is no Portnoy, and he manages to escape harm, but Shoshana Almogi is Naomi's sister: when Laing ignores her appeals to cut short his advances—she is engaged to an Israeli soldier who "expects a virgin at marriage"—Shoshana finally announces: "I don't know if you're expert at Judo," she says. "But from here I could throw you into the lake with no trouble."[22]

    In the newer tough Jewish fiction, these emanations of male

fantasies have been replaced by a new, distinctly less familiar Jewish type—and a more familiar American type. In contrast to their predecessors, the new tough Jewish women have been to the health clubs and have traveled in the fast lane, emerging taller, more lithe, more seductive, and more interested in sex. Gay Courter's recent *Code Ezra* (1986), an espionage thriller set in the Middle East in the late 1970s, for example, is singular in presenting three women in leading and tough roles: Aviva, "the olive-skinned Sabra," as the publisher's blurb reports; Lily, "the Dutch Jewess who had survived the Nazis with her cool blonde beauty intact and her heart twisted with hate and hunger for revenge"; and Charlotte, "the American heiress whose Vassar background and WASP social circle were the perfect cover for her dedication to the Israeli cause." Male dominance remains central in the form of the plot's major puzzle: which one of these striking women has betrayed their unit chief and sometime lover, Eli. But the mere fact that the stories and feelings of women occupy so much of the novel makes *Code Ezra* unusual in the tough Jewish subgenre.[23]

One representative of the new tough Jewish woman has already been introduced: Diana Mann in Joel Gross's *This Year in Jerusalem*, whose itinerary takes her from Beverly Hills to the armed underground in Palestine. A comparable physical type is found in Tara Kafir, a Mossad agent in Sabi H. Shabtai's *Five Minutes to Midnight* (1980).[24] Born in Hungary, Tara and her parents managed to escape the Holocaust and find refuge in Palestine. When the novel's hero, Sam Sartain, first sees her, the reader is introduced to a "ravishing dark beauty," aged thirty-eight, who is "neither a professional model nor an actress, though she was often mistaken for one." Her cover in the United States is as a "representative of some of the top fashion houses in Israel" and as the chief of a flourishing import-export firm.

Tara Kafir moves only among the "crème de la crème of New York and Washington society." The watch she periodically checks is a Tiffany. She will eventually make romantic contact with hero Sartain, but for the moment she is busy with her fellow Mossad agent, the handsome Itzik, preparing for an evening of political contacts under the guise of socializing at a Madison Avenue hotel. She is the spirit of the tough Jewish woman.

The man entered the room hesitantly. It was obvious that he felt rather uncomfortable in his formal attire.

"You look absolutely wonderful," Tara said with an affectionate smile. "Please Itzik, turn around,"she switched to Hebrew, one of the six languages she spoke. "C'mon don't be shy, let's see."

As the young man awkwardly, and rather reluctantly, swiveled around, Tara assessed the tall, wiry youth. His dark hair and deep tan set off his ice blue eyes. "Great!" she exclaimed. "Believe me, you look good enough to model in one of my shows. . . . Of course, you can't do it with that Beretta of yours . . . every bulge shows, you know." She winked and laughed heartily. (pp. 106–8)

Tara Kafir knows her men and her guns. So do many of the other tough women who make appearances in the new fiction, although their images and roles are notably different, for they are Arab women. They figure in two categories in this discussion: as women and as Arabs.

A larger and more typical role is played by Nouri Farraj in E. Howard Hunt's *Gaza Intercept*. Physically, Nouri Farraj is a replica of Tara Kafir in *Five Minutes to Midnight*: tall, lithe, dark, buxom. In fact, when we first meet Nouri Farraj, she appears to be a tough and gorgeous Jew (Reba Mizraki) disguised as an Arab stewardess. Neither the reader nor the novel's hero, Mossad-man Jay Black (né Jacob Schwartz), knows that Reba Mizraki is actually Nouri Farraj, a tough Arab disguised as a tough and gorgeous Jew, and so forth. Nouri Farraj is actually a key operative in a Palestinian terrorist group called Al-Karmal, which is bent on demolishing Israel with neutron warheads. When her cover is eventually blown, she shoots to kill, leaving Jay Black, whose heart she had won, for dead. He survives and outlives her, as does Israel.

Nouri Farraj's evolution as a nationalist revolutionary and terrorist is briefly as follows: She is the child of a rape, and the man who had violated her mother was a Jew. As a young girl in what is now the Gaza Strip, she, too, was raped by one of "five Jewish outcasts" who broke into the family's tent. She managed to stab her attacker to death and to flee for help. The next morning "she had been allowed to cut the genitals from the Jew she had killed, and watched while the living four were buried to their heads in the heated sand."

Brilliant, beautiful, and permanently bitter, she is sent to the American University in Beirut on an Arab League scholarship, pursues her thirst for knowledge, and commits herself to the Pan-Arab cause. First inspired by PLO leader George Habash, "whose dialectics she absorbed as a desert plant drinks rain," she eventually joins the militant splinter group Al-Karmal, in whose service she carried out several assassinations while sharpening her skill at disarming her victims with her seductive powers. At Barnard College in New York she "began her scheduled transition into a double life. Earnest language student by day, by night Arab orator at gatherings in Village lofts, smoke-filled with hashish resins. And she learned how to switch identities as occasion required." Nouri Farraj familiarized herself with the culture of "her father's people, a father she had never known," and though she came to recognize the "intellectual attraction of his race," she always rekindled her hatred by recalling how she and her mother had been violated. While she is drawn to Jay Black, she knows only one of them will survive (pp. 233–45).

The Nouri Farraj-Tara Kafir physical prototype appears again in Lewis Orde's *Munich 10*, this time as Rima Bakri, another stunning, hard-hearted Palestinian guerrilla. *Munich 10* actually offers a confrontation between a tough Arab woman, Rima Bakri, and a tough female friend of the Jews, Samantha Sutcliffe, the widow of an Israeli athlete slain in 1972 in Munich. The two women meet in a Palestinian refugee camp that Samantha visits under her cover as a pro-Palestinian British movie star. Under Bakri's icy gaze, Sutcliffe delivers a brief speech in English to a group of schoolchildren.

Here as in much of the new fiction, the scenes involving Arab characters are marked by the complete absence of the freely articulated emotions and convictions that invariably typify the Jewish scenes. Thus, we read: "From the platform Rima introduced Samantha, and there was a well-rehearsed round of applause." Characteristically, the idea that the Palestinian children might have greeted a visitor they perceived to be a friend without prompting—or that Israeli children might engage in "well-rehearsed" or manipulated behavior—is not considered. "Unable to do anything but smile in response, Samantha stood beisde Rima, feeling inadequate next to this powerful woman who had suffered so much . . . until she remembered how she, too, had suffered after Munich." Following her brief remarks, Samantha Sutcliffe "realised from the spontaneous applause that greeted her statement that the children were as politically motivated as the adults; before they learned the three R's, they were taught to hate. She stepped back as the camera man began to film the class in session" (p. 192).

In Chaim Zeldis's *Forbidden Love* Arab females are uniquely presented, as gentle, pure naïfs. They are the Palestinians Layleh Malik and her mother, S'ad. Layleh and a sensitive young Jew, Uri Arnon, share a forbidden love. S'ad is the loving but otherwise passive wife of Mahmoud Malek, a pacifist intellectual. This gentle utopia is marred by S'ad's brutal brother, Fawzi. Layleh and S'ad are among the few Arab females who play more than incidental roles in the tough Jewish novels set in the recent Middle East.

Rambowitz and Arabs: Tough Jewish Racism

These passages portraying Arab women introduce one of the most distressing aspects of the whole tough Jewish fictional subgenre: the systematically hostile and often racist depictions of Arab characters of both sexes, especially males. Compared to typical representations of Arab men, for example, the portrayals of Rima Bakri and Nouri Farraj are almost favorable. The two women are stereotypes of desirable women: exotically dark yet sufficiently westernized for the American male taste. Their serpentine sexuality invites the reader into sexual fantasy. For example, that Nouri Farraj and Jay Black the Mossad agent enjoy their sexual encounters raises the utopian hope of Arab-Jewish harmony. But such hopes are quickly and thoroughly dashed. Indeed, such sexual encounters are highly structured political events. For Jay Black, the tough but charming and honest Jew, spontaneously opens himself to Nouri Farraj, nearly succeeding in defrosting her hate-filled Arab heart.

Whereas his sexual desire is authentic, hers is an ideological instrument.

The same political structuring of sex operates in one of the rare instances of spontaneous, nonideological Arab sexuality I have come across in these novels. Even then, however, the context appears clearly intended to repel the reader, reminding her or him of the Arab's inevitable deformity and perversity. Deborah, the main female character in Alfred Coppel's *Thirty-four East* (1974), finds herself a prisoner of Palestinian terrorists, her guard being one Leila Jamil. [25] Like the sexual dynamic that unfolds between the two women, the psychological dynamic also seems aimed at reinforcing the image of Jewish decency and normalcy—an image supported by repetition of pictures of the Jews' bitter and twisted Arab counterparts.

Thus, even as a prisoner in mortal danger, Deborah thinks to herself with sympathy and understanding that "no person should have to spend a lifetime the way Leila Jamil had spent hers, in hijacking, bombing, murdering, and always running." Leila Jamil senses Deborah's thoughts, which does not generate sisterly contact but instead sends the Arab woman into a fit of rage: in this literature the Arab character *necessarily* responds in such a fashion to what is portrayed as an equally ineluctable phenomenon, namely, Jewish decency. Fueled by the very core of her Arab being, then, Leila Jamil throws herself at Deborah, and captor and captive struggle wildly:

Then as the two women grappled, something happened that Deborah could scarcely credit, something that made her feel sick. Jamil thrust her hand inside Deborah's shirt and found her breasts, and with shocking suddenness her anger was transformed into a gasping, starved passion. She pressed her mouth against Deborah's neck, biting and sucking. The thin, iron-hard fingers clutched Deborah's breasts painfully. Deborah stared at her assailant with disbelieving eyes. She knew that homosexuality was common among Arabs, but she had never before encountered it in a woman. Her revulsion started as a deep, convulsive shudder and grew to a racking feeling of disgust as the Arab woman tried to force her to the floor. (p. 257)

Arab men are portrayed even more negatively. In a troubling echo of Nazi imagery, which often depicted Jewish males as fat, drooling polluters of Aryan womanhood, Arab males are typically portrayed in the tough Jewish fiction as vehicles whose insatiable lust and lechery is matched only by their taste for violence, especially against Jews. In enough of the works depicting Arabs, the portrait gallery includes one or more porcine and sex-crazed Palestinian terrorist. In contrast to Nazi imagery regarding Jewish sexuality, however, Arab lechery is not presented as being aimed at Jewish women. In J. C. Winters's *Berlin Fugue*, for example, we meet a representative minor figure of the sort who slinks across the pages of a number of the new novels. Faris Ghantous is a

Palestinian of markedly hangdog expression [who] was one of the bodyguards of Ali Hassan Salameh, architect of the Munich Massacre. He was, truth to tell, a nonentity. He was also singularly stupid. Unfortunately, Ghantous' lack of mental agility was counterpointed by an overly active libido that would not be denied. After six months in Paris guarding the Red Prince [Salameh], who continually enjoyed the connubial comforts of his ravishing second wife, Ghantous was desperate. French women of even the lowest kind despised Arabs, and money, even lots of it, seemed not to affect them at all. (p. 19)

On reading such examples of racism presented en passant, one wonders whether French women "of even the lowest kind" look more favorably on Moroccan, Yemenite, or, for that matter, Parisian Jews. In any case, with the exception of the Jewish rapists who appear briefly in E. Howard Hunt's *Gaza Intercept*, no Jew is ever presented in anything resembling the image of Faris Ghantous. With *both* Arab and Jewish characters, however, sexuality is intimately linked to ideology: tough Jewish sexuality is central to the Jews' new political virtues and their self-realization as a people of pride and dignity; Arab sexuality is represented, in equally politicized terms, as a component of the politically criminal character of the Arab world. The sexuality of Jews is part of their normalization; that of Arabs, part of their depravity.

More adept and dangerous than the hapless Faris Ghantous is the figure of Fawzi, brother of S'ad Malik. Fawzi is responsible for the murders of his sister, her daughter, and her husband in Chaim Zeldis's *Forbidden Love*. Physically, however, Fawzi is a replica of Faris Ghantous. In addition to their barely controllable libidos, Arab characters in the tough Jewish novels are physically stereotyped in other ways, too: They are dirty and they smell. In Orde's *Munich 10*, Samantha Sutcliffe and Alan Tayfield are about to be photographed during their visit to a Palestinian refugee camp. "The chairman of the Palestinian Liberation Organization stood between Samantha and Tayfield, his arms around their shoulders. Tayfield grinned blankly into the camera; the only thought that came into his mind was that someone in the group did not use deodorant often enough. It was not himself, and it certainly was not Samantha. Mentally he ticked off another reason to loathe Arafat" (p. 213).

Even Comrade Buenaventura, a Cuban agent working closely with Palestinians to detonate a nuclear device over Tel Aviv in *The Gaza Intercept*, finds them repulsive: "As usual, the Cuban thought, and hoped that after today he would never have to work with Arabs again. Africans were bad enough," he reflects, "but Arabs were in a class by themselves for ignorance, slovenliness, and indiscipline. Just look at the terrorist soldiers puking their guts out though the sea had been calmer than anyone had any right to expect. Only two or three of them could hold their heads upright" (p. 284).

Such portrayals are not at all exceptional in the numerous tough Jewish texts in which Arabs do appear, though these novels also include "good Arabs," for example, the Malik family, who are the equivalents of the "good Jews" and the "good Negroes" in other systems of stereotyping. The good Arabs are consistently represented in a manner that underlines their marginality in the Arab world, and this exceptionality in turn highlights the typical, namely, the "bad Arab"—the Arab who, like the Nazi, is the sworn enemy of the Jews but who, unlike the Nazi (but like the Nazi's Jew) is dirty, foul smelling, lecherous, and, as we have just seen, not even seaworthy.

There is of course some irony that both Jews and their non-Jewish sympathizers today apply to others the very stereotypes that have been attached to Jews since the late nineteenth century. In this connection, it needs to be said that critics of Israel and Zionism often overstate the parallels between Nazi perceptions of Jews and present-day Zionist perceptions of Arabs. But Zionists and other supporters of Israel are quick to emphasize the continuity between Nazi and Arab perceptions of Jews.

The depiction of Arabs in the tough Jewish novels may not be an entirely accurate reflection of perceptions within the American Jewish population at large. One hopes it is not. At the same time, it surely expresses and reinforces a widespread and well-rationalized conviction that Arabs per se, rather than particularly Arab regimes or specific forces within the Arab world, are vile creatures who by their very nature hate Jews and seek to destroy them. The matter can be put more starkly: the radically dehumanized images of Arabs one finds in many of the tough Jewish novels may encourage the uncritical reader to receive with equanimity actual reports in the daily press of Arab injuries and deaths in Beirut, the Gaza Strip, or the West Bank. If this is the case, American Jews (and Americans generally) ought to reconsider the matter lest they embrace both the racism and hopelessness to which their forebears and relatives have historically been so horribly subjected.

The analogy with Nazism, provocative and scandalous as it may be, should be taken seriously. Rupert Wilkinson offers a pertinent suggestion, indicating that "European fascist attacks on Jews tended to portray them as flabby and decadent but collectively dangerous."[26] This is very much the manner in which Arabs are portrayed in the tough Jewish fiction analyzed in this work. According to Wilkinson, this paradoxical, seemingly contradictory perception is typical of "political movements that are sharply concerned with strength and weakness—especially those that combine assumptions of superiority with fears of victimization" (p. 21). Zionism, it appears, is just such a movement.

Such stereotyping of Arabs is of course not peculiar to Jews. It has found wide currency, having become indeed typical of many Western perceptions of Middle Eastern peoples. This is one of the theses in Ali Banuazizi's eloquent critique of perspectives on the Iranian "national character" among academic social scientists. As in the more subtle cases Banuazizi dissects, so in the imagery found in the new, tough Jewish fiction, "the characteristics in question flow from a general model of an 'underdeveloped man' who inhabits an 'underdeveloped world.' "[27] This is one of the unstated assumptions of the representations of Arabs in the tough Jewish novels which, to follow Banuazizi's argument one step further, thus play their part in culturally confirming and reproducing the "underdevelopment" they purport to analyze or portray.

The challenge in this context has been well stated by Edward W. Said in *The Question of Palestine* (1979), which deals not with Arabs generally but with Palestinians in particular and Israel's relations with them. In his bleak appraisal of prospects for a break in the gridlock of hatred and war in the region, Said sees little hope that significant change will be forthcoming from the Israeli government—Menachem Begin was prime minister at the time—"in the absence of a *conceptual*, much less an institutional, *apparatus for coming humanely to terms with the Palestinian actualities*" (p. 112; emphasis added).

That the "conceptual apparatus for coming humanely to terms with the Palestinian actualities" seems lacking in this country as well surely has more basic sources than the images of Arabs in the tough Jewish novels. Yet, these texts have played a role. I offer a final example: the most recent of Leon Uris's grand historical sagas, *The Haj* (1984).[28] An unquestionably bold undertaking, the novel seeks to tell the story of the Jewish-Arab confrontation in the Middle East from the 1920s through the mid-1950s from a Palestinian standpoint, specifically that of the Haj, Ibrahim. In view of the author's reputation and the book's compelling and topical theme, it is not surprising that it became a best seller. It was a Literary Guild selection and was serialized in *Cosmopolitan*. Among the comments hailing the book on the inside cover of the paperback edition is Gerald Green's proposal to "make *The Haj* required reading for the entire membership of the United Nations," and the remark by the *El Paso Times* that "no serious study of the Middle East would be complete without the perspective of this book."

If any United Nations representatives read Uris's novel and gained insight into the crisis in the Middle East, they are likely to have done so only because the novel opens a large window on the problem of American perceptions. In its more than five hundred pages, there is much material on Palestinian life, experiences, and customs. But surely events are not viewed through Palestinian eyes in this book. While Uris's novel is far richer in detail than any of the other texts discussed here, it shares their basic impulses. It reiterates the very same hostile, often hate-filled view of Palestinian society and its values that typifies those other texts.[29]

The decisive judgment, summarizing the entire inquiry in what is intended to be a memorable crescendo of concluding insight, is delivered in the final pages by a Palestinian, Dr. Mudhil. This articulate, westernized intellectual—attributes that make him all the more credible for American readers—commiserates with the Haj's desperate and bitter son and makes an effort to explain to the young man the seemingly deadly maze in which Arab life has trapped itself. The narrator is Ishmael, the son; the date is 1956; war between Egypt and Israel has just broken out:

He held my head in his lap and stroked me and I sobbed until nothing was left. A wild burst of dying sunlight flooded the room and we remained in darkness.

"Why?" I whispered, "why?"

"You were three beautiful people who loved each other fiercely. But you were born into a culture which has no place for such love to express itself. We are accursed among all living creatures."

"What is to become of us all?" I said, as much a groan as a question.

He was silent for ever so long. I watched the outline of his shadow swaying, moaning.

"You must tell me, Dr. Mudhil."

"I shall tell you," he said softly, in agony. "We do not have leave to love one another and we have long ago lost the ability. It was written twelve hundred years earlier. Hate is our overpowering legacy and we have regenerated ourselves by hatred from decade to decade, generation to generation, century to century. The return of the Jews has unleashed that hatred, exploding wildly, aimlessly, into a massive force of self-destruction. In ten, twenty, thirty years the world of Islam will begin to consume itself in madness. We cannot live with ourselves . . . we never have. We cannot accommodate the outside world . . . we never have. We are incapable of change. The devil who makes us crazy is now devouring us. We cannot stop ourselves. And if we are not stopped we will march, with the rest of the world, to the Day of the Burning. What we are now witnessing, Ishmael, now, is the beginning of Armageddon." (pp. 522–23)

Uris's perception of the Arab world—and his counterpointed perception of the Jews—betrays a distorted understanding of love and hate. "The only thing we [Arabs] lack," says Dr. Mudhil, shortly before making the remarks cited above, "is the one thing the Jews have in abundance. . . . Love. Yes, the Jews love one another" (pp. 505–6). The context is Mudhil's explanation of the difference in the way Arabs and Israelis treat their respective refugees: The Jews, motivated by an abundant spirit of love, refuse to let their own live in squalor; with boundless energy, they mobilize, develop, and build. Arabs, driven by hatred and lethargy, turn a blind eye on the abject misery of Palestinian refugees.

Leaving aside the historical lapses—for example, Jews have been known to let "their own" live in squalor; nor are they incapable of hatred. While Arab states have done far worse than ignore the plight of Palestinian refugees—the Uris/Mudhil claim regarding motives or causes (inbred hatred and lethargy) is without foundation. And the idea of love is radically narrowed to encompass concern only for members of one's own religious or ethnic group: "the Jews love one another." The idea of love and compassion for the stranger, for the other, has vanished, as has the notion of love as a universally human possibility and hope. Uris has done more than narrow, or nationalize, love. He has dissolved it altogether by placing it in the service of hatred of the other, in this case, of the Arab.

Raising Tough Jews

As a subgenre, the tough Jewish novels can be considered a dynamic new mass-circulation curriculum aimed at transforming Jewish American and American consciousness. Several of the novels focus directly on the theme of what can be called tough Jewish education, particularly education of the young. There are, moreover, a number of novels and stories for children and teens that can be placed in the frame of Rambowitz fiction. It is to these matters of pedagogy and children's stories that I now want to turn.

We saw in Orde's *Munich 10* how Palestinian children in a refugee camp are taught to hate before learning the three R's. Jewish children, presumably, are taught differently. The reader is free to conjure up familiar images of secular Jewish youths hard at work in public schools, continuing the old Jewish tradition of study, academic excellence, and the cultivation of humane values; or of young religious Jews immersed in Torah and prayer.

On the whole, of course, the Jewish scholar, mystic, and intellectual give way in the tough novels to men (and women) of action; the spectacles and slouch of the bookish student yield to the sharp and almost invariably blue eyes and martial bearing of Haganah and Mossad men; the yeshiva student's pallor is replaced by the sabra's tan. Decades ago, Arthur Koestler voiced distress at what he perceived to be a disastrous educational shift taking place in Jewish life in Palestine. Joseph, the chief character in *Thieves in the Night*, is an Oxford-educated intellectual who is transformed into an Irgun terrorist in Palestine in the mid-1930s.[30] The process of conversion is not smooth; Joseph is initially disconcerted by much of the new Jewish experience into which he is drawn, not least an instance involving the education of the young:

I almost forgot the episode which frightened me most. It was a story one of the young Tarzans told me with a grin when he saw me through the open door of my room working on [the English diarist] Pepys. It was about a friend of his, born and educated in the Commune of Herod's Well. When the boy was thirteen, his father made him a gift of a fountain pen. When he was seventeen, he wrote a letter to his father which said: "Dear Daddy, today I have finished school. So I shall not need that pen any more and am sending it back to you." (p. 128)

To this Joseph adds: "That was an extreme case. But it is no use denying that these young Tarzans are a step backward and that it will take a series of generations until we catch up again. It is a deliberate sacrifice, but that does not make it less depressing. Rousseau was lucky that the French did not take him seriously; had they followed his advice and all become shepherds and tillers of the soil, he would have hanged himself" (p. 128). The pedagogical imagery and models one finds in the Rambowitz fiction push me to similar responses.

The following examples are representative. Recall, for in-

stance, Fred Lawrence's *Israel*, in which the strapping, Aryan-
looking Chaim Kol arrives in Palestine after fighting tsarist
pogroms and marries the sabra Rosie Glaser. Herschel Kol,
their impressive offspring, grows up to join the Irgun. Regarding the decisive moment in Herschel's education, Lawrence, borrowing from Jabotinsky, is emphatic: " 'A gun,'
Herschel thought," as his father embraced him and the boy
glimpsed what was strapped to the larger man's shoulder. "His
father's beard was tickling his face and he sobbed his greetings
between kisses. My father is a Jew, but he has a gun like the
Turks. I thought Jews could only farm and let others hurt
them, but my father has a gun. He fights." Lawrence specifies
the lesson: "Seven-year-old Herschel did not have words to
express what had happened to him, but he had just made the
transition from a resigned, long-suffering Jew to a Zionist" (pp.
338–39).

Gershon Winkler's *Hostage Torah* (1981) is a novel for
young teenagers.[31] It is billed as the first in a series of adventures
of the "EMES [truth] Junior Interpol." Its hero is young Simcha Goldman, a Brooklyn yeshiva student who uses the wisdom of the Torah to crack an Arab terrorist plot. In the process,
the remarkable Simcha brings a young secular Israeli Jew and
an assimilated American Jewish college professor to new aware-
ness of their Jewishness. The novel is dedicated to "all the
spiritual hostages who have yet to find their way." The author's
acknowledgment suggests that the book is intended to meet
the "urgent needs of contemporary Jewish youth." The message is crystallized in the following, almost incidental passage
in which the reader learns the career plans of Simcha's
nephew, Shimmie. Simcha has arrived in Tel Aviv and is met
at the airport by his aunt, uncle, and nephew, who had emigrated to Israel. They joke about Tel Aviv traffic:

Aunt Sarah laughed and shut her eyes as Uncle Reuven pulled in
between two trucks on the two-lane road. Simcha told everyone the
news from Brooklyn, and all about his flight. Shimmie was thrilled
that Simcha had met the son of a high-ranking *Shin-Bet* [the Israeli
equivalent of the FBI] officer (he wanted to be a spy when he grew
up), and aunt Sarah was pleased by Simcha's answers to Moshe's
questions. "It's a great gift," she remarked, "to be able to commu-
nicate with someone unversed in the Torah. It's much too easy to
appear smug. That's what your uncle stresses in yeshiva—learning
Torah not just for the sake of learning, but also in order to teach it
to others." (p. 26)

"He wanted to be a spy when he grew up." Lodged between
the convivial atmosphere and the seriousness of Torah wisdom,
this passing note on Cousin Shimmie's aspirations is not without an element of unintended high comedy. Precisely because
it is presented in so incidental a manner, and so normally, it
serves as a striking indicator of the shift from gentle to tough
Jewish imagery, from "My son, the doctor" to "My son, the
Shin Bet agent."

A still more striking indicator (though it is not aimed at a
young audience) is the model of Jewish child rearing one finds
in Peter Abrahams's *Tongues of Fire* (1982).[32] Here it is already
too late for Jewish parents to prepare their child for a career
with the Shin Bet. *Tongues of Fire*, a macabre work of political
futurism, opens with the fading embers of Israel itself, following its destruction by Egyptian and Syrian forces. Now under
Arab control, the land has been renamed Palestine. Isaac Rehv
is one of the few survivors, all of whom have made their way
to the United States, where a small, bedraggled Israeli government-in-exile is set up in a Vermont cabin, unsupported
and barely recognized by the American government. Rehv,
who served with the Israel Defense Forces in their heroic but

futile effort to stave off the apocalypse, is also a brilliant scholar specializing in Arab culture and history. Having lost his wife, daughter, and country, Isaac Rehv is a man beyond anguish, driven by a simple, almost psychotically calm drive for revenge.

While scraping by in Manhattan, Rehv hatches his plan. He needs a male baby who will grow up to destroy the Jews' Arab enemies. Strictly speaking, his plan will not involve a Jewish, but only a so-called half-Jewish, child. Scouring the Times Square subculture, Isaac Rehv finds a black prostitute in perfect health whom he pays to bear his child. The plan requires an infant who can be molded into an Arab, indeed into a charismatic and titanic Islamic force, a Mahdi, who will draw to him the entire Arab world and then lead it not to salvation but to destruction. Using his military and survival skills, and his knowledge of Arab and Islamic life, Isaac Rehv spends two decades cultivating his son, a tough Jewish Pied Piper, for the final round of the holy war. The child, Paul, is, indeed, successfully planted in the Arab world and we watch his meteoric rise. *Tongues of Fire* closes with the death of Isaac Rehv at the hands of a CIA agent: at the last moment, Isaac experiences the doubts of a loving Jewish father, but these are canceled with his death. And Paul Rehv, the Mahdi, is about to carry the plan into its final phases.

Does Isaac Rehv's sudden, last-minute hesitation, his impulse simply to be with his son and away from the endless horror, constitute a critique of the entire plan of revenge? Or is the reader to imagine, presumably with satisfaction, the plan's fulfillment? Or, more likely, is the novel itself a nightmare triggered by a bad reality and destined, in its small way, to make it worse?

The final example of a new Jewish elementary curriculum, an actual children's book, is both more clear and more creative.

Captain Jiri and Rabbi Jacob (1976) is an adaptation by Marilyn Hirsh of an old Jewish folktale.[33] Rabbi Jacob is a beloved Cracow teacher who lived long ago. What troubles him is that the students (boys and girls) in his yeshiva are harassed and frightened each day by Jew-hating youths. Although he applies himself diligently, the poor rabbi cannot devise a solution. Meanwhile, Captain Jiri, the rugged but kindly officer of the guard, has a parallel problem in Prague, where he and his men protect the bridge into the city. When not at their posts serving the good people of Prague, his charges are awash in whiskey and fisticuffs. Like Rabbi Jacob, Captain Jiri is at his wits' end.

One night, Guardian angels visit the troubled men, delivering a message of great import. In a very specific location, a treasure awaits each one. But the angels appear to have erred: Rabbi Jacob is told to go to a certain bridge in Prague, while Captain Jiri is instructed to journey to a certain rabbi's house in Cracow. Each does as he is told. Their paths actually cross en route, but neither has any knowledge of the other. The angels' error, however, leads to their real message, for while Captain Jiri finds no treasure, he gets an idea from watching the rabbi's young students studying, writing, and debating. Rabbi Jacob likewise finds no gold, but on seeing the Captain's men, proud and intimidating in their uniforms, he finds a solution to his dilemma.

Eventually, the two men meet and together confer with the angels, who advise them that now they can also find their treasures. With his gold, Captain Jiri purchases books, musical instruments, and teachers to introduce his men to new pastimes. Rabbi Jacob has uniforms made for his students, and he equips them with small pikes. They are thereafter able to ward off their tormentors and go about their work in the yeshiva. "Captain Jiri and Rabbi Jacob met every so often to discuss their experiences with angels. Captain Jiri advised Rabbi Jacob on training the children, and Rabbi Jacob brought Captain Jiri some new books to read. They were happy that their guardian angels had made a mistake, or they would not have become friends" (n.p.).

Perhaps because the circumstances in *Captain Jiri and Rabbi Jacob* are not those of war and terror, the lines between self-defense, retaliation, revenge, and aggression are more easily drawn than they might be in other contexts. Rabbi Jacob's students do not become tough Jews but Jews who are able to defend themselves from harm when the need arises. This they learn from the Gentiles, who in turn are inspired by the Jewish example to set out on a cultural journey. The tale ends on a note of interaction and friendship. In these respects, *Captain Jiri and Rabbi Jacob* actually stands outside the frame of the images examined here and, indeed, is a kind of critique of those images.

Tough Jews and the Politics of Apocalypse

My discussion of the recent tough Jewish novels closes with remarks on their composite political profile. At first glance, this might seem redundant since the subgenre as a whole is fundamentally political, aimed at awakening and solidifying the Zionist consciousness of its readers. The unremittingly negative imagery of Arabs is also part of this picture. There are, however, more specific political dimensions to the novels that fall along the left-right spectrum. This is rugged terrain, and one should beware of relying on familiar generalizations and first impressions.

Jewish neoconservatism inevitably enters the discussion; among American Jews it shares with the tough Jewish novels both an unbending fidelity to Israel and deep hostility to the political Left.[34] The novels and the neoconservatives emerged together from the excitement and anxieties generated between the 1967 Arab-Israeli War and the 1972 massacre at the Munich Olympics, as well as from such domestic, American developments as tensions between Jewish and African Americans and the emergence within the New Left of pro-Palestinian and anti-Zionist views. That the tough Jewish novels are the literary expression of Jewish neoconservative politics is a hypothesis worth exploring, if for no other reason than to indicate that, in the last analysis, it is a hypothesis that does not quite work.

There is certainly a partial and significant fit between the two phenomena, some contours of which have just been suggested. Moreover, those tough Jewish novels that are set in Palestine before the founding of Israel or in New York's Jewish neighborhoods of the same era (1900–1948) mesh smoothly with neoconservative impulses and values in their revisions— and distortions—of at least one important historical feature: the role of socialism. If the novels were one's only source of information about the formation of Zionism and the imagery of the tough Jew (and this is doubtless the case with numerous readers), one would not know that socialism and socialists had played the major roles in *both* instances. Of Josef Trumpeldor, David Raziel, and of course Jabotinsky, much is said; of the followers of such Jewish socialists as Ber Borochov, Aaron David Gordon, and Gustav Landauer, next to nothing. More notable still is the absence from nearly all of the novels of David Ben-Gurion and, more generally, the historically dominant branch of Zionism, namely, Labor.

A curious example of the convergence of tough Jewish

thinking and neoconservatism is provided by an organization called the Jewish Institute for National Security Affairs (JINSA). While at work on the texts discussed in these pages— late 1984, early 1985—I received in the mail a JINSA fund-raising appeal; the design of its envelope caused me momentarily to believe in the power of uncanny forces. Against a light blue background it depicted the white silhouette of a tank, on the side of which was a light blue Star of David. In large white print adjacent to the silhouette were the words "How I learned to love a tank." Just at that time, of course, I was steeped in my collection of tough Jewish novels, the covers of which depicted ancient Jewish gladiators, Haganah and Irgun commandos, Mossad agents, Uzi submachine guns, armed Arabs, armed Jews, sinking ships, bombs, and related images. The actual content of the JINSA envelope proved less dramatic and more serious. The contribution return form actually included a disclaimer of the "love a tank" theme. "I'll never love a tank," the copy runs, "but I do love Israel. Enclosed is my gift to insure the safety of both our countries" (Israel and the United States). The accompanying brochure describes JINSA's work, its origins in the aftermath of the 1973 Yom Kippur War, and its goals of informing the Jewish community of security issues affecting the United States and Israel and of maintaining communication with government and military leaders in order to stress Israel's strategic importance. It cites a number of the institute's intelligence coups and endorsements from the Israeli defense minister, Moshe Arens, among others. JINSA's board of advisers was dominated by neoconservatives including Jack Kemp, Jeanne Kirkpatrick, Michael Ledeen, and John Silber.

The ideological fit, not to mention the shared worldview and imagery, between such a document and the tough Jewish novels is certainly striking. But that symmetry is not the end of the story. First, the post-1967 loyalty to Israel, and the sense of pride in both Israeli and Jewish toughness, is not limited to neoconservatives—nor, for that matter, to Jews. The feelings of loyalty and pride *traverse* the American Jewish political spectrum and are found not only among conservatives but among liberal and left-wing Jews as well. As one surveys this spectrum, of course, the particular forms of loyalty to Israel and to Jewish toughness differ significantly, just as the emotions involved express themselves in decidedly divergent ways and in varying degrees of intensity. Thus, although there is a convergence between some dimensions of the tough Jewish imagery and neoconservatism, to confine the whole of the imagery to that political corner is to miss the scope of its appeal.

A second point in the relationship between the tough Jewish novels and neoconservatism turns on their respective attitudes toward intellectuals. Rupert Wilkinson has noted that during this century American notions of toughness have gradually shifted "from anti-intellectualism to celebrations of performance that included the intellectual and artistic." Especially pertinent is Wilkinson's observation that the cold war furthered the general tendency to link intellectual activity and toughness. He speaks perceptively of the "new toughness" of systems analysis and multidisciplinary research, which, with their orchestrations and fine-tunings, "fed an aesthetic of mastery and control." Jews, too, he remarks in this context, "acquired a tougher public image, not only from Israel's military and frontier successes but from the new connections between toughness and brains."[35] The Jewish Institute for National Security Affairs and *Commentary* are outstanding examples of this development. The shift from a bodily to a brainy imagery of toughness is not reflected in the Rambowitz novels however. There preoccupations with Jewish bodies dominate.

Third, the tough Jewish pulp fiction itself often departs from neoconservatism in another major respect: its attitude toward America. The Jewish Institute for National Security Affairs, for example, is a representative neoconservative organization in its abiding faith in the American-Israeli partnership. The magazine *Commentary*, the voice of Jewish neoconservatism, is likewise characterized by its blend of fervent Zionism with an equally fervent Americanism. No such fusion of Zionism and Americanism exists for the tough Jews of the Rambowitz novels. Some of the spy thrillers do depict examples of American-Israeli partnership, but they are occasional and on the whole not impressive. The American Kirk Stewart and the Israeli Motti Barak, for example, join hands and hearts in working to foil the neo-Nazi coup in John Muir's *American Reich*. In Ken Follett's *Triple*, Nat Dickstein receives support from American friends, but the image of Dickstein and Israel confronting their enemies alone conveys the more significant political message. Indeed, the salient motif emerging from the tough Jewish fiction is that, when it comes to the fate of the Jews and Israel, America, like the rest of the world, cannot be trusted.

Like neoconservatism, numerous of the tough Jewish novels display a decidedly apocalyptic vision of a final reckoning between an empire of virtue and one of evil. For neoconservatism, however, apocalypse involves an ultimate encounter pitting America *and* Israel *together* against the Soviet Union (and the Arab states). The pertinent works of tough Jewish fiction present a different vision, one in which the *Jews alone* face yet another holocaust. In the cry Never again! is the fear that it will occur again. And when it does, America, as before, will not move to prevent it. The politics of the tough Jewish novels, then, has definite links to neoconservatism but also passes beyond neoconservatism toward a politics of Jewish apocalypse.

One glimpses this theme in some passages already discussed, for example, David Laker's outburst in John Rowe's *Aswan Solution*, following the staged Arab terrorist assault on the jeep carrying Laker and his beloved Miriam Heller. "They did it because we were Jews," he screams. "They want to do it to all Jews. Even in America, the Jew hate's just buried. And I want to be able to fight as a Jew—save the Jews. America can get fucked." The Mossad agent who had staged the episode precisely to win Laker's heart for the Israeli cause seeks to correct him: "But America *can't* get fucked. I know how you feel. I deeply sympathize, but we can't all fire rifles and all belong to the Israeli army. We need Jews in America with their moral and financial support, just as much as we need soldiers here" (p. 96).

America's relation to the fate of Israel seems to be at issue, with Laker giving vent to the politics of Jewish apocalypse and the Mossad agent speaking in the voice of *raison d'état* and the America-Israel partnership. The debate, however, is only apparent: the idea that Laker should return to America to raise support for Israel is mere charade; the Mossad agent knows that he will be doing nothing of the sort. Indeed, the agent wants the talented engineer to stay in Israel to work on the plan to destroy the Aswan Dam and with it, Egypt.[36] This Laker does. As the book ends, war with Egypt begins; to win it, Israel and David Laker destroy the Aswan Dam and the flood waters are released.

The Aswan Solution closes on an uncharacteristically ambiguous note, not least because the holocaust in question hits Egypt, not Israel—albeit a preemptive holocaust to save Israel from a devastation the United States cannot be relied on to prevent. But Israel achieves this physical survival at the price of its spiritual death. In any case, Israel is alone and lost. David Laker's final reflections, as he is flown by helicopter from the crumbling Aswan Dam, disclose his anguish but also affirm his belief in the tough Jew:

Israel had gone to war to try to survive, and it had seemed a justified war. But how could Israel and the world judge an Israel capable of such unparalleled destruction? Would Israel be judged like Nazi Germany as the genocidal mad dog of the Middle East? Like Russia, the ravenous bear, purging millions through the Gulag sewer? Or like America, the righteous white knight, exterminating the Japanese of Hiroshima and Nagasaki, those fried yellow whitebait [!], the necessary sacrifice to end that war and start a peace?

Could there possibly be peace for Israel after a war of such dimensions? Not only Egypt had been destroyed. The essence of the Jewish moral case, the terrible suffering of two thousand years had been destroyed, too. But what the hell did that matter, anyway? Laker asked himself, defensively angry. Who wanted to belong to God's chosen people when God had seemed to abandon those people for so long? The evidence seemed overwhelming that the only prophets to follow were the fighting ones: the ones who understood Napoleon's dictum, that God fights on the side of the big battalions. . . .

Then Laker began to weep at the monstrous horror of it all. He saw himself with historic clarity: a man in a speck of plane fleeing the death of Egypt, a man womanless, a man encapsuled in brilliant technology and guilt, a man of lost religion, a man groping for sensible morality, a man captive to a terrible history, a tribal man swept inexorably along like the drowned Egyptians below. (p. 251)

The politics of Jewish apocalypse (and the dissolution of the American-Israeli bond) finds less ambiguous expression in

Peter Abrahams's *Tongues of Fire*, featuring Isaac Rehv and the instrument of Jewish vengeance he has bred, his son, Paul. Significant here is the unrelentingly bitter portrayal of the United States. In contrast to its depictions by neoconservatives, the American government in this novel has refused to intervene in the Arab assault that destroys Israel and cooperates readily with the Arab victors afterward. The State Department then permits the handful of Israeli survivors no more than a dilapidated Vermont cottage in which to house a government-in-exile and accepts the renaming of the conquered territory as Palestine. Worse still, Israeli survivors in America are kept under surveillance by the CIA and are deported to Palestine (for certain execution) when they violate the strict conditions of residence. Throughout the novel, Isaac Rehv is shadowed by a CIA agent who corners and kills his prey on the last page. Jewish fears of a second Holocaust and of American betrayal eclipse all images of an inviolable American-Israeli alliance.

E. Howard Hunt develops the same theme in *The Gaza Intercept*, in which Mossad operative Jay Black is at work trying to quash the plan of the militant Palestinian group Al-Karmal to detonate neutron warheads over Israeli cities. When the American government realizes that the Arab group has gained possession of the secret documents and stock that will enable it to utilize the warheads, a top-level emergency meeting is called. "With the President in his Oval Office were the Secretaries of State and Defense, the Chairman of the Nuclear Regulatory Commission, the Director of the CIA and the Chairman of the Joint Chiefs of Staff." The question of how to prevent Israel's destruction is precisely the one that is not atop their agenda. The CIA director suggests that his information points to no links between the Al-Karmal gambit and the Soviet Union; the terrorist group is proceeding in accord with "its own narrow purposes." The decisive passage follows:

"How narrow?" the President asked.
The Director dabbed moisture from his upper lip. "An attack on the Jewish state."
"Not involving NATO or the Soviets?"
"Apparently not, Mr. President."
For the first time during the meeting, the President seemed to relax. (pp. 178–79)

"Well," the American President finally announces, "you better tell them. We owe them that much. And with our warning it's possible they can work things out for themselves." Thanks to Mossad agents, but no thanks to the United States, the Al-Karmal plan is at the last moment averted. Along the way, however, the Israeli government is not passive. Having been warned, Menachem Begin and his chiefs of staff convene their own emergency conference to set in motion Israel's reprisal plan, Operation Trumpet, which directs strikes against Damascus, Baghdad, Tripoli, and Amman.

The Israeli leaders must then reckon with the likelihood that American satellites will detect the activation of Operation Trumpet, enabling the American government to short-circuit the plan. Ezer Weizman proposes that the Americans be informed of a training exercise, adding that "this is their fault, anyway: sending neutron warheads abroad and failing to guard them properly. So if the American weapon is used against us I don't want the paradox of Americans trying to keep us from retaliation." The decision is made: if Al-Karmal detonates its warheads, Operation Trumpet will be set in motion. Menachem Begin then pronounces the benediction: "Rising slowly he walked toward his desk, poured a small glass of water and swallowed an anticoagulant pill. Then he turned to the minister of defense and said huskily, 'Let Eretz Israel strike back even from the grave!' " (pp. 178–79). In that pithy sentence we have the heart of the politics of the tough Jewish novels.

PART FOUR

Toward a Conclusion

WITH THE THEME of apocalypse and the vision of Jewish retaliation "even from the grave," my reflections on the emergence of tough Jewish imagery near their conclusion. In that particular vision and in the figure— literally, the body—of Menachem Begin some of the main motifs of these reflections are condensed. Like his successor and fellow Irgunist Yitzhak Shamir, Begin has come to stand for Jewish toughness in its more drastic political forms. Yet their bodies, not unlike Nat Dickstein's in Ken Follett's *Triple*, evoke the stereotypically scrawny, ashen Jewish weakness of their Polish roots, rather than the strength of the brawny, Judeo-Aryan Rambowitz type. Their spoken English, too, is suggestive, for it reflects not only their adopted Hebrew but their native Yiddish as well, which lends, in a way the undiluted Hebrew accent does not, a scrawny, almost whiny sound to the invariably and unbendingly tough content of their words. Begin and Shamir embody the fusion of Jewish toughness and weakness.

In his bracing reappraisal of Zionism, *The Zionist Dream Revisited*, Amnon Rubenstein offers a suggestive way of making sense of this in the Israeli context. His argument is that the outcome of the Six Day War has proven to be a Pyrrhic victory, having generated within Israel a deep crisis over the Zionist dream of transforming the frightened Jew into the confident Hebrew.[1] Far from normalizing the historically ghettoized and beleaguered Jewish situation, the Jewish state, with the victory of 1967 as the ironic turning point, has actually begun to reconstitute that older situation. Since 1967, Rubenstein proposes, the self-assured Hebrew nation has itself begun to assume the attributes of a threatened Jewish ghetto. Instead of transcending the ghetto, Israel is becoming the "successor to the Jewish community of older times" (p. 81).

In contrast to its historical predecessors, the Israeli Jewish ghetto is heavily armed and backed by the United States, and it has victims of its own—facts discussed by Rubenstein in his preface on the 1982 invasion of Lebanon and the Israeli role in the Maronite Phalangists' massacre of Palestinians in the refugee camps of Sabra and Shatilla. His analysis of recent developments in Israel enables us to see that just as the post-1967 Rambowitz fiction was generating mighty Hebrew heroes for American consumption, small (but in Rubenstein's view expressive) numbers of Israelis had begun to think of themselves as Jews, in some instances exchanging the tanned, trendy Tel Aviv style in favor of the waxen, neo-shtetl look, even dropping the hardy Hebrew names their parents had adopted and reappropriating the eastern European Jewish names of their grandparents (pp. 153–54).

Remarkably, the tough Jewish novels that envisioned a betrayed and isolated Israel going up in the flames of a final holocaust intuited the development to which Rubenstein points: the paradoxical premise of the tough Jew that I have been emphasizing in these pages, that is, his (and her) inescapable tie to Jewish victimization. The return of the historical Jewish ghetto consciousness in Israel has made itself felt even at the official level. In mid-October 1989, in connection with U.S. pressures on the Israelis to enter talks with the Palestinians, Prime Minister Shamir, for example, was quoted at a Likud rally in the West Bank settlement of Ramle as having proclaimed that Israel is without friends in the United States.[2] In view of both U.S. policies and attitudes among the American public at large as well as among American Jews, this remark is absurd. As an expression of the dynamics of Jewish toughness, however, it makes sense.

Such connections can be taken a step further. On the visible, media-attended, political scene in the occupied territories, which many Jews call Judea and Samaria, the soldier of the Israel Defense Forces remains the classic bearer of tough Jewish imagery. In recent years, however, a new figure has arrived. I have in mind the largely Orthodox Jewish and quite often American immigrant activists in the West Bank settlements. As they appear in the media, such figures are clearly tough Jews but, like Shamir and Begin, just as clearly not of the Rambowitz type. They are, rather, what could be called new old Jews of the sort journalist Chaim Pearl describes in the opening pages of this study. Their physical aesthetic is precisely eastern European rather than Greco-Roman or Aryan. In the settlements one often sees pale, gaunt faces, deep-set, nervous eyes, and on the men beards, earlocks, and, as Pearl noted, automatic weapons. Such imagery, such bodies, like Shamir's statement regarding Israel's mortally threatened isolation in an anti-Semitic world, evoke the Jewish situation on the eve of the Nazi Final Solution and thereby vindicate in advance the actions of today's beleaguered Jews.

To be sure, this is far from the only politico-cultural current in Israel, and it is not yet clear that it is the dominant one. Nor is there unanimity on these matters among American Jews. Consider a case that not only speaks pointedly to the issues raised in these pages but also involves the real life of one of the authors of the Rambowitz novels. Chaim Zeldis, whose *Forbidden Love* was discussed in part 3, was outraged when, in the face of the Palestinian *intifada*, American Jews refused to come forward with a "groundswell of support for Israel." In response, Zeldis and his wife, Nina, not to be outdone by the heroes of tough Jewish fiction, went on aliya, that is, "went up" or "home" to Israel. Instead of massive support, Nina Zeldis comments in a recent interview in the *Jerusalem Post*, "we got Woody Allen." And Woody Allen, Chaim Zeldis interjects, is "the quintessential rabbit-Jew. That guy trembles in his boots. He's so cowardly!" Zeldis continues, "He's never even visited Israel, yet he signs that ad in the *New York Times* criticizing Shamir. Him and Philip Roth and Saul Bellow and all the rest. They're all self-hating Jews. Totally insecure with their Jewishness and with living in America. They just enrage me."[3]

It is a sign of different tendencies among Jewish Americans—the sort of tendencies Chaim Zeldis finds so distressing—that in recent years the production of tough Jewish novels has begun to diminish, having reached something of a peak in the early 1980s. In addition to dwindling numbers, several of the most recent works contain different political markings than their predecessors' and critical impulses that, not long before, one found only extremely rarely, Emanuel Litvinoff's *Falls the Shadow* being virtually the sole example. Not only do both Gay Courter's *Code Ezra* (1986; discussed in part 3) and Howard Kaplan's *Bullets of Palestine* (1987), for example, present relatively uncensored accounts of the Sabra and Shatilla massacres—representing the extent and ghastliness of the killing, placing it in the political center of the story, and not exonerating the Israelis—but each does so from the standpoint of Palestinian characters who also play significant and sympathetically portrayed roles.[4]

Bullets of Palestine is in this last regard a radical departure from the patterns of the Rambowitz novels examined in part 3. Next to Shai Shaham, an Israeli agent, Kaplan presents the figure of Ramzy Awwad, a Palestinian poet and former terrorist, who has not only rejected terrorism, but eventually actually joins with Shaham in a collaborative effort to capture Abu Nidal. The Israeli is made to see the 1982 massacre from the standpoint of Ramzy Awwad, who had lived through it. One can, I think, actually speak of a new direction in the tough Jewish fiction. At least it can be said that *Bullets of Palestine* is not as isolated as Litvinoff's *Falls the Shadow* was a half decade ago. Kaplan's novel, for example, is joined by William Bayer's *Pattern Crimes*[5] and Roger L. Simon's *Raising the Dead*.[6]

The latter work features Moses Wine, a Jewish American detective working in Israel. Sometimes satirically, at other times sincerely, the highly intellectual Wine is preoccupied with the *differences* between American and Israeli Jews, and generally speaks on behalf of a kind of humane skepticism. *Raising the Dead* is in part a tough Jewish novel about tough Jewish novels. In connection with what he sees as the naïveté of American Jews, for example, Detective Wine contrasts the Israel of his experience with that of the images he had absorbed from the film *Exodus* (p. 87). Wine's own leftish views—he is critical of "the militarism of the state, the economic reliance on arms sales, the aid to South Africa and the contras, the treatment of Palestinian refugees, . . . the spying on the U.S., the pervasive fundamentalism, the conservative social structure and the decline of the socialist ideal"—are answered by Israelis. But at least there is a political debate, which, however, excludes Palestinians (p. 124).

Pattern Crimes, likewise, is not dominated by an unfailingly virtuous Zionism. William Bayer's affection for Israel is clearly deep, as is Howard Kaplan's and Roger L. Simon's. Nevertheless, *Pattern Crimes*'s main characters, all passionately loyal Israelis, articulate a range of insider expressions of disenchantment and political criticism. The novel's police and secret service ambience is full of talk of the "It's not the same now, is it?" sort, with "now" being the years since 1967. "Remember how we all adored Arik [Sharon]?" one operative sighs. "Then Lebanon," he continues. "I was there. It stunk. Bastard! We didn't know it then. '67! That's when everything started going wrong" (p. 82). Elsewhere, Israel, "this pretty young virgin we married almost forty years ago," is seen as a "tarted-up old whore" (p. 161). "The break-down of civility in Israeli public life" is evoked and specified—"corruption, scandals, cabinet meetings that ended in insults, physical shoving on the floor of the Knesset, lawlessness, tribalism, violence, pervasive cheating, rage, and greed" (pp. 77–78). And outbursts such as the following come from the lips of patriots: "Everyone knows Shin Bet has murdered prisoners. Everyone knows about Mossad assassination squads" and Israeli "embassy officials in Washington [who] recruit American Jews to spy on their own government" (p. 180). Behind the evil in Bayer's novel is an alliance of retired Israeli army officers, Orthodox Jews, and American fundamentalist Christian ministers.

Bayer, moreover, effects a reversal as basic as Howard Kaplan's. In this instance, however, it pertains not to Palestinians, but to tough Jews themselves. In pursuing a series of macabre murders, hero David Bar-Lev, a Jerusalem detective, gradually discovers that his own deceased father and brother are implicated. The brother, Gideon, an Israeli paratrooper who commits suicide in a plane crash, and his comrades have the distinction of being the first homosexual tough Jews in the entire subgenre. If that were not sufficiently original, however, David Bar-Lev's interpretation of Gideon's role in the story is, when placed next to the body politics of the fiction examined in part 3, simply remarkable—not least in its fit with the themes developed here. "He was a soldier," detective Bar-Lev says of his brother, "and my mother loved him for it." He goes on:

The sharp uniform, the perfect hair-cut, the beautiful clean-shaven chin. He was the favorite warrior son with the strong tanned arms and legs. He was also—and it hurts me to say this— a bit of a fascist, too. He was particularly vicious in hand-to-hand combat training, and he gloried in the Israeli war machine. The helmet visors, the zippered flight suits, the cult of manliness. Muscled flesh, polished paratrooper boots, smart salutes—the whole esprit of the pilot corps. You wonder why he didn't run away. Where could he go? Cyprus? England? The United States? Without his aircraft, without the cult, he was nothing and he knew it. Fact is, he had no place to go except into the sky . . . so that was where he flew. (p. 273)

What I like best about both this passage and the context in Bayer's novel from which it comes is their exemplary disruption of familiar images. The possibility of a gay Israeli fascist is, after all, a departure from what postmodern critics call the master narratives, and, it could be added, the master stereotypes, by which sense has been made of modern life. Yet, in its very strangeness, such a notion suggests another, that of a world without power, violence, and the cult of manliness. A critique of tough Jews ought, then, to begin and end with a summons gently to abolish the conditions that generate toughness itself.

NOTES

PART 1

1. Ariel Sharon, with David Chanoff, *Warrior: An Autobiography* (New York: Simon and Schuster, 1989).
2. Chaim Pearl, "Tora and Terror," *Jerusalem Post*, International Edition, June 24–July 1, 1984, 16.
3. Milton Himmelfarb, "In Light of Israel's Victory," *Commentary*, October 1967, 53.
4. Edward Tivnan, *The Lobby: Jewish Political Power and American Foreign Policy* (New York: Simon and Schuster, 1987).
5. *The Story of Chanukah* (Southeastern, Pa.: Stoneway, Ltd., 1983), n.p.
6. Ken Follett, *Triple* (New York: Signet Books, 1979).
7. Philip Roth, *The Counterlife* (New York: Farrar, Straus, Giroux, 1986), 75.
8. Philip Roth, *The Facts: A Novelist's Autobiography* (New York: Penguin Books, 1988), 28.
9. Sigmund Freud, *The Interpretation of Dreams*, trans. James Strachey (New York: Basic Books, n.d.), 197. See the discussions in Marthe Robert, *From Oedipus to Moses: Freud's Jewish Identity*, trans. Ralph Manheim (New York: Doubleday, 1976),

111–19, and Carl E. Schorske, *Fin-de-Siècle Vienna: Politics and Culture* (New York: Random House, 1981), 189–93.

10. Arnold L. Goldsmith, *The Golem Remembered, 1909–1980: Variations of a Jewish Legend* (Detroit, Mich.: Wayne State University Press, 1981), 22.

11. Gershom Scholem, *Sabbatai Sevi: The Mystical Messiah, 1626–1676*, trans. R. J. Zwi Werblowsky (Princeton: Princeton University Press, 1973), 284–85.

12. William J. McGrath, *Freud's Discovery of Psychoanalysis: The Politics of Hysteria* (Ithaca, N.Y.: Cornell University Press, 1986), 313–16.

13. Robert, *From Oedipus to Moses*, 41–42.

14. Cited in McGrath, *Freud's Discovery of Psychoanalysis*, 314.

15. As McGrath indicates (ibid., 314–15), Freud was in this instance anticipating Carl Schorske's analysis of both Herzl and the populist, anti-Semitic leaders Karl Lueger and Georg von Schoenerer. See Carl Schorske, "Politics in a New Key: An Austrian Trio," in his *Fin-de-Siècle Vienna*, 116–80.

16. Isaac Deutscher, *The Non-Jewish Jew and Other Essays* (New York: Oxford University Press, 1968).

17. John Hoberman, *Sport and Political Ideology* (Austin: University of Texas Press, 1984).

18. Jean-Paul Sartre, *Anti-Semite and Jew*, trans. George J. Becker (New York: Schocken Books, 1965), 117–18. The work originally appeared in France in 1946 under the title *Reflections sur la question juive* (Reflections on the Jewish question). I have borrowed from that title for my own subtitle as a gesture of my admiration for Sartre's book.

19. John Murray Cuddihy, *The Ordeal of Civility: Freud, Marx, Levi-Strauss and the Jewish Struggle with Modernity* (New York: Basic Books, 1974).

20. Jean Baudrillard, *America*, trans. Chris Turner (London: Verso, 1988).

21. Daniel Boorstin, *The Image: A Guide to Pseudo-Events in*

America (1961; reprint, New York: Atheneum, 1975), 107.

22. Uris's comments in the interview with the *New York Post* are cited in Philip Roth, "Some New Jewish Stereotypes," in his *Reading Myself and Others* (New York: Farrar, Straus, Giroux, 1975), 138. The published essay was originally delivered as a speech in 1961.

23. Roth, "Some New Jewish Stereotypes," 138–39.

24. Leon Uris, *Mitla Pass* (New York: Doubleday, 1988), 304.

25. Tivnan, *The Lobby*, 50–51.

26. Ibid., 63.

27. Roth, "Some New Jewish Stereotypes," 137.

28. "The Six-Day War and Jewish Power," *New Republic*, June 8, 1987, 7–10.

29. Tivnan, *The Lobby*, 69.

30. Albert Vorspan, "Jewish Umbrellas and Dissent: Baby, It's Raining Outside," *Tikkun*, May–June 1988, 72. The "Umbrellas" in the title refer to Jewish umbrella organizations, such as the NJCRAC.

31. Ruth Wisse, *The Schlemiel as Modern Hero* (Chicago: University of Chicago Press, 1971), 72–73. If Ruth Wisse herself shared any of this ambivalence at the time—and she seems to have—she no longer does, as her recent denunciation of American intellectuals with doubts about Israeli policy in the Middle East makes clear. In a passage of particular insensitivity, she refers to Palestinians as "people who bleed and breed and advertise their misery," and warns Israel's intellectual supporters against undue fretting since the Jewish state is not implicated in this misery, which "for forty years now the Arabs have foisted . . . on their Palestinian 'brothers' as the crucial element in the war against Israel." "Israel and the Intellectuals: A Failure of Nerve?" *Commentary*, May 1988, 19–25.

32. Sol Weinstein, *Loxfinger. A Thrilling Adventure of Hebrew Secret Agent Oy-Oy-7: An Israel Bond Thriller* (New York: Pocket Books, 1965). Patrick Pardy, a graduate student in the

history department at Boston College, kindly brought this book to my attention.

33. Michael Selzer, *The Wineskin and the Wizard: The Problem of Jewish Power in the Context of East European Jewish History* (New York: Macmillan, 1970), 18. Selzer's religious, eastern European–based, and pacifist criticism of Zionism deserves renewed attention. I learned much from him at an early stage of this work. As later pages make clear, the pre-Zionist history of European Jewry is not as free of tough Jews as his book suggests. Nor do I share the notion of Jews as a chosen people, a non-Zionist version of which Selzer passionately upholds.

34. Tivnan, *The Lobby*, 61.

35. To the blacks and Jews one could add the New Left of the 1960s. For reasons that parallel those just noted, some participants, including women, in the initially nonviolent student and youth movement would, after 1968, become what amounted to the left wing of the new tough style and conduct. Again, the Weatherman group is the best-known example.

36. Jonathan Kaufman, *Broken Alliance: The Turbulent Times between Blacks and Jews in America* (New York: New American Library, 1988).

37. Podhoretz's essay is reprinted in *The Commentary Reader*, ed. Norman Podhoretz (New York: Atheneum, 1966), 376–87.

38. Bruno Bettelheim, *The Informed Heart: Autonomy in a Mass Age* (Glencoe, Ill.: The Free Press, 1960).

39. Hannah Arendt, *Eichmann in Jerusalem: A Report on the Banality of Evil*, rev. ed. (New York: Viking Press, 1984).

40. Arendt's *Eichmann in Jerusalem* was the more notorious of the two because of her claims that Adolf Eichmann, the chief commandant at Auschwitz, was not a sadistic monster but an example of the "banality of evil" and that some Jewish community leaders had not only failed to resist the Nazi killing bureaucracy, but had cooperated with it. The main criticisms of the latter claim are Jacob Robinson, *And the Crooked Shall*

Be Made Straight: The Eichmann Trial, The Jewish Catastrophe, and Hannah Arendt's Narrative (Philadelphia: Jewish Publication Society, 1965), and Isaiah Trunk, *Judenrat: The Jewish Councils in Eastern Europe under Nazi Occupation* (1972; New York: Stein and Day). Instructive commentary on the storm unleashed by Arendt's book is provided by Elizabeth Young-Bruehl, *Hannah Arendt: For Love of the World* (New Haven: Yale University Press, 1984), 328–78. See also Stephen J. Whitfield, *Into the Dark: Hannah Arendt and Totalitarianism* (Philadelphia: Temple University Press, 1980), 208–47. For critical analysis of Bettelheim's views, see the compelling study by Terrence Des Pres, *The Survivor: An Anatomy of Life in the Death Camps* (New York: Oxford University Press, 1976), 157–77.

41. Leon Jick, "The Holocaust: Its Uses and Abuses," *Brandeis Review* Spring 1986, 25–31.

42. For a good dissection of the role played by this need for the Holocaust in Israeli political culture, see Avishai Margalit, "The Kitsch of Israel," *New York Review of Books*, November 24, 1988, 20–24.

PART 2

1. Isaiah Trunk, *Jewish Responses to Nazi Persecution: Collective and Individual Behavior in Extremis* (New York: Stein and Day, 1982), x. The volume was first published in Yiddish in 1979.

2. Yehuda Bauer, *The Jewish Emergence from Powerlessness* (Toronto: Toronto University Press, 1979), 33. Among the recent studies of this theme are Reuben Ainsztein, *Jewish Resistance in Nazi-Occupied Eastern Europe: With a Historical Survey of the Jew as Fighter and Soldier in the Diaspora* (New York: Barnes and Noble, 1975); Yehuda Bauer's highly critical review of Ainsztein in *American Historical Review* 81:4 (October,

1976): 896–97; Bauer's own A *History of the Holocaust* (New York: Franklin Watts, 1982), esp. chaps. 8 ("Life in the Ghettoes") and 11 ("Resistance"); Lucy S. Davidowicz, *The War against the Jews, 1933–1945* (1975; New York: Bantam Books, 1981), 327–479; Yisrael Gutman, *The Jews of Warsaw, 1939–1943: Ghetto, Underground, Revolt,* trans. Ina Friedman (Bloomington: Indiana University Press, 1982); and Trunk, *Jewish Responses.*

3. Trunk, *Jewish Responses,* ix.
4. Georges Friedmann, *The End of the Jewish People?* trans. Eric Mosbacher (1965; New York: Doubleday, 1967), 225–26. Prior to World War II and the Nazi mass murder, Friedmann had evidently paid little attention to the fact that he was a Jew. His visit to Israel and the book cited here were part of his post-Holocaust reappraisal. As he saw things, however, Israel was less of a Jewish state than a state that was tending, as the book's title proposed, toward an end of the Jewish people; toward becoming a society of "Hebrew-speaking Gentiles."
5. Amnon Rubenstein, *The Zionist Dream Revisited: From Herzl to Gush Emunim and Back* (New York: Schocken Books, 1984), 134.
6. David Biale writes that in Israel, beginning in the 1950s, "archeology became a national mania as Israelis literally dug for the roots of their past." *Power and Powerlessness in Jewish History* (New York: Schocken Books, 1986), 153.
7. Yehoshafat Harkabi, *The Bar Kokhba Syndrome: Risk and Realism in International Politics* (Chappaqua, N.Y.: Rossel Books, 1983). For an informative discussion of the debate generated in Israel by Harkabi's book, see Jonathan Frankel, "Bar Kochba and All That," *Dissent,* Spring, 1984, 192–202.
8. "The Six-Day War and Jewish Power," *New Republic,* June 8, 1987, 7–10.
9. Quoted in Werner Keller, *Diaspora: The Post-Biblical History*

of the Jews, trans. Richard Winston and Clara Winston (New York: Harcourt, Brace & World, 1969), 67.

10. See the long introductory essay, "Fighters or Fatalists," in Ainsztein, *Jewish Resistance in Nazi-Occupied Eastern Europe,* which was cited earlier in connection with studies of Jewish resistance to the Nazi Final Solution, and Biale's *Power and Powerlessness.*

11. Josephus, *The Jewish Wars* (New York: Viking Penguin, 1985), 398.

12. See Biale, *Power and Powerlessness,* 74; and Jacob Katz, *Exclusiveness and Tolerance: Studies in Jewish-Gentile Relations in Medieval and Modern Times* (New York: Schocken Books, 1962), 82–92.

13. See Linda Gordon, *Cossack Rebellions: Social Turmoil in the Sixteenth Century Ukraine* (Albany: State University of New York Press, 1983).

14. Isaac Bashevis Singer, *The Slave* (New York: Fawcett, 1980). *The Slave* was originally published in 1962. By the novel's second half, Jacob and Wanda have not only consummated their love, but they actually leave the farm and return to Josefov, which the Jews have restored several years after the massacres. Singer, after having explored the dynamics of seventeenth-century Polish anti-Semitism, turns in the novel's later sections to the responses to Wanda by Josefov's Jews. In that connection, he presents an unforgettable criticism of a community whose members apparently follow with great rectitude every formal commandment of Judaism, while treating Wanda with the same hatred of otherness that drives anti-Semitism itself.

15. The main character in Singer's short story for children, "Reb Asher the Dairyman," is big, strong, and, in connection with a life-threatening fire, brave. But he is also gentle, not a fighter. See *A Day of Pleasure: Stories of a Boy Growing up in Warsaw* (1963; New York: Farrar, Straus, Giroux, 1969), 51–58.

16. Paul R. Mendes-Flohr and Jehuda Reinharz, eds., *The Jew in the Modern World: A Documentary History* (New York: Oxford University Press, 1980), 357–59.
17. Mark Twain, *Concerning the Jews* (Philadelphia: Running Press, 1985), 29. The essay was first published in *Harper's New Monthly Magazine*.
18. See also Frank L. Byrne and Jean Powers Soman, eds., *Your True Marcus: The Civil War Letters of a Jewish Colonel* (Kent, Oh.: Kent State University Press, 1985). A sample from 1862: as commander of the Union steamer *Ft. Wayne*, Colonel Marcus Spiegel, an American of German Jewish heritage, writing his wife, recounts an uplifting Friday service at a synagogue on shore—"I think I was a devout Israelite"—and then conveys his pride: "Just think: your Liege Lord in Command of Steamer Fort Wayne, one of the finest steamers ever floated [on the] Mississippi River; 500 as good men and 21 officers under him who look upon him as *the man*; every accommodation you could imagine and everybody his friend and think for one moment, *is he not bully? Eh? Say? . . .*" (p. 181; emphases in original). In a revealing passage in his forward to the volume, Jacob R. Marcus of the American Jewish Archives writes that the letters show how the "Children of Israel could succeed in the profession of arms, a field of endeavor that had been alien to them since the days of the Maccabees when a handful of patriots defeated the Syrian armies. The war [1860–64] taught Jews to have faith in themselves, to forget the disabilities under which they had labored in Germany. The new Jew who emerged from the fratricidal conflict in the U.S. was a complete American. He believed in himself; he inisisted on equality; he had emancipated himself from the ghetto mentality. For immigrants, for Jews, the war was an Americanizing forcing house" (p. viii).
19. See the excerpt and comments in Mendes-Flohr and Reinharz, *Jew in the Modern World*, 271–73. See also Moshe Zimmer-

man, *Wilhelm Marr: The Patriarch of Anti-Semitism* (New
York: Oxford University Press, 1986). On the larger theme of
the rise of racial anti-Jewish thought, see George L. Mosse,
Toward the Final Solution: A History of European Racism (New
York: Howard Fertig, 1978).

20. See John W. Boyer, *Political Radicalism in Late Imperial Vienna: Origins of the Christian Social Movement, 1848–1897*
(Chicago: University of Chicago Press, 1981); and Peter Pulzer,
The Rise of Political Anti-Semitism in Germany and Austria
(New York: Wiley & Sons, 1964). On the liturgical and iconographic dimensions of nationalist movements in modern Germany, and the role of anti-Semitism within them, see George
L. Mosse, *The Nationalization of the Masses: Political Symbolism and Mass Movements in Germany from the Napoleonic
Wars through the Third Reich* (New York: Howard Fertig,
1975).

21. The left-wing revolutions in Europe after World War I, the
Spanish Civil War, the antifascist resistance and partisan struggles in World War II, and the Communist parties in Eastern
Europe in the late 1940s and 1950s were all political stages on
which armed, fighting Jews had substantial parts. As tough and
as self-consciously Jewish as such women and men may have
been, however, they fought under banners of internationalism,
antifascism, and socialism rather than under the Zionist flag.
While the leftist segment of Jewish toughness is significant, it
is definitely eclipsed by the simultaneous development of Zionism (which, of course, includes socialists). Part 3 addresses the
more recent phenomenon of tough Jews on the political right.

22. See Cecil Roth, ed., *The Concise Jewish Encyclopedia* (New
York: New American Library, 1980), 365.

23. Richard Deacon, *The Israeli Secret Service* (1977; New York:
Taplinger Publishing, 1985), 15. That it is not easy to see what,
other than a father he never knew, makes Sidney Reilly a Jew
does not trouble Deacon, who also seems unaware of the not

necessarily friendly implications of his comment cited above. For that comment appears in connection with an account of the remarkable case of Ievno Azeff, a Jew who worked as an agent of the tsarist secret police, Ochrana, within the revolutionary terrorist underground, often serving both causes with equal skill and succeeding in escaping exposure until after his death during World War I. Deacon writes: "Purists may argue that the case of Azeff has nothing whatsoever to do with the history of the Israeli Secret Service. In one sense this is true, but as an important factor of background to the subject the Azeff affair is vital to an understanding of how such a tiny country could develop so up-to-date and efficient an Intelligence Service. Azeff was not a typical Jewish agent of the great powers prior to 1914, but his enterprise, courage, attention to detail, patience, objectivity and ruthlessness exemplify the Jewish natural talent for espionage. When the Jewish state was created after World War II, these qualities were to be found in abundance among many agents of Haganah and other Palestinian organizations; unlike Azeff, they had a burning patriotic motive for their actions" (p. 15). Even in context, the remark hovers very close to anti-Semitism; if one excludes courage from these supposedly natural Jewish attributes, one is left with a classic, if only partial, anti-Semitic list. That lends an ironic twist to the fact that Deacon's remark (and his book as a whole) is a contribution to the post-1967 blossoming of the tough Jewish stereotype.

24. Harriet and Fred Rochlin, *Pioneer Jews: A New Life in the Far West* (Boston: Houghton Mifflin, 1984).

25. Gloria Goldreich, *West to Eden* (New York: Avon Books, 1987).

26. Twain, *Concerning the Jews*, 13–14.

27. Jena Weissman Joselit, *Our Gang: Jewish Crime and the New York Jewish Community, 1900–1940* (Bloomington: Indiana University Press, 1983).

28. Albert Fried, *The Rise and Fall of the Jewish Gangster in America* (New York: Holt, Rinehart and Winston, 1980).

29. See Steven Aschheim's excellent *Brothers and Strangers: The East European Jew in German and German Jewish Consciousness, 1800–1923.* (Madison: University of Wisconsin Press, 1982).

30. The shtetl legacy of Jewish nonviolence is a recurrent theme in Barbara Meyerhof's study of life among elderly Jews in Venice, California. See her *Number Our Days* (New York: Simon & Schuster, 1978).

31. Once again, I include myself among those who would until recently have taken such formulations entirely for granted.

32. That Moritz Spiegelberg also provides grist for any anti-Semitic mill need not occupy us here. See the excellent discussion in Hans Mayer, *Outsiders: A Study in Life and Letters*, trans. Denis M. Sweet (Cambridge: MIT Press, 1982), 283–381. The original German edition appeared in 1975.

33. George L. Mosse, *German Jews beyond Judaism* (Bloomington: Indiana University Press, 1985), 15.

34. Friedrich C. B. Ave-Lallement, *Das Deutsche Gaunerthum* (The world of the German gangster) (Leipzig: F.A. Brockhaus, 1858). The subtitle of this two-volume work is "In its social-political, literary, and linguistic formation, including the present." I am grateful to George Mosse for calling this work to my attention. Jews, it should be said, constitute only a part of Ave-Lallement's research. Nor is he interested in what might have been the specifically Jewish roots or implications of the Yiddish-speaking criminal underworld he studies. His investigations are especially interesting precisely because he seems not at all surprised by the phenomenon of Jewish gangsters.

35. Some simply did not care, Joselit notes, citing the example of the Jewish tenement owner who permitted rings of prostitution in his buildings. The tendency to deny and suppress in the service of sustaining a vital self-image has played a substantial

role in Jewish American responses to numerous Israeli policies in the Middle East and elsewhere—just as it has in American responses to, for example, American policies in Southeast Asia or Central America, and in the public responses in many Arab countries toward their governments' policies on Palestinians, not to mention Jews.

36. See Joselit, *Our Gang*, 170, 201 n. 17; and Rupert Wilkinson, *American Tough: The Tough Guy Tradition and American Character* (Westport, Conn.: Greenwood Press, 1984). With the exception of one matter that will be discussed in part 3, Wilkinson's intriguing work says nothing about Jews in connection with the American "tough guy" tradition. This, of course, says *something* about the erasure from both Jewish and the larger American public consciousness of the imagery of the Jewish gangster. Nor, other than references to novels by Saul Levinson and Eleazar Lipsky, will one find a Jewish component in Geoffrey O'Brien's *Hardboiled America; The Lurid Years of Paperbacks* (New York: Van Nostrand Reinhold, 1981).

37. Gerald Green, *The Chains* (New York: Bantam Books, 1981).

38. Mike Gold, *Jews without Money* (New York: International Publishers, 1930). For background to Gold's novel, see Elizabeth Ewen, *Immigrant Women in the Land of Money: Life and Culture on the Lower East Side, 1890–1925* (New York: Monthly Review Press, 1985).

39. See Joan Baum, "Amboy Dukes," *Tikkun* May–June, 1988, 22–24. My colleague James Cronin, an expert on the fiction of juvenile delinquency, called this to my attention.

40. Budd Schulberg, *What Makes Sammy Run?* (1941; New York: Random House, 1952).

41. Harold Robbins, *A Stone for Danny Fisher* (1951; New York: Pocket Books, 1979).

42. See Albert Prago, *Jews in the International Brigades* (New York: A *Jewish Currents* Reprint, 1979).

NOTES

43. Frederic Arnold, *Kohn's War* (New York: Signet, 1984).
44. Marge Piercy, *Gone to Soldiers* (New York: Fawcett Books, 1987).
45. Jonathan Frankel, *Prophecy and Politics: Socialism, Nationalism, and the Russian Jews, 1862–1917* (London: Cambridge University Press, 1981), 488. I am much indebted to this great work of scholarship.
46. On this whole theme, see Mosse, *Toward the Final Solution,* esp. 94–127.
47. See the many samples in Norman L. Kleeblatt, ed. *The Dreyfus Affair: Art, Truth and Justice* (Berkeley: University of California Press, 1987). This is the catalog, including extensive scholarly commentary, of the exhibition organized by the Jewish Museum, New York City, in late 1987.
48. Gustave Le Bon, *The Crowd: A Study of the Popular Mind* (New York: Viking Penguin, 1981).
49. David Roskies, *Against the Apocalypse: Responses to Catastrophe in Modern Jewish Culture* (Cambridge: Harvard University Press, 1984), 83. I have learned much and borrowed freely from this remarkable book.
50. Shlomo Lambroza, "Pleve, Kishinev, and the Jewish Question: A Reappraisal," *Nationalities Papers* 12:1 (Spring 1984): 117–27.
51. Quoted in Walter Laqueur, *A History of Zionism* (New York: Schocken Books, 1976), 123.
52. Quoted in Lambroza, "Pleve, Kishinev, and the Jewish Question," 125.
53. In 1905 troops awaiting shipment to the battle lines of the Russo-Japanese War often participated in pogroms, either by way of warm-up or simply to pass the time.
54. Irving Howe and Eliezer Greenberg, eds., *A Treasury of Yiddish Stories* (New York: Viking Press, 1954), 60–61.
55. "Kola Street" appears in Howe and Greenberg, *A Treasury,*

260–75. The passages cited above are from p. 262. See the comments on "Kola Street" in Roskies, *Against the Apocalypse*, 142–43. .

56. Fishel Bimko, "The Draft," in Joachim Neugroschel, trans. and ed., *The Shtetl* (New York: Richard Marek, 1979), 471–80.

57. The *ba'al-guf*, Roskies concludes, "represented this new Jew in his earlier, rudimentary state: a man who acted alone, on impulse, but remained fiercely loyal to the tribe" (p. 142). Following a lead suggested by Ruth Wisse, Roskies observes further that the *ba'al-guf*, like his counterpart the schlemiel, "was not yet responsive to history"; did not enter into social action to change the world (pp. 142–43). To these insights, only a small note needs to be appended. In contrast to the remarks on the *ba'al-guf* stories by Howe and Greenberg in the 1950s, the more pointed and fully developed commentary from 1984 by Roskies is itself part of the more recent, post-1967 Jewish "transvaluation of values" and is dependent on it. While the many historical and sociological differences between them cannot be ignored, Roskies, like Sholem Asch, Fishel Bimko, and Isaac Babel, is on the lookout for tough Jews. Irving Howe and Eliezer Greenberg were not.

58. Isaac Babel, *Red Cavalry*, trans. Nadia Helstein (New York: Knopf, 1929). The original Russian edition appeared in 1926.

59. Leo Rosten, *The Joys of Yiddish* (New York: Washington Square Press, 1968), 435–36. Notice that the able young scholars *do* become expert marksmen, as any good members of a chosen people would. Then there is the one about the American who, on a visit to Israel, attends the unveiling of a tomb to the unknown soldier. After many speeches, the canvas is lifted, exposing a stone on which is inscribed: Chaim Isadore Cohn. Born: Poland, 1903. Died: Israel, 1955. How can this be? the American asks his host; this is no unknown soldier. There's his name, his birthdate. Oh, the Israeli interjects with a shrug: as

a *tailor* he was known; but as a soldier—*nah!* See Rosten, p. 320.

60. Primo Levi, *If Not Now, When?* trans. William Weaver (New York: Summit Books, 1985), 116. The original Italian edition appeared in 1982.

61. Clive Irving, *Promise the Earth* (New York: Ballantine Books, 1982), 67.

62. Arthur Koestler, *Promise and Fulfillment: Palestine, 1917–1949* (New York: Macmillan, 1949), 67–69.

63. The richest account of the early-twentieth-century migration to Palestine of the Russian Jewish spirit of self-defense and the accompanying imagery of a new type of proud, hardy, fighting Jew is Frankel, *Prophecy and Politics*, 366–452. See also Bernard Avishai's important *The Tragedy of Zionism: Revolution and Democracy in the Land of Israel* (New York: Farrar, Straus, Giroux, 1985), 99–132; and Laqueur, *History of Zionism*, 270–337. If Clive Irving's *Promise the Earth* indirectly corrects the lapse in the joke about the *yeshiva bucherim* by noting the fighting element in the Russian Pale, it also injects a new distortion. This anticipates a theme developed more fully in part 3, but it can be said here that Irving's novel virtually suppresses the roles of labor and left-wing Zionism in spearheading the transplantation of tough Jewish theory, practice, and imagery from Russia to Palestine.

64. Amos Elon, *Herzl* (New York: Holt, Rinehart and Winston, 1975), 60–63.

65. Ibid., 54–56, 77.

66. Arthur Koestler, *Arrow in the Blue: An Autobiography* (1952; New York: Macmillan, 1961), 87.

67. Interestingly, not long after Nordau's call for a Jewish physical culture movement, Mao Tse-tung, then a young student, published his first essay (1917), which summoned his contemporaries to retrieve their bodies from colonial control and strengthen them, and thus their collective political will,

through regular exercise, especially swimming. See "A Study of Physical Education," in *The Political Thought of Mao Tsetung* ed. Stuart R. Schramm (New York: Praeger, 1970), 152–60. In Mao as in Nordau, much emphasis is placed on the degradation of the body as a central experience of the subordinated people for whom they speak. In both cases as well, the counterstrategy of physical culture is cast in collective-political rather than individualistic body beautiful terms. On the role of sports and physical culture in nationalist and other modern political movements, see the suggestive work of John Hoberman, *Sport and Political Ideology* (Austin: University of Texas Press, 1984). See also Mosse, *Nationalization of the Masses*, 127–36.

68. It appeared originally in the *Jüdische Turnzeitung* (Jewish Gymnasts Gazette) and is translated in Mendes-Flohr and Reinharz, *Jew in the Modern World*, 434–35. This is the source of the passages cited here.

69. In the spring of 1985 a fund-raising appeal was circulated by the United States Committee of Sports for Israel, seeking support for the Maccabiah Games, which are held every four years in Israel and are often called the Jewish Olympics. Mark Spitz, the American swimmer who in 1972 broke the record for most gold medals won by an individual in the International Olympic Games, is the letter's signer. Spitz is Jewish. Reflecting the transformations that had unfolded since Nordau's day, especially since 1967, he notes that "back when I was a competitor, it never would have occurred to me that there was anything remarkable about the idea of Jews being strong and athletic." He had not realized, Spitz adds, that "this was a relatively recent tradition. I'd never heard of 'muscle Jews,' the term used by Dr. Max Nordau when he spoke to his Zionist colleagues . . . about the necessity for Jews who were as fit physically as they were intellectually." Spitz goes on to note that he cannot "imagine how Israel could ever have come into

existence if Jews hadn't taken Dr. Nordau's advice to heart. By the time I came along, the term 'muscle Jew' had become redundant!" At the games, Spitz closes on this ringing note, Jews of the world will "once again . . . return to our ancestral home to celebrate this new kind of Jew who is no longer weak and vulnerable, to reaffirm their solidarity with one another and with the state of Israel." In considering the circuitous line from Max Nordau to Mark Spitz, particularly the closing lines of the latter's appeal, it is difficult not to notice the absence of even a gesture to *human* solidarity across state, religious, and other lines. My point is not to burden a mere fund-raising letter with so weighty a criticism. On the contrary, it is to indicate that the radical constriction of focus and sensibility in Spitz's words is today quite typical and widely taken for granted. The Spitz comments are from Fund-raising Material from United States Committee/Sports for Israel (275 South 19th St., Philadelphia, Pa. 19103).

70. Quoted in Daniel Levine, "David Raziel, the Man and His Times" (Ph.D. diss., Yeshiva University, 1969), 27–28.

71. On Rabbi Kook, see Shlomo Avineri, *The Making of Modern Zionism: The Intellectual Origins of the Jewish State* (New York: Basic Books, 1981), 187–97.

72. Levine, "David Raziel," 142–43.

73. The first systematic discussion of Jewish self-hatred is by Theodor Lessing, the German Jewish thinker, who experienced it himself as a young man, later becoming a Zionist before his murder by Nazis in 1933. See *Der Jüdischer Selbsthass* (Berlin: Jüdischer Verlag, 1930). See also the analysis of the "inauthentic Jew" in Jean-Paul Sartre, *Anti-Semite and Jew* (New York: Schocken, 1965), 83ff. The most recent investigation, focusing largely on literary examples, is Sander Gilman, *Jewish Self-Hatred: Anti-Semitism and the Hidden Language of the Jews* (Baltimore: Johns Hopkins University Press, 1986).

74. Freud seems not to have been interested in *Sex and Character*

as a document of Jewish identity: his interest lay in Weininger's reflections on the theme of bisexuality. Wilhelm Fliess, Freud's colleague and intimate friend, was distressed by the publication of Weininger's book, convinced that the young man had stolen and published Fliess's own theories of the bisexual nature of humans. See Gilman, *Jewish Self-Hatred*, 250–51. See also Peter Gay, *Freud: A Life for Our Time* (New York: W.W. Norton, 1988), 154–56.

75. Avishai, *Tragedy of Zionism*, 120.
76. Ibid.
77. Betar is also the acronym for Brit Trumpeldor, the Jewish Legion unit named for its fallen cofounder, Josef Trumpeldor. According to Arthur Koestler, the Betar camps in Europe "served as a reservoir and training corps for Palestine terrorists" of the Irgun. Koestler, *Arrow in the Blue*, 120.
78. Quoted in Joseph B. Schechtman, *Fighter and Prophet: The Vladimir Jabotinsky Story, The Last Years (1923–1940)* (New York: Thomas Yoseloff, 1961), 425. This is an informative but virtually uncritical work. Schechtman was for many years Jabotinsky's secretary. See also Kahane, *Jewish Defense League*, 131–33, where Jabotinsky's "learn to shoot!" is enthusiastically invoked.
79. James Patterson, *The Jericho Commandment* (New York: Crown Publishers, 1979).
80. Gay Courter, *Code Ezra* (New York: New American Library, 1986), 180–82.
81. Gloria Goldreich, *This Promised Land* (New York: Berkley Books, 1982), 255–331.
82. Fred Lawrence, *Israel* (New York: Dell, 1984), 295ff.
83. Arthur Koestler, *Thieves in the Night* (1946; New York: Berkley Medallion, 1960).
84. Koestler, *Arrow in the Blue*, 114–15.
85. On Deir Yassin, see the eyewitness account of the results of the massacre in Jacques de Reynier, "Deir Yassin" (April 10,

1948), reprinted in *From Haven to Conquest: Readings in Zionism and the Palestine Problem until 1948*, ed. Walid Khalidi (Washington: Institute for Palestine Studies, 1987), 761–66. While Reynier's account does not prove that the Haganah had agreed with the Irgun on the strategy of taking Deir Yassin, it does show that once the slaughter was over, Irgunists were scarce and Haganah troops controlled the town. See also Menachem Begin, *The Revolt*, rev. ed. (New York: Nash Publishing, 1972), 162–65. The first edition of Begin's book appeared in 1948. Conor Cruise O'Brien, *The Siege: The Saga of Israel and Zionism* (New York: Simon and Schuster, 1986), 280–83, is less critical of the Jewish role in Deir Yassin than is Simha Flapan, *The Birth of Israel: Myths and Realities* (New York: Pantheon Books, 1987), 94–96, 164–65. The most detailed, and highly sympathetic account of the Irgun and Stern Gang is J. Bowyer Bell, *Terror out of Zion: Irgun Zvai Leumi, LEHI, and the Palestine Underground, 1929–1949* (New York: St. Martin's Press, 1977).

86. On the *Altalena* episode, see Koestler, *Promise and Fulfillment*, 245ff; Avishai, *Tragedy of Zionism*, 180ff; and Begin, *The Revolt*, 154–76.

87. See the provocative if somewhat cramped analysis in Lenni Brenner, *Zionism in the Age of the Dictators: A Reappraisal* (Westport, Conn.: Lawrence Hill & Co., 1983), 265–70.

88. Avineri, *Making of Zionism*, 171.

89. Cited in Schechtman, *Fighter and Prophet*, 79.

90. Cited in Avineri, *Making of Zionism*, 173.

91. Schechtman, *Fighter and Prophet*, 415–16.

92. Cited in Avineri, *Making of Zionism*, 172.

93. Ibid, 173–74.

94. See the summary in Schechtman, *Fighter and Prophet*, 409–14.

95. Avineri, *Making of Zionism*, 173.

96. Quoted in Amnon Rubenstein's outstanding study, *The Zionist*

Dream Revisited: From Herzl to Gush Emunim and Back (New York: Schocken Books, 1984), 4.

97. Ibid., 23–24. Rubenstein refers to "Facing the Statue of Apollo" (1899) by Saul Tchernichowsky, one of the new Hebrew-language poets of the Russian Pale. The poet describes himself facing the pagan god—"the youth-god, sublime and free, the acme of beauty!" In the battle between the pagan god and the Jews, Tchernichowsky writes, "I am the first of my race to return to you" (p. 24).

PART 3

1. Kurt Dittmar, "Die jüdische 'Renaissance' in der Literatur der USA nach 1945," *Juden und Judentum in der Literatur*, ed. Herbert A. Strauss and Christhard Hoffmann (Munich: Deutscher Taschenbuch Verlag, 1985), 373.

2. "Rambowitz" is the invention of Dr. Max Pensky of the philosophy department at SUNY, Binghampton.

3. John Rowe, *The Aswan Solution* (New York: Doubleday, 1979), 38, 96, 197–98. David Laker's reference to Neanderthals—he wants to "get those bastards," the supposedly Arab terrorists; to "pay those Neanderthals back"—is worth brief comment. For the same image is evoked in reverse in *A Perfect Peace* (1982) by Israeli novelist Amos Oz, who has long been critical of the militaristic dimensions of Zionism. At one point in Oz's story, an old kibbutznik angrily ruminates on the ways in which Israel has distorted Jewish and even Zionist traditions. For him, in effect, David Laker would be one of the "Jewish Neanderthals, Cro-Magnon heroes, moronic rednecks, circumcised Cossacks, biblical Bedouins, Tartars of the Hebrew faith." Will the Jewish future, the old militant wonders, consist of "no more Marxes, Freuds, and Einsteins; no more Menuhins and Jascha Heifetzes; not even any more Gordons, Borochovs,

and Berls [A.D. Gordon, Ber Borochov, Berl Katznelson were socialist Zionists from Russia early in the century]—no, from now on nothing but sunburned, ignorant, illiterate warriors, Joabs, Abners and Ehuds." Amos Oz, *A Pefect Peace*, trans. Hillel Halkin (San Diego and New York: Harcourt Brace Jovanovich, 1985), 155.

4. My friend Michael T. Gilmore called this to my attention.

5. No other country, including Israel, has seen a comparable flowering of tough Jewish fiction, although this in itself is not surprising since there are more Jews in the United States than anywhere else. While numerous tough Jewish novels have been available on reading racks in Israel's Ben-Gurion Airport as well as in bookstores and hotel lobbies in Jerusalem and Tel Aviv, they are imports into Israel and presumably aimed at a tourist market. Amnon Rubenstein indicates, however, that a common theme in many Israeli children's books is one of "the Jewish immigrant boy, seeking the company of healthy Sabras, [who] is always portrayed as a pale weakling, gradually losing his ashen look and acquiring true manly Sabra qualities." See Amnon Rubenstein, *The Zionist Dream Revisited: From Herzl to Gush Emunim and Back* (New York: Schocken, 1984), 135. In the same vein, Edward Said has noted the presence in Israeli children's literature of stories depicting "valiant Jews who always end up by killing low, treacherous Arabs, with names like Mastoul (crazy), Bandura (tomato), or Burka (tomorrow). As a writer for *Haaretz* said (September 20, 1974), children's books 'deal with our topic: the Arab boy who murders Jews out of pleasure, and the pure Jewish boy who defeats 'the coward swine!' " See Edward W. Said, *The Question of Palestine* (New York: Random House, 1980), 91.

6. A good summary of le Carré's views on the Middle East is found in Peter Lewis, *John le Carré* (New York: Frederick Ungar Publishing, 1985), 184–93.

7. Emanuel Litvinoff, *Falls the Shadow* (New York: Stein and Day, 1983).

8. Fred Lawrence, *Israel* (New York: Dell Publishing, 1984).

9. Joel Gross, *This Year in Jerusalem* (New York: New American Library/Signet, 1983).

10. William Caunitz, *One Police Plaza* (New York: Bantam Books, 1985).

11. E. Howard Hunt, *The Gaza Intercept* (New York: Stein and Day, 1981).

12. Douglas Muir, *The American Reich* (New York: Charter Books/ Berkley Publishing Group, 1985).

13. Wayne Karlin, *Crossover* (New York: Harcourt Brace Jovanovich, 1984).

14. A Jewish James Bond? According to Isser Harel, a Latvian-born Jew and first head of the actual Mossad, which was created in 1951, Agatha Christie's detective novels passed muster, but Ian Fleming's spy thrillers did not. "My boys," Harel is reported to have said, "make so-called heroes like James Bond look like amateurs." See Dennis Eisenberg, Uri Dan, and Eli Landau, *The Mossad: Israel's Secret Intelligence Service. Inside Stories* (New York: New American Library/Signet, 1978), 15. The American romance with post-1967 tough Jews has also generated a number of laudatory journalistic accounts of the Israeli intelligence services, of which the volume just cited is one. See also Stewart Steven, *The Spymasters of Israel* (New York: Ballantine Books, 1980). Originally published in England in 1977, Richard Deacon's *The Israeli Secret Service* (New York: Taplinger Publishing, 1985) has also been issued in this country. Eli Ben-Hanan, *Our Man in Damascus: Elie Cohn* (Israel: Steimatzky, n.d.) is distributed here.

15. George Jonas, *Vengeance* (New York: Bantam Books, 1984).

16. Gloria Goldreich, *Leah's Journey* (New York: Berkley Books, 1979).

17. Chaim Zeldis, *A Forbidden Love* (New York: Berkley Books, 1983).

18. Gloria Goldreich, *This Burning Harvest* (New York: Berkley Books, 1983).

19. Lewis Orde, *Munich 10* (New York: Kensington Publishing/ Zebra Books, 1982).

20. Gerald Green, *Karpov's Brain* (New York: Bantam Books, 1982).

21. J. C. Winters, *Berlin Fugue* (New York: Avon Books, 1985).

22. Lionel Davidson, *The Menorah Men* (New York: Harper & Row, 1966), 87.

23. Gay Courter, *Code Ezra* (New York: New American Library, 1987).

24. Sabi H. Shabtai, *Five Minutes to Midnight* (New York: Dell Publishing, 1980).

25. Alfred Coppel, *Thirty-four East* (New York: Popular Library, 1974).

26. Rupert Wilkinson, *American Tough: The Tough-Guy Tradition and American Character* (Westport, Conn.: Greenwood Press, 1984).

27. Ali Banuazizi, "Iranian 'National Character': A Critique of Some Western Perspectives," in *Psychological Dimensions of Near Eastern Studies*, ed. L. Carl Brown and Norman Itzkowitz (Princeton, N.J.: Darwin Press, 1977), 239.

28. Leon Uris, *The Haj* (New York: Bantam Books, 1985).

29. Edward W. Said's scathing comments on *The Haj* are on target. See "An Ideology of Difference," *Critical Inquiry* 12 (Autumn 1985): 38–58.

30. Arthur Koestler, *Thieves in the Night* (New York: Berkley Books, 1960).

31. Gershon Winkler, *The Hostage Torah* (New York: Judaica Press, 1981).

32. Peter Abrahams, *Tongues of Fire* (New York: Pocket Books, 1982).

33. Marilyn Hirsh, *Captain Jiri and Rabbi Jacob* (New York: Holiday House, 1976).

34. See the critical commentaries by Earl Shorris, *Jews without Mercy: A Lament* (New York: Anchor Press/Doubleday, 1982), and Alexander Bloom, *Prodigal Sons: The New York Intellectuals and Their World* (New York: Oxford University Press, 1986).

35. Wilkinson, *American Tough*, 103–4.

36. This can also be read, against what seem to be John Rowe's intentions, as a depiction of a cynical Israeli manipulation of an honest, ingenuous, and brave American Jew.

PART 4

1. Amnon Rubenstein, *The Zionist Dream Revisited: From Herzl to Gush Emunim and Back* (New York: Schocken Books, 1984).

2. *The Boston Globe*, October 19, 1989, 21.

3. *Jerusalem Post Independence Day Magazine, Jerusalem Post International edition*, May 10, 1989, vi.

4. Howard Kaplan, *Bullets of Palestine* (New York: Gold Eagle, 1987).

5. William Bayer, *Pattern Crimes* (New York: New American Library, 1988).

6. Roger L. Simon, *Raising the Dead* (New York: Warner Books, 1988).

BIBLIOGRAPHY OF TOUGH
JEWISH NOVELS

Abrahams, Peter. *Tongues of Fire*. New York: Pocket Books, 1982.

Arnold, Frederic. *Kohn's War*. New York: Signet, 1984.

Bayer, William. *Pattern Crimes*. New York: New American Library, 1987.

Caunitz, William J. *One Police Plaza*. New York: Bantam, 1985.

Cohen, Irving R. *The Passover Commando*. New York: Crown, 1979.

Coppel, Alfred. *Thirty-four East*. New York: Popular Library, 1974.

Courter, Gay. *Code Ezra*. New York: New American Library, 1986.

Davidson, Lionel. *The Menorah Men*. New York: Perennial Library, 1966.

De Hartog, Jan. *Star of Peace*. New York: Signet, 1984.

Deighton, Len. *Funeral in Berlin*. New York: Berkley, 1964.

Follett, Ken. *Triple*. New York: Signet, 1979.

Fredman, John. *The Wolf of Masada*. New York: Avon, 1978.

Gann, Ernest, K. *Masada*. 1970. Reprint. New York: Jove, 1981.

Goldreich, Gloria. *Leah's Children*. New York: Jove, 1985.

——. *Leah's Journey*. New York: Berkley, 1978.

——. *This Burning Harvest*. New York: Berkley, 1983.

——. *This Promised Land*. New York: Berkley, 1982.

——. *West to Eden*. New York: Avon, 1987.

Green, Gerald. *The Chains*. New York: Bantam Books, 1981.

——. *Karpov's Brain*. New York: Bantam Books, 1982.

Gross, Joel. *This Year in Jerusalem*. New York: Signet, 1983.

Guild, Nicholas. *The Linz Tattoo*. New York: McGraw Hill, 1986.

Harrison, Harry. *The QE2 is Missing*. New York: Tor Books, 1980.

Hunt, E. Howard. *The Gaza Intercept*. New York: Stein and Day, 1984 [1981].

Irving, Clive. *Promise the Earth*. New York: Ballantine Books, 1982.

Kaplan, Howard. *Bullets of Palestine*. New York: Gold Eagle, 1987.

Karlin, Wayne. *Crossover*. New York: Harcourt Brace Jovanovich, 1984.

Klawans, Harold L. *The Jerusalem Code*. New York: Signet, 1988.

Koestler, Arthur. *Thieves in the Night*. 1946. Reprint. New York: Berkley, 1960.

Kriss, Gary. *Final Option*. New York: Lynx Books, 1989.

Lawrence, Fred. *Israel*. New York: Dell, 1984.

Le Carré, John. *The Little Drummer Girl*. New York: Knopf, 1983.

Litvinoff, Emanuel. *Falls the Shadow*. New York: Stein and Day, 1983.

Muir, Douglas. *American Reich*. New York: Charter Books, 1985.

Orde, Lewis. *Munich 10*. New York: Zebra Books, 1982.

Patterson, James. *The Jericho Commandment*. New York: Crown, 1979.

Piercy, Marge. *Gone to Soldiers*. New York: Fawcett, 1987.

Robbins, Harold. *A Stone for Danny Fisher*. New York: Pocket Books, 1979 [1951].

Rowe, John. *The Aswan Solution*. New York: Doubleday, 1979.

Shabtai, Sabi H. *Five Minutes to Midnight*. New York: Dell, 1980.

Shapiro-Rieser, Rhonda. *A Place of Light*. New York: Pocket Books, 1983.

Simon, Roger L. *Raising the Dead*. New York: Warner Books, 1988.

Talmy, Shel. *The Web*. New York: Dell, 1981.

Uris, Leon. *Exodus*. 1958. Reprint. New York: Bantam Books, 1981.

———. *The Haj*. New York: Bantam Books, 1985.

———. *Mila 18*. New York: Bantam Books, 1981 [1961].

———. *Mitla Pass*. New York: Doubleday, 1988.

Willis, Ted. *The Lions of Judah*. 1979. Reprint. New York: Playboy, 1981.

Winkler, Gershon. *The Hostage Torah*. New York: Judaica Press, 1981.

Winters, J. C. *Berlin Fugue*. New York: Avon, 1985.

Zeldis, Chaim. *Forbidden Love*. New York: Berkley, 1983.

INDEX

Abrahams, Peter, 177, 218–20, 228

Ainsztein, Reuben, 87–91, 95–99, 102, 104

AIPAC. *See* American Israel Public Affairs Committee

Aleichem, Sholom, 62, 70

Alexander II (Tsar of Russia), 128

Allen, Woody, 3, 63, 65, 199, 236

Altalena (ship), 159–60

The Amboy Dukes (Schulman), 118–19

American Israel Public Affairs Committee (AIPAC), 6–7

American Reich (Muir), 186–87

American Zionist Federation, 122

Annenberg, Moses, 106

Anti-Semite and Jew (Sartre), 45

Arab-Israel War of 1967. *See* Six Day War (1967).

Arab-Israel War of 1973. *See* Yom Kippur War (1973)

Arab League, 160

Arab riots (1929), 152

Aranowicz, Yehiel, 55

Arendt, Hannah, 70, 81, 82, 94

Arens, Moshe, 223

Arnold, Frederic, 120

Asch, Sholem, 133

The Aswan Solution (Rowe), 172–74, 195, 226–28

Auschwitz, 17, 52

Auto-Emancipation (Pinsker), 129

The Autobiography of Solomon Maimon, 110

Ave-Lallemont, Friedrich Christian Benedict, 111–12

Avineri, Shlomo, 161–62

Avishai, Bernard, 150, 151

Babel, Isaac, 134–36

Banuazizi, Ali, 211–12

Bar Kokhba, Simon, 28, 83–87, 88, 117, 130

Bar Kokhba Gymnastic Club, 142–44

Barak, Motti, 225

Baudrillard, Jean, 53
Bauer, Yehuda, 80
Bayer, William, 237–40
Begin, Menachem, 17–18, 150, 154, 158–60, 233, 235
Bellow, Saul, 236
Ben-Gurion, David, 139, 154, 223
Berlin Fugue (Winters), 194–95, 208–209
Bettelheim, Bruno, 70, 73, 81, 82, 94
Beyond the Melting Pot (Moynihan), 63
Biale, David, 87–91, 95, 102
Bialik, Chaim Nachman, 130
Bialystok Pogrom, 131
Bimko, Fishel, 133–34
Bingham, Theodore, 113, 122
Black Panther Party, 65–66
Boer War, 99
Boorstin, Daniel, 53–54, 56
Borochov, Ber, 222
Broken Alliance: The Turbulent Times Between Blacks and Jews in America (Kaufman), 69
Brown, H. Rap, 64
Buchhalter, Lepke, 106
Bullets of Palestine (Kaplan), 237
Bund, 127–28, 131–32, 140
Bureau of Social Morals, 122
Bush, George, xii

Camus, Albert, 64
Captain Jiri and Rabbi Jacob (Hirsh), 220–21

Caunitz, William, 178, 179, 185–86
The Chains (Green), 116–18, 195
Chmielnitski, Bogdan, 28, 92–94
Christian Social Party (Germany), 101
Civil War (U.S.), 103
Code Ezra (Courter), 153–54, 202, 236–37
Concerning the Jews (Twain), 98, 100, 105
Coppel, Alfred, 207–208
Cossacks, Ukraine, 92–97
The Counterlife (Roth), 22
Courter, Gay, 153–54, 202, 236–37
Crossover (Karlin), 187–88
The Crowd: A Study of the Popular Mind (Le Bon), 126–27
Crusades, 89–90

Dalitz, Moe, 105
Darkness at Noon (Koestler), 155
Davidowicz, Lucy, 81
Davidson, Lionel, 201–202
Dawn (Wiesel), 55
Deacon, Richard, 103
Deighton, Len, 176
Deir Yassin massacre, 158–59
Delaney, John, 123
DeNiro, Robert, 5
Deutscher, Isaac, 35
Diaspora, 27–28, 145, 188, 195
Dittmar, Kurt, 171–72

Dreyfus, Alfred, 30, 43, 99, 101, 125–26, 141, 149, 164, 166

Earp, Wyatt, 104
Eastman, Monk, 106
Eichmann in Jerusalem: A Report on the Banality of Evil (Arendt), 70, 94
Eichmann trial, 81, 82
Einstein, Albert, 34, 65
Eleazar, Simon ben, 83, 91–92
Elon, Amos, 140–41
The End of the Jewish People? (Friedmann), 81–82
Entebbe raid, 5–6
Exodus (Uris), 5, 10–11, 54–56, 57–59, 174, 176, 193

The Facts: A Novelist's Autobiography (Roth), 23
Falls the Shadow (Litvinoff), 180–82, 236–37
Fein, "Dopey" Benny, 106
Fiddler on the Roof, 62, 65
Five Minutes to Midnight (Shabtai), 202–203
The Fixer (Malamud), 62, 65
Fleming, Ian, 60
Follett, Ken, 9–22, 71, 176, 178–80, 225, 233
Forbidden Love (Zeldis), 189–90, 193–94, 206, 209, 236
Frankel, Jonathan, 123–25, 131

Fredman, John, 172, 177, 200–201
French Revolution, xi, 99
Freud, Jakob, 26–28, 30, 40–41, 47, 72
Freud, Sigmund, xiii, 22, 24–29, 30–47, 135, 140, 148
Fried, Albert, 105, 117–18, 122
Friedmann, Georges, 81–82
Friedman-Yellin, David, 158

Gann, Ernest K., 177
Garibaldi, Giuseppe, 150
The Gaza Intercept (Hunt), 176–77, 186, 203–205, 209, 210, 228–30
General Jewish Labor Union. *See* Bund
Glazer, Nathan, 63
The Godfather (Puzo), 66, 116
Gold, Mike, 118
Goldreich, Gloria, 104, 175, 177, 183–84, 189, 190, 195–97, 200
Goldsmith, Arnold L., 27–28
The Golem Remembered, 1909–1980: Variations of a Jewish Legend (Goldsmith), 27–28
Gone to Soldiers (Piercy), 120–21
Goodbye Columbus (Roth), 63
Gordon, Aaron David, 222
Gordon, Waxy, 106
Grand Central Palace rally (New York), 123–24
Green, Gerald, 116–18, 176, 191–92, 195, 212
Greenberg, Eliezer, 132

INDEX

Gross, Joel, 184, 190, 197, 202
Gutman, Yisrael, 80

ha-Nagid, Samuel, 90
Haganah, 140, 151, 158, 160
The Haj (Uris), 176, 212–15
Halperin, Moyse Leib, 130
Hannibal, 25–27, 29, 31–33, 37–38, 42
Harkabi, Yehoshafat, 84–87
Hashomer, 139
Helfand, Chaim, 132
Herzl, Hans, 31–32
Herzl, Theodor, 31–32, 47, 140–42, 149–51, 154, 156, 162–64, 192
Herzog, Elizabeth, 108
Himmelfarb, Milton, 5
Hirsh, Marilyn, 220–21
Hitler, Adolf, 17, 30, 127, 140, 148, 160, 192
Holocaust, 16–17, 58, 71, 73, 81, 171–72, 188. *See also* Nazis
Holocaust (film), 176
Hostage Torah (Winkler), 217–18
Howe, Irving, 113, 117, 132
Hunt, E. Howard, 176–77, 178, 179, 186, 203–205, 209, 210, 228–30

If Not Now, When? (Levi), 137
The Image: A Guide to Pseudo-Events in America (Boorstin), 53–54

The Informed Heart (Bettelheim), 70, 94
The Interpretation of Dreams (Freud), 24–25, 30, 37, 40, 47
Irgun, 151, 158–59
Irving, Clive, 138
Israel: formation as state, 57, 159; invasion of Lebanon (1982), 13, 88, 234
Israel-Arab War of 1967. *See* Six Day War (1967)
Israel-Arab War of 1973. *See* Yom Kippur War (1973)
Israel Defense Forces, 52, 84
Israel (Lawrence), 182–83, 192–93, 217
Israeli Secret Service (Deacon), 103

Jabotinsky, Vladimir, 146–67, 192, 222
Jahn, Friedrich, 143
JDL. *See* Jewish Defense League
The Jericho Commandment (Patterson), 152–53
Jewish Defense Association (New York), 123–24
Jewish Defense League (JDL), xiv, 152
Jewish Institute for National Security Affairs (JINSA), 6, 223–25
Jewish Legion, 150
Jewish lobby. *See* American Israel Public Affairs Committee
Jewish Museum (New York), 61, 117

Jewish Responses to Nazi Persecution (Trunk), 85
The Jewish War (Josephus), 83, 91
Jews Without Money (Gold), 118
Jick, Leon, 71
JINSA. *See* Jewish Institute for National Security Affairs
Johnson, Paul, 179
Jonas, George, 188–89
Jonathan Institute, 6
Joselit, Jena Weissman, 105–109, 106–15, 112–15, 122
Josephus, 83, 91
Judah Maccabee, 7
Judean Regiment, 150
Jung, Carl Gustav, 35

Kahane, Meir, xiv, 66, 150, 152
Kant, Immanuel, 110
Kaplan, Howard, 236–38
Karlin, Wayne, 187–88
Karpov's Brain (Green), 191–92
Katz, Jacob, 91
Kaufman, Jonathan, 69
Kemp, Jack, 6, 224
Kennedy, Robert, 65
King, Martin Luther, Jr., xii, 64, 65
Kirkpatrick, Jeane, 6, 224
Kishinev Pogroms, 123, 144, 150, 166
Koestler, Arthur, 139, 141, 154–61, 216–17
Kohn's War (Arnold), 120

Kook, Rabbi Abraham Isaac, 146–47
Korean War, 79

Lambroza, Shlomo, 130, 131
Landauer, Gustav, 222
Lansky, Meyer, 105, 115
The Last Angry Man (Green), 176
Lawrence, Fred, 182–83, 192–93, 217
Le Bon, Gustave, 126–27
Le Carre, John, 176
League of Anti-Semites (Germany), 101
Leah's Journey (Goldreich), 189, 195
Lebanon, Israeli invasion of (1982), 13, 88, 234
Ledeen, Michael, 6, 224
Leone, Sergio, 5
Lessing, Gotthold Ephraim, 110
Leumi, Irgun Zvai, 145
Levi, Primo, 136–38
Levine, David, 147
Life is With People: The Culture of the Shtetl (Zborowski and Herzog), 108
Likud bloc, 150, 154, 235
Little Drummer Girl (Le Carre), 176
Litvinoff, Emanuel, 180–82, 236–37
Loew, Judah, 28
Loxfinger: A Thrilling Adventure of Hebrew Secret Agent Oy-Oy-7: An Israel Bond Thriller (Weinstein), 60–61
Luxemburg, Rosa, 34–35

Magnes, Judah, 122–25
Mailer, Norman, 120
Maimon, Solomon, 109–10
Malamud, Bernard, 62, 65
Marcus, Josephine ("Josie") Sarah, 104
Maronite Phalangist massacre of Palestine. *See* Sabra and Shatilla
Marr, Wilhelm, 101
Marshall, Louis, 122
Marx, Karl, 34, 102–103, 160
Masada, 61, 83
McGrath, William, 31–32
Meir, Golda, 188
Mendelsohn, Moses, 110
Mendes-Flor, Paul, 101
Mendoza, Daniel, 103
Menorah Men (Davidson), 201–202
Middle Ages, 88–90, 92–97
Mila 18 (Uris), 70, 174, 176, 178, 199–200
Mitla Pass (Uris), 55–56, 176
Moses, 31, 35
Moses and Monotheism (Freud), 35
Mossad, 3
Mosse, George L., 110
Moynihan, Daniel Patrick, 63
Muir, Douglas, 186–87
Munich Olympics massacre (1972), 188, 222
Munich 10 (Orde), 190–91, 205–206, 209–10, 215
Mussolini, Benito, 127

The Naked and the Dead (Mailer), 120

Napoleon, 37, 40, 142
Nathan the Wise (Lessing), 110
National Jewish Community Relations Advisory Council (NJCRAC), 59
Nazis (National Socialist German Workers' Party), 16, 18, 30, 57, 66, 70, 71, 73, 79–83, 85, 101, 161, 162, 211, 235. *See also* Holocaust
Neither Victim nor Executioner (Camus), 64
Netanyahu, Benjamin, 6
Netanyahu, Jonathan, 6
New York Kehilla, 122
Newman, Paul, 56, 58
Nietzsche, Friedrich, xi
Nitzberg, Irving "Knadles", 106
NJCRAC. *See* National Jewish Community Relations Advisory Council
Nordau, Max, 47, 142–47, 149, 151, 156, 166, 192

O'Brien, Conor Cruise, 179, 180
Old Testament, 84
Once Upon a Time in America (film), 5
One Police Plaza (Caunitz), 185–86
Orde, Lewis, 190–91, 205–206, 209–10, 215
Orwell, George, xii
Our Gang (Joselit), 106

Palestine Liberation Organization (PLO), 69, 188

Palestinians, 4, 17, 29, 50, 52, 73

Pattern Crimes (Bayer), 237–40

Patterson, James, 152–54

Pearl, Chaim, 5, 235

Petlyura, Simon, 161

Piccone, Paul, xi

Piercy, Marge, 120–21

Pinsker, Lev, 129

PLO. *See* Palestine Liberation Organization

Podhoretz, Norman, 69

Portnoy's Complaint (Roth), 199, 201

Preminger, Otto, 56, 57

Promise and Fulfillment (Koestler), 157–58

Promise the Earth (Irving), 138

Puzo, Mario, 66, 116

The Question of Palestine (Said), 212

Raid on Entebbe (film), 5

Raising the Dead (Simon), 237–38

Raziel, David, 145–47, 158, 182–83, 222

Red Cavalry (Babel), 135, 136

Reilly, Sidney, 103

Reinharz, Jehuda, 101

Reles, Abe, 106

Revisionist Zionist World Organization, 151, 153

The Rise and Fall of the Jewish Gangster in America (Freid), 117–18

Risorgimento, 150

The Robbers (Schiller), 109

Robbins, Harold, 119

Robert, Marthe, 31

Rochlin, Fred, 103–104

Rochlin, Harriet, 103–104

Rosenbloom, Sigmund Georgievich. *See* Reilly, Sidney

Rosenthal, Herman "Beansy", 113–14, 122

Roskies, David, 129–32, 134

Ross, E. A., 107

Rosten, Leo, 136–38

Roth, Philip, xiii, 22–24, 25, 26, 36, 42–48, 56, 57, 63, 72, 199, 201, 236

Rothstein, Arnold, 106

Rowe, John, 172–74, 195, 226–28

Rubenstein, Amnon, 82, 166, 233–34

Russian Pale of Settlement, 124, 129, 131, 134, 139, 166, 178

Russian Revolution, 103, 123, 130

Sabra and Shatilla, 13, 234, 237

Said, Edward W., 212

Sartre, Jean-Paul, 45, 49, 67, 72, 161

Schechtman, Joseph, 163

Schiff, Jacob, 122

Schiller, Friedrich, 109

The Schlemiel as Modern Hero (Wisse), 59–60, 63
Scholem, Gershom, 28
Schulberg, Budd, 119
Schultz, Dutch, 106
Second Zionist Congress, Switzerland (1898), 142
Selzer, Michael, 61–62, 78
Sex and Character (Geschlecht und Charakter) (Weininger), 148–49, 166
Shabtai, Sabi, 202–203
Shamir, Yitzhak, 150, 154, 233, 235, 236
Shapiro, Gurrah, 106
Sharon, Ariel, 4, 188
Shatilla-Sabra massacre. *See* Sabra and Shatilla
Shaw, Irwin, 120
Shosha (Singer), 11–12
Shulman, Irving, 118–19
Siegel, Bugsy, 106
Silber, John, 224
Simon, Roger L., 237–38
Singer, Isaac Bashevis, 11–12, 15–16, 18, 33–36, 50, 62, 65, 93–95
Six Day War (1967), 5, 13, 57–62, 65, 69, 71, 72, 94, 116, 172, 174–75, 181, 201, 222, 234
The Slave (Singer), 93–95
Spanish-American War, 98
Spinoza, Baruch, 26, 34
Stern, Avraham, 161
Stern Gang, 151, 158–59
Stewart, Kirk, 225
Stoecker, Adolf, 101

Stone for Danny Fisher (Robbins), 119
Stuyvesant, Peter, 96

"Texas Rasslin", 21
Thieves in the Night (Koestler), 155–56, 216–17
Thirty-Four East (Coppel), 207–208
This Burning Harvest (Goldreich), 190, 196–97, 200
This Promised Land (Goldreich), 183–84, 195, 197–99
This Year in Jerusalem (Gross), 184, 190, 197, 202
Tivnan, Edward, 7, 55–57, 63
Tongues of Fire (Abrahams), 177, 218–20, 228
Torah, 87
Treblinka, 17
Triple (Follett), 9–22, 71, 176, 225, 233
Trotsky, Leon, 103
Trumpeldor, Josef, 150, 154, 222
Trunk, Isaiah, 80–81, 85
Twain, Mark, 98, 100, 105

Ukrainian Cossacks (1648–1650), 92–97
Union of American Hebrew Congregations, 59
Uris, Leon, 5, 10–11, 54–56, 57–58, 70, 73, 174, 176, 178, 193, 199–200, 212–215

*Vengeance: The True Story of an Is-
    raeli Counter-Terrorist Team*
    (Jonas), 188–89
Vietnam War, 64, 65
Vorspan, Albert, 59

War of Independence (U.S.), 98,
    99
Warheit, 106–107
Warrior (Sharon), 4
Warsaw Ghetto, 80, 82
Weathermen, 66
Weininger, Otto, 148–49, 166, 192
Weinstein, Sol, 60–61
Weizmann, Chaim, 151, 154
West Bank, 235
West to Eden (Goldreich), 104
What Makes Sammy Run? (Schul-
    berg), 119
Wiesel, Eli, 55
Wilkinson, Rupert, 115, 211, 224
Winkler, Gershon, 217–18
Winters, J. C., 194–95, 208–209
Wisse, Ruth, 59–61, 63
The Wolf of Masada (Fredman),
    172, 177, 200–201

World of Our Fathers (Howe), 113
World Zionist Organization, 140,
    142, 151

Yad Vashem, 82
Yom Kippur War (1973), 4, 6, 175,
    223
Young Lions (Shaw), 120

Zborowski, Mark, 108
Zealots, 82, 83
Zeldis, Chaim, 189–90, 193–94,
    206, 209, 236
Zelig, "Big" Jack, 106
Zevi, Sabbatai, 28, 87
Zion Mule Corps, 150
The Zionist Dream Revisited (Rub-
    enstein), 233–34
Zionist movement, 30–33, 47–51,
    56–57, 78, 101, 120, 125, 127–
    28, 132, 139–49, 150, 165–66,
    222–34
Zola, Emile, 43
Zwillman, Longy, 106